"I knew I'd adore *Friendships Don't Just* .... It's tough to make friends as an adult, and women are often made to think we've done something wrong if new pals don't come easily. Shasta Nelson does a great job of breaking down how to identify the friendships you need, how to go about forging new relationships, and how to turn those relationships into true friendships. I'd recommend this book to anyone who is looking to make new friends or strengthen their existing friendships. In fact, there is no one who won't benefit from reading *Friendships Don't Just Happen!*"

—RACHEL BERTSCHE, AUTHOR OF
MWF SEEKING BFF: MY YEARLONG SEARCH FOR A NEW BEST FRIEND

"As CEO of GirlFriendCircles.com, Shasta Nelson has made bringing women together her life's work. Now, Shasta has written an inspiring book that empowers women to reach out and connect as individuals. *Friendships Don't Just Happen!* is a call to action, offering women practical tips and tools to find and nurture meaningful friendships. The perfect workbook for someone who wants to work on their friendships!"

—IRENE S. LEVINE, PhD,
PROFESSOR OF PSYCHIATRY, NYU SCHOOL OF MEDICINE, AUTHOR OF
BEST FRIENDS FOREVER: SURVIVING A BREAKUP WITH YOUR BEST FRIEND

"As I was reading *Friendships Don't Just Happen!*, I had this profound wish that someone had shared all of this amazing information with me when I was much younger. This book should be required reading for women of all ages and especially for mothers of daughters."

—CHRISTINE BRONSTEIN, CEO OF A BAND OF WIVES,
EDITOR OF *NOTHING BUT THE TRUTH SO HELP ME GOD:
51 WOMEN REVEAL THE POWER OF POSITIVE FEMALE CONNECTION*

"Loving friendships are essential to feeling fulfilled and well nourished. And this is one AWESOME book that walks us through really well laid-out steps of creating and nurturing supportive and lifelong friendships that too few of us have been taught or shown."

—CHRISTINE HASSLER, AUTHOR OF
20 SOMETHING, 20 EVERYTHING AND 20 SOMETHING MANIFESTO,
SPEAKER AND COACH

"At a time when so many people are 'friending' one another online yet reporting feelings of loneliness, *Friendships Don't Just Happen!* reminds us that friendships worth creating are done with intention and significance."

—DALE V. ATKINS, PHD,
PSYCHOLOGIST, AUTHOR, MEDIA COMMENTATOR

"Women read books on parenting, romance, and diet all the time, but when was the last time we read about our friendships? . . . We've never been taught about the types of friends, healthy expectations, incremental vulnerability, and the steps of developing friendships. This book was so eye-opening and hope-filling. Read this book, get one for your mom, sister, friend, clients . . . the art of friendship is seeing a revival thanks to Shasta Nelson!"

—ANGELA JIA KIM,
FOUNDER OF SAVOR THE SUCCESS AND SAVOR SPA

"When it comes to getting the girlfriend love you need (and we all need it!), Shasta Nelson has the path. No longer do you need to wish you had close, soulful relationships with other women; with this book as your guide, you are empowered to create them! This book is SO good, so thorough, and so perfect!"

—CHRISTINE ARYLO, SELF-LOVE TEACHER,
AUTHOR OF *MADLY IN LOVE WITH ME: THE DARING ADVENTURE TO BECOMING YOUR OWN BEST FRIEND*

"Shasta sums up what it takes to make and sustain relationships, and validates all my neuroses about this subject. She teaches us how to nurture friendships, how to focus on what can be a most important thing in our lives . . . OUR GIRLFRIENDS!"

—MELODY BIRINGER, FOUNDER OF WWW.THECRAVECOMPANY.COM

"When it comes to friendships, there is no better person to learn from than Shasta Nelson. Her book is a beautiful reminder of how important it is to maintain healthy friendships throughout our lives, as many women tend to put themselves and their friendships last on the to-do list! . . . I highly recommend this book for every woman who yearns for a meaningful, lifelong connection to her girlfriends!"

—JENNIFER TUMA-YOUNG,
AUTHOR OF *BALANCE YOUR LIFE, BALANCE THE SCALE*

"*Friendships Don't Just Happen!* not only strengthens and deepens current friendships, but it starts with reminding us how normal it is to actually need new friends regularly through life. It can be hard to admit when we need more friends, and even harder still to know how to develop meaningful friendships. I love how Shasta Nelson walks us through every step of the way."

—DEBBA HAUPERT, FOUNDER OF GIRLFRIENDOLOGY.COM

friendships

don't just happen!

friendships

don't just happen!

The Guide to
CREATING *a*
MEANINGFUL CIRCLE
of
GIRLFRIENDS

shasta nelson

Turner Publishing Company
200 4th Avenue North • Suite 950 • Nashville, Tennessee 37219
445 Park Avenue • 9th Floor • New York, New York 10022
www.turnerpublishing.com

*Friendships Don't Just Happen!: The Guide to Creating a
Meaningful Circle of GirlFriends*

Cover design: Laura Beers
Book design: Kym Whitley

Library of Congress Catalog-in-Publishing Data
Nelson, Shasta.
Friendships don't just happen! : the guide to creating a meaningful circle of girlfriends / Shasta Nelson. -- 1st Edition.
pages cm
ISBN 978-1-61858-014-6
1. Friendship. 2. Girls--Psychology. 3. Interpersonal relations. I. Title.
BF575.F66N45 2013
155.3'3392--dc23
2012037540

Printed in the United States of America
13 14 15 16 17 18 19 0 9 8 7 6 5 4 3 2 1

*It is because of my girlfriends
that I wanted to write this book,
Some of whom are mentioned in my stories on these pages,
All with whom it has been a privilege to co-create
friendships.*

*It is because of two men that I could write this book,
My dad, Jeff Emery, for helping me launch
GirlFriendCircles.com, and
My husband, Greg Nelson, for fueling this dream and
loving this girl.*

table of contents

PART 1: FROM LONELINESS TO FRIENTIMACY

Chapter 1: Admit the Desire: *I Value New Friends!*.......5

Chapter 2: Learn the Circles of Connectedness: *What Are the Five Types of Friends?*.......21

Chapter 3: Determine the Need: *Evaluating My Friendship Circles*.......41

Chapter 4: Anticipate the Frientimacy: *Developing the Intimacy We Crave*.......59

PART 2: FIVE STEPS TO TURNING FRIENDLY PEOPLE WE MEET INTO FRIENDS WHO MATTER

Chapter 5: Be Open: *Making New Left-Side Friends*.......75

Chapter 6: Initiate Consistently: *Every Friendship Needs Momentum*.......105

Chapter 7: Add Positivity: *Bringing Joy to Our Friendships*.......127

Chapter 8: Increase Vulnerability: *Risking Rejection for Frientimacy*.......147

Chapter 9: Practice Forgiveness: *It's the Lesson of Relationships*.......169

PART 3: FRIENDSHIPS DON'T JUST KEEP HAPPENING: BE INTENTIONAL

Chapter 10: Follow Grace: *Responding to the Five Friendship Threats*.......195

Chapter 11: Activate Friendship: *Moving from Inspiration to Action*.......225

Acknowledgments.......239
Bibliography.......241

friendships
don't just happen!

part one

FROM LONELINESS TO FRIENTIMACY

ADMIT THE
DESIRE:
*I Value New
Friends!*

JULIANA
ANN
LYNNE
ROBIN
JACQUELYN
NANCY
CHRISTINA
KYM
ANGIE

T here is a lie out there that real friendship *just happens.*

When I was new to San Francisco eight years ago, I still remember standing at a café window on Polk Street watching a group of women inside, huddled around a table laughing. Like the puppy dog at the pound, I looked through the glass, wishing someone would pick me to be theirs. I had a phone full of far-flung friends' phone numbers, but I didn't yet know anyone I could just sit and laugh with in a café.

It hit me how very hard the friendship process is. I'm an outgoing, socially comfortable woman with a long line of good friendships behind me. And yet I stood there feeling very lonely. And insecure. And exhausted at just the idea of how far I was from that reality for which I was yearning.

I knew I couldn't just walk in there and introduce myself to them. "Hi! You look like fun women, can I join you?" I would have been met with stares of pity. No one wants to seem desperate, even if we are. We don't have platonic pickup lines memorized. Flirting for friends seems creepy. Asking for her phone number like we're going to call her up for a Saturday night date is just plain weird. All the batting of my eyelashes wasn't going to send the right signals. I wanted to give them my friendship résumé, my vast references from past friends who adore me, assuring them how lucky they would be to call me a friend.

But it doesn't work that way. And so I turned away from the scene of laughter and walked away.

No, unfortunately, friendships don't just happen.

WE VALUE BELONGING

Friendship may not happen automatically, but what we crave about them sure seems to! We all want to belong—that need to be connected to others is an inherent feeling that comes with being born. We live our entire lives trying to fit in, be known, attract acceptance, and experience intimacy. We desperately want to have others care about us. This book is about that hunger. And more pointedly, it is about listening to it and learning how to fulfill it.

Much is written and taught about romantic love and parent-child relationships. We buy armloads of books on these subjects that feel so urgent and life consuming. Yet, when it comes to our friendships—relationships that will outweigh in quantity the number of kids and spouses most of us will have—we tend to take a much more laid-back approach. We end up just hoping that we'll meet the right women, at the right time, and both know the right way to act. While some of us have seen good modeling of healthy platonic friendships, the vast majority of us are left hoping that it just comes intuitively, as though we should know how to make and keep good friends. Few of us have been taught what we need to know.

When it comes to friendships it is all too easy to either idealize them or devalue them. Neither approach is very helpful.

Wearing our rose-colored glasses, we picture these perfect tribes of women who always show up for each other no matter what obstacles, life stages, or relationships enter the picture. From some of our favorite TV shows, we have found ourselves wishing for a group that knows us and loves us, accepting us just as we are. It didn't matter how opposite sexually active Samantha and prim-and-proper Charlotte were from each other on *Sex and the City*, or how tough and sarcastic Dorothy was in contrast to the naïve ways of pushover Rose on *The Golden Girls*, they rarely judged and always loved each other. Whether it's the single life of those on *Friends*—where they could all swap each other as roommates and dates while keeping their sense of chosen-family intact—or the married-with-kids lives of *Desperate Housewives*, in which neighbors go from playing poker and delivering baked goods to raising kids and going through divorces and affairs—friendship is always highlighted as the one relationship that is constant through all of life's ups and downs.

For the majority of us who view these tight groups as the ideal friendships, there are also some who view female friendship more like those depicted in the reality spin-offs such as *The Real Housewives of Atlanta, New Jersey, Orange County,* or any of the other handful of featured cities. Most of us can't help but roll our eyes at that unhealthy depiction. If that's "real" friendship, we'll take a pass, thank you very much. Competitive, catty, dramatic, and filled with backstabbing rivals, shows such as these have made the words *toxic friend* and *frenemy* all too common.

And those hurtful actions aren't limited to TV. In her book *Blueprints for Building Better Girls,* Elissa Schappell shares horror stories of how mean some friends can be to each other when growing up. In the first chapter of her book she introduces Heather, a teen who was unlucky enough to be the first to develop breasts in her class, a wrongdoing that branded her with a reputation that suggested immorality. Her female friends were jealous of her arrival into puberty before them and her male classmates scrawled her name on bathroom walls. (Speaking from experience, I can attest that being the last to develop isn't much fun either.)

It's inconceivable to get through childhood and adolescence without scars of embarrassment, feelings of rejection, and an overall sense of never quite feeling like we fit in with whomever we deem "the popular girls."

These reality shows and painful childhood stories reinforce some of our own memories of friends who disappointed us over the years; and if we're not careful, we risk devaluing what friendship can be in our attempt to protect ourselves from what we don't want it to be. Some of us point to unhealthy relationships as evidence that we don't need a group of close friends, believing drama and friendship are one and the same. We might resist the idea of girlfriends because we picture the stereotypical high school cliques. We might see ourselves as above sitting around and gossiping like other girls. We may not see ourselves as girlfriend-types since we don't like fashion, lattes, or the color pink. Maybe our gag reflexes are even triggered over the romantic-sounding love-fests that other girls champion with poetic euphemisms and syrupy sayings. Or, maybe we just shrug our shoulders and claim to not be joiners.

And yet, for all our foibles and painful memories, here we are. Still wishing we had a wee bit more love and support in our lives. Sure, we might love someone romantically, and we love our kids, parents, and siblings more than anything, but there is another type of relationship we crave.

We mustn't lose hope in intimate female friendships. Just because we've been disappointed doesn't mean we can't also be impressed, and just because some women are mean doesn't mean others won't want our happiness. For example, just because the divorce rate is high doesn't mean there aren't happy lifelong marriages, and just because I may have had a bad divorce doesn't mean my next marriage can't be fulfilling. It's the same with friendships. It doesn't matter what our previous experiences have been as much as it matters what we're willing to create now. What we're willing to invest. What we're willing to do.

No one said making friends was easy, automatic, simple, or pain-free. Very few things in life are effortless—certainly not the things that matter.

But let's be clear: female friendships matter.

WE VALUE HEALTH AND HAPPINESS

In fact, female friendships matter to our health and happiness almost more than anything.

There are numerous studies and articles that link a circle of supportive friends to lower stress levels, greater happiness, prevention of diseases, faster recovery rates from surgery and accidents, and greater chances of reaching life goals. Who among us doesn't want those benefits? In fact, most of what we do every day is actually an attempt to achieve one of these results!

The Happiness Project, by Gretchen Rubin, was a *New York Times* bestseller largely because happiness is something most of us would like to increase in our lives. While Rubin lists many fabulous methods for boosting our joy, she is adamant that friends play the most significant role in our pursuit of happiness: "One conclusion was blatantly clear from my happiness research: everyone from contemporary scientists to ancient philosophers agrees that having strong social bonds is probably the most meaningful contributor to happiness."

As a life coach, the question I always ask my clients, regardless of their stated goal, is "Tell me about your friends." The response is always revealing. Whether they want to lose weight, get a new job, make a decision about a relationship, or start their own business, who they have supporting them and influencing their definition of "normal" is a major contributor to their success or failure.

Beyond friendships adding to the list of improving life success and happiness, experts also assert that supportive relationships improve our odds of survival by fifty percent. Our social connections are on the "short list" of factors that can be used to determine our odds of living or dying, at any given age.

In a study out of Brigham Young University, the researchers examined nearly 150 previously published longitudinal studies that measured how the frequency of human interaction affects health outcomes. They concluded that low social interaction can be compared to the damage caused by smoking fifteen cigarettes a day, being an alcoholic, or not exercising. Ponder all the attention we give to our weight in this culture and sit with the fact that feeling disconnected is twice as dangerous as obesity (and what if it's not the obesity itself that is as damaging as the shame and isolation that often accompany that label?). We have laws and government-funded health campaigns designed to motivate us to stop smoking and at least twelve grades of school curriculum to teach us the importance of exercise (not to mention fitness centers and multibillion dollar industries devoted to producing magazines and books about it), but we have some catching up to do when it comes to understanding exactly how important a circle of friends can be to our *health.*

Editors of *PLoS Medicine* explain the research with a rather startling statement: "The idea that a lack of social relationships is a risk factor for death is still not widely recognized by health organizations and the public." This tells us that our friendships are not a nice-to-have as much as they are a necessity.

Many studies reveal that friendship has an even greater effect on health than a spouse or family member. A landmark study of 3,000 nurses with breast cancer found that women without close friends were four times as likely to die from the disease as women with at least ten friends. Having a spouse didn't rank with survival rates. In a *New York Times* article on the importance of friendship to our health, Rebecca G. Adams, a professor of sociology at the University of North Carolina, Greensboro, gave this statement: "There is just scads of stuff on families and marriage, but very little on friendship. It baffles me. Friendship has a bigger impact on our psychological well-being than family relationships."

In addition to all the physical and psychological benefits, I think one of the greatest outcomes of relationships is learning to expand our ability to love. To love people requires that we keep growing personally. It's impossible to engage with other humans without seeing the places in our own lives where we need to learn greater patience, increased acceptance, and continued forgiveness. In our friendships there is no blood relation or marriage license holding us together, rather we're simply acknowledging that we are willing to give and receive with each other. That willingness will change us for the better.

Since I'm not anticipating any city putting up billboards next to their anti-smoking efforts saying, "Make a friend. Save your life." anytime soon, I figure we better take on the cause for ourselves.

WE VALUE UNDERSTANDING

The first action toward that "make-a-friend, save-a-life" cause is awakening to the fact that we can't just sit and wait for friendship to happen to us. We can't wait for it to feel automatic.

Misunderstanding #1: How Friendship Used to Happen Automatically

We're tempted to think that friendships just happen because we have memories of friendships that felt automatic, easy, natural, and effortless.

My childhood best friend was Amy K. We'd race to the playground at recess, knowing that whoever made it to the swings first would save one for the other. We'd swing high in unison while we sang "Believe It or Not," the theme song for a show neither of us had ever seen. Two little girls, belting out the lyrics, knowing we did believe in "us."

We'd soon giggle over inside jokes, whisper secrets about boys, and beg our parents for permission to spend the night at each other's homes. Playing all day long on a weekend never felt like enough time. We believed the pact we made to be forever friends.

I no longer make a habit of swinging and singing with my friends, but something about childhood memories makes me wistful, wishing for that kind of time and loyalty that I don't remember ever working on creating.

But even then friendships didn't just happen.

Friendship may have felt like it just happened to us when we were kids at recess, campers in the same cabin, playmates on the same street, or suitemates in the same college dorm. What *did* just happen was consistency. Seeing each other regularly without our ever scheduling it in. We played with the same kids over and over, every day, all day long sometimes, without ever having to find the time to fit them in. We were required to go to school, we had to sleep in cabins with other campers, we couldn't play games in the streets by ourselves, and it was cheaper in college to live with a roommate. Repetitive time together is what happened automatically back then, not friendships. There's a difference.

Some of us still get that consistency with people we work with—it's why we are more likely to become friends with people at work with whom we'd otherwise probably never hang out again if we just met them randomly. We see them regularly and that makes all the difference.

When we can recognize that we don't need to wait for friendships to happen, we can figure out ways to add consistency with a few chosen people. Without built-in consistency we have to be more intentional to find an hour here and an hour there to connect with our friends.

Our friendships did not just magically appear out of nowhere; they were birthed and fostered in a container of consistent time together.

Misunderstanding #2: What Friendship Is Supposed to Be

I think another of the factors that makes this constant friendship search so hard is that we're raised with the belief in a BFF—our Best Friend Forever—with the emphasis on Forever.

But Amy K. moved away when we were in the fourth grade.

Furthermore, I know nothing more about my high school best friend's life now than what she says in her Christmas card. One of my college roommates and I have only seen each other once since graduation, long ago. My former neighbors on the eighteenth floor in Seattle have all moved to the far corners of the country. I lost one of my best girlfriends after my divorce. I still grieve over that one. The truth is that friendships change.

Dr. Irene Levine, in her book *Best Friends Forever: Surviving a Breakup with Your Best Friend,* reports that most of us will make around 396 friends in our lifetime, staying in touch with only one out of every twelve. And we all know that simply staying in touch with others doesn't mean we're friends. In fact, we often stay in touch more consistently with acquaintances than we do the women we consider our real friends, especially if our close friends aren't local, which is increasingly the case as fewer of us live in our childhood or college hometowns.

More recent research pushes it one step further and shows that we are now replacing half our friends every seven years. (Think about who you'd ask to be a bridesmaid in your wedding today, and chances are half of them wouldn't be the ones you'd have asked seven years ago, or would ask seven years from now.) That statistic implores us to admit that we must keep welcoming new friends into our lives, and reminds us that we will be letting go of friendships as well.

Our lives do have a revolving door, whether we want them to or not. As friends go out the door, it's our responsibility to welcome new ones in at the same time.

We're called to a lifetime of friend-making. We don't have the option to just go back to our high school schedule, our college parties, or our favorite summer job to rebuild. We have to become skillful and hopeful in our ability to make friends as adults, in our current lives. In the midst of being a mom, moving for jobs, working from home, paying a mortgage, and feeling sleep-deprived—we need to find the energy and time to connect with a girlfriend. We had best get comfortable with quickly seeing the need!

In fact, even if we do still have a BFF from days long ago, we know now that not only do we need more than one close friend in life, but that no matter what, life stages will force that friendship to become something new, many times over. No one's life stays static, and therefore it's impossible for our friendships to be anything but dynamic. Even a long-term friendship has to find new ways of being.

I was reminded of this when one of my closest friends had her first baby a couple years ago. We both tried. She tried not to talk about the baby all the time. I bought her baby clothes and agreed to be the godmother. But it takes more than good intentions to hold a friendship through that kind of change. A few painful conversations about unmet expectations, and mutual affirmations of how important it was to both of us to make it through this life-changing event, helped us eventually find a new normal. She added a few mom-friends to her circle; I made sure I had girlfriends who were emotionally present for me when she was consumed. We made it. We're still close friends. It became something new.

More important than anything, then, is to not only know how to start new friendships, but to also know how to enhance, repair, transition, and end others. No matter how much we want that one group of friends that will never change, we will still need to know the art of holding friendships with an open hand, allowing people to come in and out of our lives with grace. The ebbs and flows should not detract from who we are, but add to who we are. For whatever time our paths cross we can be sure that those who have known us are better off for that time together.

Knowing that most friendships aren't forever invites us to forgive ourselves for those relationships that didn't live up to the fairy tale. It's not that we shouldn't strive to be loving and committed in our relationships, but for most of them the word *forever* simply won't apply. We must give ourselves as much grace as we can, separating our ideas about our likability from whether or not our friendships prove to be permanent. The two are not the same.

The truth is that we all want to be beautiful, happy, powerful, loving, and friendly women. And we're all doing the best we can on that journey. But that doesn't mean that all of us can travel together, intimately, forever. We have undoubtedly lost a few friends. Two likable women can have valid reasons to move on and still be likable. It's normal. That doesn't reflect on our ability to make new friends and love others well.

Misunderstanding #3: How a Lack of Friends Reflects on Us

It is hard to say, "I need friends."

We associate loneliness or a sense of social disconnection with *those* people. We picture some angry, hurt, unfriendly, socially awkward, and unlovable woman sitting in a dark house, with the curtains closed, alone. Maybe with a dozen cats.

We aren't rushing to picture ourselves as needing new friends. Instead, our egos remind us how likable we are, how friendly and fun we can be, and how much we have to offer someone. With defensive speed, we'll begin to name a few people we'd call friends, brushing away the nagging voice that prompts us to admit it's been a while since we've talked to them. Our self-image equates loneliness with unlikability, as though the two go hand in hand. They do not. The most beautiful, loved, respected, powerful, outgoing, social, networked, busy, famous, important, and wealthy among us know loneliness. Sometimes more so.

Nonetheless, the admission that we need new friends can be hard to confess. We're afraid that we might somehow be misinterpreted as meaning, "No one likes me," or "I have no friends." We don't want to look like we're lonely, much less actually *be* lonely. We don't want to have needs that aren't yet met. We don't want to risk taking it personally—perhaps making ourselves feel worse that it's our fault that we're in this situation.

We're more at ease saying that we need more money, need to lose weight, or need to find balance in our lives. We're even perfectly willing to tell people we're single and looking for love. (I still remember when we hid the fact that we had met our dates online! Today we comfortably accept that twenty percent of all couples meet on sites like match.com, and there's almost more shame in someone being unwilling to try it than not.) But admitting that we might need more friends still stops most of us in our tracks. We are shy to admit when we're on the search.

"The perception is that being proactive about making friends is inauthentic," says Rachel Bertsche in her book, *MWF Seeking BFF: My Yearlong Search for a New Best Friend*. Two years after moving to Chicago she decided to intentionally friend-date for a year in an attempt to create a local BFF. Her story was like a coming-out in a world that isn't yet used to us publicly admitting that we are on the friend hunt.

But needing new friends is normal.

It's normal in the same way that needing to move to a new town to start school or to start a new job is normal; in the same way many of us will go through more than one significant romantic relationship even after we hoped we'd found "the one." Life does change. Our relationships change. Our needs change—for all of us, no matter how good we are, how balanced we are, or how healthy we are. Life changes are what we all experience.

Life changes, indeed, seem to be the one constant in life. No matter how good the friendships are that we co-create, it seems we often will still have that sign in our window that says, "Now hiring."

I needed new friends in graduate school back in Michigan where all my seminary classes seemed to be made up of men. Two years later when I moved to Seattle to pastor my first church, I had to do the friendship hunt all over again—this time made harder due to the new title that seemed to scare off many women. A couple years later when I went through my divorce, I discovered that the event seemed to throw my friends all up in the air and it took several months to really see who landed where. That life change seemed to cause a friendship shuffle in a way I would have never been able to predict. Another move to Southern California would invite the opportunity all over again to figure out how to make new friends in my new life. And then I was standing there on Polk Street in San Francisco wondering if I had it in me to do it yet again.

And I'm not alone in this need.

There are many wake-up calls alerting us to the times we may need new friends. Moves are not among the least of them. With Americans moving on average every five years, we barely have time to enjoy the friends we just made before it seems either they or us are moving away.

My youngest sister, Katrina, talked several of her college friends into moving to Portland after they all graduated, which helped her not need to make as many new friends in a new city. I thought that strategy was brilliant until she and her husband moved to Amsterdam a couple years later and it became clear that she couldn't convince all her friends to move every time she did.

My other sister, Kerry, moved her young family to Tampa a few years ago for her husband's job and—even with jumping into mother's groups, home association boards, and parent-teacher associations—has found it hard to replace the friends she left behind. She quickly found women who were friendly, but it took several years before she felt the support of a local best friend.

The friend search doesn't get easier with age, either. My stepmom shared honestly about the depression she faced in her fifties when she uprooted her life from decades in Colorado to an entirely different culture in Michigan. She says it took about five years to form the deep friendships she enjoys now. And my Nana, in her eighties, still writes to me of loneliness in her retirement center, where she moved several years ago after becoming a widow, to be closer to her sister. Even having a family member nearby doesn't replace all the lifetime friends she may never see again.

Beyond moves, there are countless other life changes that can just as easily trigger the desire to invite new people into our lives. Relationship break-ups and divorces are among the top wake-up calls, followed by life stages such as marriage, kids, empty nest, and retirement. Sometimes, though, it's a shift in our schedules and priorities as we change jobs, decide to work from home, or choose to explore a new hobby or interest. Often it's a life-changing experience, such as a health diagnosis that stuns us, an alarming event that leaves us shaken, a crisis that feels looming, or a huge loss that kicks us in our gut, that turns our focus toward "what really matters." And sometimes it's less about a change in our lives and more about the fact that our friends' lives have changed—they all had kids, moved to the suburbs, aren't married anymore, changed religions, retired, or became unavailable due to their own dramas—and we realize we need to step back into active friend-making.

All of these are simply stages of life that most of us go through. While a couple of our friendships might survive as we make these changes and transitions, the truth is that we all need to be constantly replenishing our circle of friends to ensure that it's meaningful for who we are now. As we mature, grow, and dream, we are in a constant process of becoming. There should be no shame attached to the fact that life changes will inspire us to connect with different women, in different ways, at different times.

Needing new friends is normal.

Misunderstanding #4: What Friendship Actually Takes

I think one of the other reasons we hold too long to the myth that this process should feel automatic is because it makes us feel better if we don't currently have the friendships we want. We can simply shrug our shoulders and blame fate, assuming we just haven't met the right woman for this stage of our lives yet. It somehow seems easier to keep waiting for someone to fall from the sky who already knows us and loves us, than to figure out how to meet strangers and become friends without the help of recess.

But it's damaging to keep pretending that friendships are something done to us, rather than something we make happen. Damaging because nearly half of us report being only one confidante away from social isolation. Many of us don't even have that one confidante. This is a significant factor in the increasing depression in women. It's why we seem more net-worked than ever, and yet, ironically, lonelier. It's why we know more people, and yet seem to be known by none. We just keep hoping and waiting.

We all know how many potential friendships haven't become realized because we dropped the ball. We waited for someone else to pursue us. We waited for someone else to "just make it happen." We waited for them to want us. We waited too long to follow up, and then felt silly getting back in touch. In other words, we waited for friend-making to feel easier, more natural, and more automatic.

We'd never admit that we're hoping that she just miraculously shows up on our doorstep announcing that she is our new best friend. But in some ways we want just that. We want to know her when we see her. And we want her to know it in the same second that we do so that we don't ever risk it not feeling completely mutual. And then we hope that somehow our busy schedules will just free up, that she'll fit right into our openings, and that we can just go on singing our theme song, "Believe it or not, it's just me."

But friendships don't just happen. We make them happen.

And not only have we done it before, but we must do it again.

From Polk Street to Present

And I did do it again.

I didn't ever walk up to a group of women in a café and offer myself as their newest addition, but I did eventually create my own local circles of friends.

I will forever love my far-flung friends across this country who "go back" with me—women who knew me intimately at another time. But at some point we also have to start at the beginning with a few new ones.

And this book is about that entire process.

CHOOSE TO HOLD FRIENDSHIP WITH OPEN HANDS

Anyone who hangs out with me for long will hear me say "hold it with an open hand." It's a hand gesture where each hand is cupped, palms up, relaxed in a way, and yet intentional enough that I could bring water to my lips with those fingers if needed. The very act of making those open hands has become my own little mantra in life, inviting my heart to reflect the handmade sign.

For when I see those open hands, I am reminded of all that they can do, and conversely what they cannot.

If my hands are open, then that means they are *not* limp, by my side, unwilling, unnoticing, or incapable of being ready to receive.

If my hands are open, they are *not* clinging, fists tight, trying to hold, control, keep, or grasp.

If my hands are open, they are *not* palms out, pushing away, putting up walls, resisting, defending, refusing to let life in.

If my hands are open, they are *not* flat and stretched, unable to hold anything of value, refusing to be a safe container for that which is given in my life.

If my hands are open, they are *not* trying to stretch the fingers ever wider to hold more and more, where as the fingers spread in greed, the gifts begin to seep out like sand through the cracks.

I want to step into life with gentle, but firmly cupped, hands, not needing to grab, push, cling, force, or refuse. Rather, I show up with a readiness that says I will look for things to hold, people to love, life to relish, moments to enjoy, gifts to appreciate.

Open hands remind me that I am deserving of goodness. I am worthy, willing, and capable. I refuse to let past rejection, fears, insecurities, and previous losses stop me from being ready to receive this time. I value living life fully and I will look for moments to cherish and love.

Open hands remind me that if I give the gifts of goodness the freedom to land in my life, then those gifts have that same freedom to fly away in their own time. I can't not control one and then try to control the other. An airport cannot choose to only accept arrivals and not departures; there are valid times for travel in both directions. I cannot force people to stay here longer, any more than I can force time to stand still. I cannot manipulate, coerce, charm, or trap gifts into lasting forever.

And should I ever be tempted to close my hand around something, I will inevitably close my hand to other gifts as well. The very gesture of trying to keep one thing can be the gesture that prevents other good things from coming our way.

Sometimes we're so focused on refusing to let go of one thing that we miss other opportunities. We hold so tight that we suffocate the very breath that we never wanted to lose. With gripped hands we squish the bug we were trying to save, melt the chocolate we wanted for later, or find fingernail marks in our skin because we clenched too hard. That which we wanted to keep, we lost anyhow. And now our hands are just messy and sore.

Open hands remind me to engage, to not give up, to expect, to hope, and to cherish. They teach me to let go, to unclench, to find peace. They offer me moments of joy and loss, inviting me to find contentment in both.

My open hands invite me to embrace, hug, and cherish the people in my life now.

My open hands remind me to feel grateful for those relationships even when they have flown away.

My open hands are a visual promise that I can anticipate a future filled with more love.

Not everything is meant to last forever. Emotional growth is about learning to hold gratitude for the blessings—those blessings that I have now, the ones I have had, and those that are still to come.

LEARN THE CIRCLES OF CONNECTEDNESS:
What Are the Five Types of Friends?

JULIANA · AILN · LYNNE · ROBIN · JACQUELYN · NANCY · CHRISTINA · KYM · ANGIE

I t's one thing to finally whisper the truth, "I need new friends." It's another to actually know what we mean when we say it.

When we say we want friends, it's usually some form of the *Sex and the City* foursome that we imagine. Not that our lives are all Jimmy Choo shoes, Cosmo's, and sex stories, but the idea of a small group of women who can be both our social life and our confidantes is appealing. It looks comfortable, safe, and meaningful.

However, how we actually use the word "friend" most frequently is in reference to anyone we feel linked to, such as, "Oh I have a friend who works there that I can introduce you to." In this day of Facebook and all things social media, the word includes everyone who we've ever met, connected with online, or who is networked to someone else we know.

There are a thousand shades of relationship between an acquaintance and a long-term best friend. The distinctions between people we're *friendly with* and *friendships we've developed* are significant.

The importance of recognizing the vast spectrum of friendship nuances not only guides us to better articulate what our personal needs are right now, but also helps us recognize that to experience the bond the *Sex and the City* women share might require us to start by just being friendly with a stranger.

WHAT ARE THE DIFFERENT KINDS OF FRIENDSHIPS?

The strength of our friendship isn't as dependent on how much we like each other, but more on how much time we spend together developing our friendship in broader and deeper ways. I developed the Circles of Connectedness Continuum to help women visualize the varying shades of relationships based on the two primary factors that create friendship: consistency and intimacy. Both are words we'll unpack more in depth in this book, but suffice it to say, consistency is regular time spent together, and intimacy is sharing that extends to a broad range of subjects and increases in vulnerability.

When we see that there are five types of friendships, we can more clearly assess each friendship to better understand what Circle it belongs in, what healthy expectations accompany friends in that circle, and how to increase the commitment to each other, if we want.

Shasta's Circles of Connectedness

The Continuum begins on the left with the most casual of friends and moves to the right as the attachment and commitment deepens.

In describing each Circle, I'll begin with the two on the left side, skipping over to the two on the right side, and ending with the one in the middle.

I'm going to ask you, at the end of this chapter, to identify your current relationships on this Continuum so you can see which Circles are full of friends and which ones might reveal some loneliness. We all tend to have some Circles that are easier for us to fill and nurture, and others that we may not even know we neglect. There are some clear parameters to each Circle, but how we categorize any given friend will depend on our subjective sense of the bond between us.

LEFT-SIDE FRIENDS

Contact Friends

We are friendly when we see them in our shared context, but we have limited consistency and limited intimacy. We are somehow linked to them because we went to school together, because a mutual friend introduced us, or because our kids play together on a local sports team. We consider these individuals as friends, in the most casual sense of the word.

This is not the same as all acquaintances, though. For example, when I attend my monthly Bay Area Coaches Association meeting, I could probably name at least twenty of the other coaches, being friendly to them all. But my Contact Friends would be the three to four other coaches that I gravitate to each month, making sure I catch up with them before or after the program. We consider each other friends, see each other monthly, have a lot in common, and respect each other—but they are Contact Friends in that our relationship is based upon seeing each other in those shared meetings. If one of us stopped attending, we haven't yet created any other structures—or ways of being together—so it's likely that we wouldn't continue connecting.

In this category there is little expectation that we would remember the name of their spouse or even know if they have kids, and we certainly aren't expected to send them birthday cards or invite them over for dinner. These aren't the friends we think to call when we're hurting or lonely. In fact we'd probably never call without a specific purpose or question in mind, and almost always in regards to the subject that we already have in common.

But that doesn't mean these aren't important friends to have. They serve fundamental purposes in our lives. For one thing, they give us a sense of belonging in the context in which we know them. We might look forward to an annual convention because we have a Contact Friend or two who will be there, saving us from being among all strangers. Attending church is more enjoyable when it gives us the chance to catch up a bit with another Contact Friend, sharing what we've each been up to since the last service. We are happy that a Contact Friend volunteers at the same place we do because she makes our participation more fun. We're appreciative to have a Contact Friend in our weekly art class because we have a friend to chat with every Tuesday night while waiting for the teacher. We're always grateful to see that Contact Friend standing in the parking lot giving us someone to talk with while we both wait for our kids to get out of school. These friends offer us a sense of safety and support in various settings.

They may also provide a network of resources. These friends may be able to get our résumé into the hands of someone they know, or they may be willing to re-tweet our upcoming seminar to all their contacts. They can recommend health care providers, tell us what they love about their gym, or rave about a new online shoe store. They will make sure we hear about interesting new restaurants, a parenting book they appreciated, or a new movie. Intimate these topics are not; helpful they most definitely can be.

All friendships start in this category. And it's safe to say that the vast majority of them will stay in this Circle. Or we may eventually drift apart if we move on to another group or setting. There is no expectation that they will all develop into deeper friends but it doesn't mean they're not real if they remain in the Contact Circle. We can honor what these friendships are in our lives just where they are.

But some, a select few, may move into the next stage.

Common Friends

We are increasing either our consistency or our intimacy with these women, getting to know them better largely in the area we have in common. The difference between women in the Common Friends Circle and the Contact Circle is that we spend time with these women in more intentional and personal ways, developing a friendship that feels more substantial. We are most likely feeling close to them because we see them more often—daily at work or weekly in a small group, or because we are building our trust—sharing more honestly and vulnerably.

To illustrate: if we saw the same woman in our yoga class consistently enough that we regularly made small talk in the locker room after class we would be Contact Friends. Showing up at class is more fun because we see someone familiar there with whom we can whine about how hard certain poses are to master and share where we bought our flattering yoga pants. For that person to develop into a Common Friend our connection would advance from engaging in locker room chitchat to the two of us drinking smoothies or tea for an hour after class on occasion.

We can find these Common Friends in moms groups, at work, at choir rehearsal, or in a club. We know these individuals well within the area we have in common. In other words, we may see them more frequently than our Contact Friends, or our conversations may feel more personal and consequential. They are definitely more than just the person we gravitate toward; they are also people we feel connected with and close to.

We're not measuring how much we like the other person, rather how much time we spend with them and whether our relationship centers more or less around one commonality.

In fact, in this Circle reside some women I admire tons. I think of Teri who's the spouse of my husband's best friend. I think of Peggy, the wife of a couple that we try to eat dinner with at least every other month. I would trust either of these women with any burden I felt and I so enjoy our time together whenever it occurs. But they show up in this Circle because I don't have a relationship with them outside of my husband. When I spend time with them, it's as couples. I know I could call them if needed and they'd be there for me instantly, but we haven't practiced being friends outside of the structure—our current way of being together—that brought us together in the first place.

In this category, no matter what the area of commonality, the bond is formed over something we share. We connect because we have found common ground.

The Common Friends Circle is a super important Circle in our lives. When we say we want new friends, we are often looking for someone who is "like me," so finding someone with a common interest is a first step.

Here are a few reasons that we seek out Common Friends:

- When all our friends seem to be dating or married, we may decide we need more single girlfriends.
- If we want to lose weight, we may look for someone to share that goal with us.
- As new mothers, we need the camaraderie of other women going through this life-changing experience at the same time.
- Because we have a certain belief system or background we may want someone who shares our values, our political viewpoints, or our ethnicity to hang out with.

- The loss of a child or another life-changing tragedy may cause us to look for friends in a support group, people who can help understand the road we're facing.

Of course there can be a range of depth and vulnerability depending on the shared experience. Context determines what we share. We will probably share more—or different—details with a friend from our AA group than we do with our weekend scrapbooking friend. We may share our fears around weight loss with our workout friend that we wouldn't share with our church friend, and we undoubtedly talk with our church friend about beliefs and questions that we'd never broach with our girlfriend at the gym. Our conversations may be deep, honest, and intimate, but our friendship will stay in the Common Friends Circle, either if the topics we discuss are limited primarily to the common interest we share or if our ways of being together are inconsistent enough to not quite feel as close to our Common Friends as we do with our friends on the Right Side of the Continuum.

For example, we may find that the woman from the yoga studio develops into a Common Friend when we get smoothies every Monday after class. We can talk about health, fitness, weight loss, favorite teachers, challenging poses, and perhaps even the impact of yoga on our spirituality. But we may find we have little else in common with her beyond our shared yoga routine. Maybe she's ten years older, divorced, holds opposite political views to our own, and is a homebody, whereas we like outdoor adventures, have young kids, and spend most of our free time with our husband. Does that mean we shouldn't be friends? Not at all. We motivate each other on our respective health journeys. It's meaningful. If we enjoy it, we should continue to relish our time together in this area of shared interest.

Friendships don't have to be all or nothing. It's not BFF or bust. Friends who matter to us in one particular life area are just as important and can feed us in that area, probably more than our best friend could. No one person will share all of our interests and go through the same life stages simultaneously with us. At different times, different women help us meet different needs. That's no small gift. We hold gratitude in our hearts for each of them.

RIGHT-SIDE FRIENDS

I'll return to the middle Circle—Confirmed Friends—in a minute. First I want to discuss the two circles on the Right Side of the Continuum. When we cross over to the Right Side, these friendships must have both strong consistency and strong intimacy. On the Left Side, those two factors were limited in our Contact Circle, or only one out of the two was present in our Common Circle.

So, jumping over to the Right Side of this Continuum, let's talk about the Circle that I call Community Friends.

Community Friends

We spend consistent time together growing the intimacy of our relation-ship. When we become Community Friends we have crossed the lines of our original relationship boundaries with a gym buddy, a book club part-ner, or a work colleague. We now share our lives beyond our initial shared common interest. When we enter into Community Friends territory, we have crossed the lines of our original relationship boundaries so that now it feels normal to invite them to a random concert, check in with them about their weekend plans, or see if they are interested in starting a book club with us.

This is an incredibly meaningful category of friends. These women help us feel rooted, they care about the things we do, and have journeyed through a bit of life with us. They are invited to our big moments in life and cheer for us as we become our best.

I see this Circle as the place where our tribe collects—where we are introducing friends to each other at our parties, expanding our social time together in new ways, and staying up to date on each other's lives in a variety of subjects. These are the people who fit in our living room when it comes time to invite our friends over to celebrate our birthday. If we heard one of them went into the hospital, we'd want to know what we could do to help. This group is bigger than our closest confidantes, but doesn't include friends who are limited to only specific areas of our lives.

Friends eventually move into this Circle when we have regularly spent time with them beyond the area we have in common. The woman we met for smoothies after yoga would stay in the Common Friend category if that were as far as the relationship progressed. But if we ended up connecting and sharing beyond the original area of bonding—yoga and fitness—then the two of us would become Community Friends. Maybe while enjoying our smoothies after class we discover that we share a love of museums but usually go alone. If we decide to start meeting at a museum once a month, then we have now broadened our relationship from "yoga friends" to something more. She now steps into a new area of our life, no longer limited to the label of how we met.

A new Community Friend could be a work colleague (Common Friend) who also loves watching *Grey's Anatomy* with us on Thursday evenings, double-dating with our hubbies on occasional weekends, and ducking out from work together to grab lunch. Maybe a friend of a friend has been a Common Friend for the last year, the mutual friend being our bond. If we start building our own one-on-one friendship with her, we might stop thinking of her as "so-and-so's friend" and more like a friend of ours—making her possibly a Community Friend now.

As we broaden our ways of being together we are ensuring that we have other things connecting us even if the original commonality changes. Adding stronger glue to our relationship communicates that this person is important enough to practice being friends in a new context, creating new structures that can hold our friendship.

So should we ever decide we can't afford yoga classes anymore, our friendship continues at the museums. If we change jobs and no longer work with her, our friendship continues since we had already taken the friendship home to TV nights. And if the friend that introduced us to each other moves away, we already know how to get together without her. Our church friend can stop attending church, but we still have a friendship that is based on other things. Our single friend can get married and we'll still want her in our life even if she no longer shares a common relationship status with us. Our kids, who met in our moms group, may not be friends or attend the same school anymore, but we will still be friends with the other mom since we built a friendship that expanded beyond the kids getting together to play. We may have retired years before she'll be able to, but our relationship can continue regardless of whether we are both in the workforce or not.

This is not to say that losing commonality is necessarily easy, or that there won't be a transition period as the relationship shifts to find a "new normal." Clearly, when a big area of bonding is no longer there, we may not see each other as much, we may change what we talk about a bit, and we may have to reset some expectations. But the point is that these are friends who matter enough to us to go through that transition.

It's sometimes hard to know ahead of time who these people will be. It's easy in our entrepreneurs' small group to think all six of us are close and that we'd be friends with any of them even if we were no longer running our own business. But more often than not—while we can wish all those friendships would survive if we no longer met with the group—if we haven't built in the structure of bonding outside of that time, then we shouldn't be surprised when they're not all knocking down our door to connect with us later.

I see it happen frequently in churches when someone stops attending and then feels hurt if no one ever follows up with her. But if the church friends were only Common Friends, where they only had weekend services in common, then it's not surprising that when one stops attending those services, their friendships dissipate. If we step outside of the one structure—a scheduled time, place, or interest—that brought us together then we are risking those relationships. If we can broaden those Common Friendships before the change occurs, we'll have a foundation on which to continue and grow our relationship outside of church. That's our responsibility, if those friendships are important to us to maintain and grow.

Sometimes it's not until after we've lost the common connection that we realize, "I miss that person." So maybe we never became friends outside of work with someone until she switched careers and we realized we wanted to forge a new way of being together. With some intention, these women can still step into our Community Circle.

Clearly, at the Community Circle stage, we are most likely meeting significant people from other areas of each other's lives, and revealing stories to one another beyond our original bonding context. We should now know the name of this friend's spouse, how many kids she has, and where she grew up. We know things about her that have nothing to do with how we met—we have shared beyond the original connection, found additional points of bonding, and established our own patterns of spending time together.

This is a Circle that not only holds meaningful and impressive women that we consider really good friends, many of them also might someday become our best friends. We are journeying through life together, sharing deeply and honestly, and enjoying each other's presence. But I reserve the last circle for the women with whom I am committed to nurturing a very consistent, meaningful friendship—it's a commitment I simply cannot make to more than three to five women at a time.

Committed Friends

We intimately and consistently share our lives with each other. The Committed Circle on the far Right of the Continuum is reserved for the friends with whom we regularly share our feelings and for whom we have a mutual commitment to be present, no matter what.

The Committed Circle is our BFF Circle, and it includes a handful of tried-and-true girlfriends. Women in this Circle are the *Sex and the City* foursome, the Monica/Rachel/Phoebe of *Friends,* the neighbors of *Desperate Housewives,* the iconic *Golden Girls*—a cluster of consistent women who are committed to us no matter what life changes bring. They don't all have to know each other, but they undoubtedly hear us talk about each other, and those who are local will definitely meet up at some of our special events.

The term Committed is purposeful. These are the friends we intentionally make room for in our life on a regular basis. These are the women for whom we would drop what we're doing, when needed, to be there for her. These are the women whose birthdays we plan around, whose relationships we know about, and whose dreams we hold close. And they do the same for us.

Women don't start out as friends in this category—even if we loved them instantly. We may have bonded as Common Friends because of our kids, or because we worked at the same place, or we were both single—but these are now the friends with whom our bond is stronger than that commonality. They could switch jobs, get married, change interests, move away, or the kids could all grow up, but we would still be in each other's lives. Regularly.

Having women friends in this Circle requires that we have developed patterns of spending time together, have shared extensively about our life, and would want to introduce important people to each other—all actions that take intention and time.

When we ache for belonging, it's typically this group that we need in our lives. If we haven't yet built our friendships up to this place of commitment, we are at risk of expecting women in the other Circles of our lives to behave in this way. This unrealistic expectation often results in hurt feelings and disappointment. But we cannot expect commitment and intimacy to just be there—both are experiences that require a process.

At best, these women have actually gone through some transitions with us. At the minimum, we believe they will do so if it's ever required. A reminder, though: in the deepest of the deep, where our BFF's—Best Friends Forever—are held, the word "forever" is still not meant to be literal. It is beautiful that in this Circle we hold the intention for that longevity, much as we do in our marriage vows, but that doesn't prevent friendships from shifting. There will be times where one or more of these women move back into other Circles.

For example, I used to have five women I'd have listed in this Circle, but when I moved away from where I met them, I simply couldn't keep up with all five of them with the same weekly frequency we were used to, and still have energy or time to make the new local friends I knew I needed. They are still in my life and I know them intimately. But, for the most part, they have moved back to the middle Circle—Confirmed Friends—which is the fulcrum on our Continuum.

Confirmed Friends

We share a history with these friends that maintains our intimacy, but our connection is not consistent. These are the friends we used to live close to and love but only talk to occasionally now. These are the women with whom we know we can pick up where we left off. They are dear to us and we will stay in touch occasionally, but they are not engaged in our daily lives and in the creation of regular new memories together.

This middle Circle is reserved for the friends with whom the relationship goes much deeper than the Circles on the Left Side—we in fact would have at one point placed them on the Right Side of our Continuum—but we no longer have the regular contact with them that we reserve for our Right-Side Friends.

These friends serve beautiful purposes in our lives: they share a history with us. They know who we used to be. They can say "Remember when . . ." and have us tapping into our former self within moments. These are women we know who, if we needed them, we could call them. We feel supported by them even if we haven't spoken in a while.

The Confirmed Friends Circle, however, is not for everyone we used to know. Rather, it is for women who were once Committed Friends, but due to life changes (usually a move) we no longer have consistency with them. But we want to stay connected. They may be childhood friends, college roommates, a fellow intern from a first job, or any woman with whom we developed a friendship but with whom we no longer interact in the same deep and regular way.

For women to be in this Circle, it is necessary to stay in touch with them, even occasionally. We may only talk once or twice a year, but we still talk. We aren't tracking all former friends, but current friends that still contribute to our sense of community, of being known. We want to be honest with that difference.

My Confirmed Friends are those I know I would call if something big happened in my life and I needed outside support. I know these women love me and would want to hear from me. We can automatically pick up where we left off, even if it's through occasional random Facebook updates, Christmas cards, or long voice mails left in a game of phone tag. The point is that, at an earlier time, we built the intimacy that allows us to still feel close even without the current consistency.

SHASTA'S FIVE CIRCLES OF CONNECTEDNESS

Shasta's Circles of Connectedness

Contact Friends: limited intimacy, limited consistency
Common Friends: an increase in either consistency or intimacy
Confirmed Friends: high intimacy, low consistency
Community Friends: increased intimacy and consistency
Committed Friends: highest intimacy, high consistency

HOW TO IDENTIFY OUR CIRCLES

Together these five Friendship Circles comprise our community. The women in each Circle serve different purposes, feeding our life in different ways. By clearly seeing what types of friends we currently have, we can step into two vital feelings: appreciation for those relationships we have fostered, and clarified hope for what we anticipate creating.

Appreciation for our current friends is significant. It reminds us that even though we may need to add more friends to our lives, it is not because we have no friends. We have been loved well in many ways, and at different times. We will want to intentionally maintain these relationships, even as we grow new ones.

And evaluating our current Circles of Connectedness will help us see what types of relationships we're hungering to still experience. For example, by acknowledging that some of the women you name as friends may actually be Common Friends ("work friends" or "moms group friends") or Confirmed Friends (with whom you haven't really connected in years) you may learn that you're longing for more local, consistent, and intimate friendships.

Identifying the different types of friends will also clarify our understanding of what we can expect from them (no wonder she doesn't remember our birthday—she's on the Left Side of the Continuum) and how we might best move certain people into preferred categories. When we can visually see that there is a process to our friendships, we can better identify which ones are perfect where they are, letting go of unnecessary expectations, and better figure out with whom we may want to increase consistency or intimacy.

Here are some tips that will be helpful for you when assigning each of your friends to the appropriate Circle.

1) Go for current, not past, status.

Remember that there will be dozens of times in life when friendships shift. So you need to consciously evaluate your friendships for what they are currently. Doing so doesn't minimize how much people have meant to you or how much you appreciate them; it simply recognizes that today's needs may be different than last year's.

Let me give you some examples from my own friendship continuum. There are a few women I used to be more consistent and more intimate with. None of them live local to me anymore. It would be easy to place them all in my Confirmed Circle just because I don't see them very often. But that would be a mistake. I need to look at the relationship we have today, evaluating for both the frequency and the intimacy of our contact.

Valerie was one of my closest friends in college. We can both look back at photos and point out how much fun we had gaining the stereotypical "freshman fifteen" together. Our memories include eating late-night cheesecake and nachos at Claim Jumpers Restaurant while studying, surviving on daily baguettes while traveling in Paris, and cooking up big pasta meals for friends at her parents' house. She was decidedly in my Committed Circle back then. Distance and marriages soon separated us, at which time she became a Confirmed Friend for several years, since we still stayed in touch sporadically.

However, two years ago we made a decision to travel to see each other at least two or three times a year; we're doing better at staying in touch now, and we're both sharing deeply and honestly about our lives. Today I'd say she's moved into my Community Friend Circle. And, if we ever lived in close proximity again, or did a better job talking on the phone more regularly she'd easily move into my Committed Circle.

Compare that to my roommate for two years in college. I still love that girl—her boldness and her vivaciousness in living fully and deeply wows me. She travels, produces TV shows, and entertains me with her blog, and yet we are no longer in touch. Our occasional comments on each other's social media pages just skim the surface. For that reason, she wouldn't even be in my Confirmed Circle since she's not someone I would call to share news with. I don't think I even have her phone number in my cell phone. So, although I do not admire her any less, and I still value all the fabulous memories we shared, today she'd be in my Contact Friends list. I consider her a friend who I could definitely contact if I needed something, but just because we used to be roommates doesn't mean we'll stay close forever.

Next, take Sherilyn as an excellent example of someone who could have easily been in my Confirmed Friends Circle since she lives halfway across the country in the suburbs of Texas. I was a classmate at seminary with her husband, and with our spouses we soon became couple-friends during graduate school and into our first churches together.

At first glance, one might think we have very little in common anymore since I'm no longer a pastor in any local church, nor married to the same man who was a part of our shared history. She's still a pastor's wife and currently a stay-at-home mom to three kids. Her stories are filled with church activities and decisions about whether she wants to homeschool her kids; my life in urban San Francisco couldn't be more different—I talk about TV interviews I'm doing this week and the struggles of running a company.

We certainly have reasons to drift apart, given how our lives have diverged. However, we made a decision several years ago to talk on the phone every Wednesday at noon. (If you're "starting from scratch" with many new friends, you may benefit from reconnecting as often as you can during this time to a Confirmed Friend—someone who doesn't live nearby but loves you because of past bonds. Having someone you can share and update and process with is important while you take the time to build new friends to that point.)

It's rare for me to have long-distance friends in that most intimate of Circles, and I certainly wouldn't want more than one or two of them to not live nearby. But because we have committed to consistency, Sherilyn knows some of the smallest details about what's going on in my life. We have important history together and sincerely respect each other's different lives. She is one of the wisest friends I have, one who trained as a life coach before that field was even trendy. And I find that it's meaningful to have a friend who isn't in the thick of things and has an objectivity that comes with that distance. Those weekly conversations keep her as one of my closest friends, definitely in my Committed Circle.

These three women could on the surface appear to be Confirmed Friends—women with whom I used to be local and intimate. But at the moment, none of them are actually in that Circle, each landing in a different place on my continuum.

Now let's look at an example of a friend who is currently in my Confirmed Circle. Tonya was also a roommate of mine—we witnessed each other falling in love and getting our hearts broken, and we helped each other pack for more than one move. Both in college and again several years ago after my divorce, she was in my Committed Circle, someone I cherished as a BFF. But now she's moved to the Confirmed Circle. We no longer update each other regularly on our lives, and when we do visit we spend more time catching up than really being intimate and revealing. But honoring her as my Confirmed Friend Circle doesn't diminish how much I adore her as one of the most sincere and sweetest women I'll ever know, admire her as a mom, appreciate how well she has loved me through some hard times, or value the plethora of memories we've made over the years. She is still someone I would call to update if something big happened in my life, and she'll still look me up every time she's in the area visiting family so we can catch up for an hour or two. And in different circumstances, we could most definitely move right back into the Committed Circle.

Does that help you as you evaluate some of your friendships by seeing how I categorize mine? It is a subjective process. Think carefully about how you're experiencing these relationships now—today—rather than thinking about how much you love these women or how long you've known them.

2) Go for reality, not potential.

On the flip side of women we've known forever are women we've just met. Again, we shouldn't categorize women based on how we feel about them, but rather on how we're actually engaging in friendship. Just because you meet someone and feel an instant chemistry doesn't make you Committed Friends. No matter how wonderful someone is, how much you have in common, how much she seems to like you too, or how much you want to get to know her—evaluate your friendship on the basis of the connection you actually have, not the one you hope to have.

Judy is a recent new friend of mine. After I complimented her on her striking red bag at a writers conference, we found ourselves looking for each other's familiar faces between workshop sessions. She is fifteen years older than I, lives outside San Francisco (where I live), and is beautiful enough to intimidate the best of us. But moments of conversation left me wanting to know her better. We have since scheduled a couple of lunches, and went so far as to introduce our men to each other over a double-date dinner in my home. I adore her and feel close to her, trusting her implicitly.

But BFF's we are not. Yet. Maybe we will be by the time you read this book! Or maybe we won't. We both have many other meaningful friend-ships, so perhaps we will remain as Common Friends who cheer each other on in our writing. (There is no one I love e-mailing updates of my book to more than her!) Or maybe, when my husband and I go spend a weekend away with Judy and her boyfriend, we'll all decide we simply have to see each other more regularly. Either way, I'm okay with how it plays out. She is someone that I could see becoming a Committed Friend, but someone I will love just as much should that not happen. The point is that when I fill out my friendship continuum, I will evaluate this friendship for what it is today, not what I think it could become. For now, she is in my Common Friends Circle because we share passions for writing good books and lov-ing great men.

Another example that comes to mind is how easy it might be for us to assume that our social group is our Community Circle, when most of them might actually belong in the Common Circle. One of my friends belongs to a group of about five families whose kids all go to the same school. They all take turns hosting Sunday barbecues, babysitting each other's kids for get-away weekends, and getting together for big football games. In some sense, our social groups may feel like our tribe—our Community Circle. But it's unlikely that everyone in these groups falls into our Community Circle, where sharing is deep and broad. It's more realistic that maybe only one or two of them fit on the Right Side, the rest being Common Friends. Know-ing they are Common Friends helps us enjoy all that we do share with each other without putting unrealistic expectations on each other. That aware-ness will explain why we don't feel safe telling all of them something pri-vate for fear it will make its way to more people, or why we don't always get together with each of them on their own. Instead, we allow most of them to stay in our Common Circle—a super valuable group of people—and we will look to see if there are a few of them we can foster a deeper relationship with outside of our group time.

We will honor friendships for where they are now, not where we wish they were or where we think they can go.

3) Go for your experience, not hers.

One thing we do well as women is take other people's feelings into consideration—sometimes to a fault. This is one exercise where you do not need to hesitate to place a woman in one category even if you think she'd place your friendship in a different circle. This exercise is personal and subjective, so the only experience we're focusing on now is ours.

There are women who might feel closer to me than I do to them. Maybe I've coached them or been their pastor, so they've shared things with me that bonds them to me. But that doesn't necessarily mean that they are the women I confide in. Or there are those who consider me a Community Friend while I consider them a Common Friend. And that's okay.

On the other side, maybe there's someone you think of as your closest friend, but you're unsure if she'd list you in her top five friends, since she seems to have so many close friends. Again, it doesn't matter who else she knows or calls a friend—the question right now is only how you experience her. If she's the first person you call to talk about life and you feel she loves you, then maybe she belongs in your Committed Circle regardless of whether she would put you there.

For now, the point of this exercise is for you to decide your experience of the relationship, not to try to guess what the other person's continuum would look like.

4) Go for honesty, not warm-and-fuzzy.

Many women want to avoid this exercise if they sense that some of their Circles are empty or low. If that's true for you, rather than avoiding it or denying it, I invite you to actually sit with it for a moment. Sadness isn't to be prevented; it's to be heard. That feeling gives you powerful information about what's important to you, what you've cherished that you've lost, and what you still hope to create. That kind of information cannot be bought! I hope you take the risk, even if it produces feelings of sadness. That's okay.

You might even feel angry as you think of certain people who used to be on your list. That, too, gives you information about losses you've grieved (or not yet grieved?), boundaries that were violated, or times you didn't speak up when you wanted to. This, too, is revealing information. And ultimately, to be in healthy friendships, we need to learn to forgive others and ourselves. So knowing there is healing to come is vital information for you.

Maybe you even feel a little fearful because you mistakenly think that this is a reflection of who you are and how lovable you are. It's not. I assure you, many times over, that every single one of us feels loneliness. And in a shifting world, we simply cannot control and hold everything in one place. We can be beautiful in our own way, talented with our unique strengths, funny in our own style, powerful in our own world—and still sometimes have empty Friendship Circles.

Just as hunger pangs, yawns, thirst, and pain are ways for our bodies to say to our brains, "feed me, put me to bed, give me water, care for this injury," being able to feel our disconnection means we are in touch with our souls and can hear the hunger for more meaningful community. This is good. Just as eating breakfast doesn't mean you won't be hungry again in a few hours, our relationships ebb and flow, and we need to be able to hear our hearts prompting us to embrace others in regular and energizing ways.

Almost every amazing weight loss story starts with the person describing that moment when they realized something had to change: they didn't fit into a certain outfit, couldn't complete a specific activity, saw a picture of themselves that shocked them, or had a doctor clearly articulate the impending consequences. What's amazing is that that moment surely wasn't the first picture they saw of themselves, wasn't the first piece of clothing they outgrew, and wasn't their first trip to a doctor's office. Denial is powerful for many for a long time.

But not for us. Not this time. There is no shame when we take this snapshot, or weigh in on the relationship scale. Whatever friendship losses we have grieved or opportunities we wish we had handled differently, the important thing is that right now we are metaphorically stepping on the scale to see our starting point. It doesn't mean we'll stay here. It means we're ready to move toward our ideal.

So embrace your feelings, whatever they are. Own them. Gather the information that comes with them. Then congratulate yourself that you're now doing something that will help you lean into more meaningful community.

IDENTIFYING OUR CIRCLES

I hope you feel ready now to start listing your friends along the Continuum.

Shasta's Circles of Connectedness

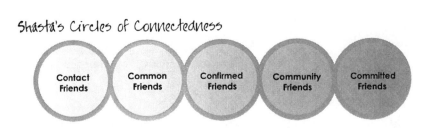

Take the first name that comes into your head and ask yourself: "Where does this person fit on this Continuum right now based on the relationship we share?" And then move through other names that come to mind, placing them all into the various Circles. (There is a free worksheet you can download at http://goodies.ShastaNelson.com/.)

This step is important. It's your way of affirming the love you've helped foster around you. It's also beautiful for helping state your desire. It's honoring to us when we can acknowledge what we feel.

This chapter and the next one provide language for where your lack of connection may be coming from. The following chapter will help you determine where you want your relationships to go. And the rest of the book is basically about moving the right friendships toward that. A year from now can look very different! I'm so glad we're on the journey.

To close, I invite you to place your hand on the names of all your friends and state out loud *"I am grateful for these people who enhance my life, and I eagerly look forward to not only growing these relationships in whatever ways will be meaningful, but also inviting new ones in."*

DETERMINE THE NEED:
Evaluating My Friendship Circles

When I moved to San Francisco, I initially felt content with my current circle of friends, although none were local. That's not to say that I didn't want to meet new people or find a social circle, but I couldn't fathom starting all over in building up the meaningful friendships I had already co-created with the friends I left behind. I feared that making new friends would not only be unsatisfying in comparison, but would also consume my limited time and energy, which I wanted to use to maintain my current friendships.

Fast-forward several months and it was a different story.

I would soon be admitting that I'd rather be sitting in a café swapping stories with real live people than coming up with witty social media updates, giving thumbs-up to my friends' photos, leaving long voice mails, and sitting down with good intentions to write that lengthy e-mail. I wanted to literally toast my new successful project, not just tell someone about it. I wanted someone to come shopping with me for the perfect dress, not just send her a photo from the dressing room. I wanted to watch a movie with someone, not just talk about it afterward.

I had amazing friends strewn across the country; nonetheless, I was a candidate for wanting friendships of a different kind. I felt the pang of loneliness.

We usually aren't lonely because our entire Continuum is empty. Instead, it's usually because one of our Circles has shifted recently and our heart is trying to tell us that we have room in our lives for more current connection.

In my case, I had amazing friends elsewhere in the country, but I still experienced loneliness because none of them lived nearby.

WHAT MY NEED MAY LOOK LIKE

Another shade of loneliness can be illustrated by the experience of my friend Daneen, a woman who is the consummate hostess, always inviting, loving, and serving people. Her roots have long been planted in the Bay Area, her connections extend far-and-wide, and her home welcomes people for many meals and tea breaks throughout the week.

One minute she had all the love and community she could have ever wanted. Fast-forward nine months, maybe less, and as the new role of impending motherhood settled in her belly, she found herself craving conversations with others who knew that specific transformative experience.

All the local friendships she had fostered were still meaningful; nonetheless, she was a candidate for wanting friendships of a different kind. She felt the pang of loneliness.

Many women can also relate to my friend Vania, a woman whose life has been filled with changing jobs, relationships, and homes in her search for what felt right. That constant influx of transition meant that it was sometimes hard to keep her friendships feeling stable. Her training as a therapist and her own uncanny ability to be brutally authentic about herself ensured that the relationships she made were deep, intimate, and honest, but they often felt inconsistent—possibly going months between get-togethers since she was often traveling, moving, or dating.

Fast-forward to a painful relationship breakup, and she looked around feeling that although she could schedule any number of lunches with women she liked, she didn't feel like she had a community that really could support her in the heartbreak she was going through. She had a list of fabulous people who would have enjoyed meeting her for drinks, but not a list of women who had witnessed the unraveling of that relationship, knew the details of her pain, and could show up in meaningful ways. She became a candidate for wanting friendship of a different kind. She felt the pang of loneliness.

Lastly, I want to highlight my friend Dannah, whose calendar overflows with people in a way that impresses even other socialites. She networks with everyone; it's hard to meet someone who doesn't know her. Tonight she'll be at an art exhibit opening, followed by a meditation class. Tomorrow it will be another match.com date, and then off to a workshop she's excited about. The next night it will be some huge charity fundraiser where she'll undoubtedly meet someone who invites her to a private wine tasting. This is a woman who knows how to have fun, how to laugh, how to live life in big and deep ways.

Rewind a year and you would see a woman known by everyone and yet at risk of being unknown in the deep ways it can often matter. While her eyes light up at all the exciting events she attends, she knows that she has to choose stability and consistency in a few of her relationships in order to foster the depth that can support her heart. Just being busy with people isn't the goal. She was a candidate for friendship of a different kind. She felt the pang of loneliness.

These stories bring three truths to the surface. First, we were all amazing women, even when we felt lonely. Our worth didn't drop one iota when we recognized that we needed to make new friends. We were still talented, deep, funny, and wise— even if, as in my case, no one around me knew it yet!

Second, we all needed new friends. But the word "new" meant different things to each of us. For me, since I was new to the area, making new friends literally meant meeting new people. For someone like Dannah, who knew a lot of people already, creating new friendships most likely meant transforming current relationships into something new, something more meaningful for her current phase of life.

And third, it bears repeating, we can do everything right to build up friendships and still find ourselves in a place where we have to do it again. Life shifts. Our needs shift. Our friendships shift.

It's important to point these truths out. I have found that often a woman will express loneliness, but then quickly try to talk herself out of it, telling me what great friends she already has. I usually smile and say, "Undoubtedly you have amazing friends. Nonetheless, like most of us, you're a candidate for adding a different kind of friendship to your life."

WHY WE MUST RECOGNIZE LONELINESS

Loneliness is rampant. Loneliness is not about social skills, likeability, or the kind of friend we can be to others. We can be popular and be lonely. We can be beautiful, friendly, and successful and be lonely. We can have a full social calendar and be lonely. We can be married and be lonely. We can be networked and be lonely.

Loneliness isn't the state of being alone, without anyone. It's *feeling* alone.

Loneliness speaks to our sense of connection. Loneliness is a signal, like the orange cones on the freeway that say, "Slow down! Take notice." Loneliness is an invitation to recognize that our hearts have more capacity to love. The same way hunger pangs tell us when we need nourishment and energy, loneliness is our heart's way of encouraging us to engage.

That's a beautiful message to receive!

Unfortunately, for most of us, when we start to feel loneliness, we start to withdraw. Isn't it ironic that our brains say, "I want to be closer to others," and our response is often to pull away? We sometimes do this because a pang of loneliness might trigger memories of times we felt sadness, grief, anger, or rejection—and without even recognizing that we're acting out of our past, we stall our present. It's almost like we involuntarily start to recoil, which results in us defending ourselves against the very thing we want. With that kind of dissonance—the distance between where we are and where we want to be—if we talk ourselves into staying where we are, we invariably are tempted to talk ourselves into being okay there, pretending we don't care about where we thought we wanted to be.

But we must care. We must not ignore our loneliness. We need to refuse to get used to it.

Furthermore, we will not sit on our couch and hope that someday she rides up the driveway on a white horse announcing herself as our long-lost BFF. Aside from the fact that we'd honestly be creeped out if it actually happened, the wait may be too long.

Dr. Jacqueline Olds, a consulting psychiatrist at McLean Hospital outside Boston who has seen patients for thirty-two years, is a prolific author on the subject of loneliness. She has frequently said, "Aside from genetics, the two most important factors in longevity are exercise and a network of friends." Add to that the myriad of medical research that shows we recover from surgeries faster, get sick less frequently, exhibit less stress, and report being happier with friends. One study on the impact our support systems can have on us was conducted at the University of Virginia where students were asked to estimate the steepness of a hill as they stood at the base of it with a weighted backpack. Those who stood beside a friend guessed the incline to be less than those who stood alone. Additionally, the longer the friends had known each other, the less steep the hill appeared.

Who among us doesn't need that? Who among us wants to look at life and see the hills as steeper than they are? Who among us wants to increase our stress and at the same time decrease our ability to cope with it? Perhaps it feels instinctive to say that we're scared to make friends, but it's also instinctive that we crave them—our bodies and hearts need them. The lonelier we are, the more we need them. The busier we are, the more we need them. The more things I want to accomplish, the more I know I need to invest in this part of my life. The healthier I want to be, the more I need to connect. We need friends.

But there's another reason that we cannot allow ourselves to withdraw and give up: and that is that our loneliness doesn't only affect us—it also hurts others.

Research from the *Journal of Personality and Social Psychology* suggests that not only is our loneliness contagious ("lonely people attract fellow 'lonelies' and influence others to feel lonely, too" which can "compound or increase those feelings of solitude"), but lonely people behave in less affirming ways towards themselves and others, which can affect people up to three degrees of separation.

This means that even if we just sit in our house night after night trying to convince ourselves that we don't need more meaningful connections, that meeting people is too awkward, or takes too much energy, that friendships bring up too much drama, exhaust us, and never feel worth it—we are more likely to show up in ways that hurt people. It means that our friendships in the other Circles could be at risk if we are unknowingly taking our loneliness out on them, devaluing them, or judging them too harshly. Whether it's updates we post on Facebook, comments we make anonymously on blogs, interactions we have with our family, or the way we relate with our colleagues, loneliness can bleed out in ways that leave other people feeling worse. Then, when those people mirror that behavior, an entire web of pain from our loneliness has been created.

And the world definitely doesn't need more of that.

Maybe our loneliness is why so many women have a reputation for being catty, judgmental, and mean to other women. Maybe it's because we aren't all as connected as we need to be for our health and happiness. Maybe that disconnectedness, and the way it causes us to treat others, is spreading. Maybe because we don't feel loved, we have a harder time giving it. Maybe we've forgotten that we can only receive that which we extend. Maybe more friendship would make this world a better place.

Let's sit with the truth for a moment: We don't need to feel rejected because we're lonely in one circle, or several. Loneliness is not a judgment against who we are or about whether or not people like us. In fact, Marianne Williamson, a prolific author, articulates one of my favorite sayings: "Whoever doesn't love you doesn't know you." We are lovable. Making friends will remind us of that.

And while the nature of loneliness makes us think that we are alone in our experience, the tragic reality is that the majority of Americans know the feeling.

How Many Friends Do You Have?

The *American Sociological Review* published research in June 2006 that showed almost twenty-five percent of Americans claim to have no confidante with whom they share deeply. Add the nineteen percent of people who claimed to only have one such person in their life (most likely a spouse or significant other) and we have almost fifty percent of Americans who have virtually no close friends outside of one relationship, leaving us deeply vulnerable after a divorce, breakup, or death. The other half of us have an average of two close friends.

How Many Friends Do We Need?

Let's compare how many close friends most of us have to how many friends most of us need.

Primologists have determined that a female baboon with a small but loyal core of female companions is less prone to jagged spikes of the stress hormone cortisol than a female who casts her social net wider, rather than deeper. Observing repeated examples within the animal kingdom, we find that females who are living longer, raising more children to independence, and showing less signs of stress and fear seem to do best with a support group of about three other females. It may or may not be a coincidence that most movies and TV shows highlight foursomes.

A study commissioned by The National Lottery to compare the happiness levels of lottery winners and non-lottery winners found that the number of friends they had was more important than the amount of money they had! The report found that "those with five friends or fewer had a sixty percent chance of being unhappy. People with between five and ten friends have a fifty percent chance of being happy. But for people with more than ten friends, the likelihood of being happy varies between fifty-five and fifty-six percent. Adding more friends than this doesn't significantly increase the possibility of happiness—so ten is the optimum number. On average, respondents who reported themselves 'extremely satisfied' with their lives had twice the number of friends of those who were 'extremely dissatisfied.'"

So, on average, most of us have zero to two confidantes in our Committed Circle. And, on average, most of us would be happiest with three to five. (Those other five—of the ten friends that the Lottery study claims is the "optimum number"—would be in my Community Circle.)

Broaden the definition to go beyond intimates or our Right-Side Friends, and various studies put us as having anywhere between fifty and several hundred in our collective Circles.

Robin Dunbar, an anthropologist, has determined that with our brain size, we can maintain 148.4 relationships "that depend on extensive personal knowledge based on face-to-face interaction for their stability." The term "Dunbar Number" was coined, and rounded up to 150.

Of course, every study defines friendships and confidantes differently, and an average never shows the distinctions between our individual personalities and felt needs. We are not statistics. And my goal isn't to place numbers in front of us like carrots in the friendship race.

My goal is to help us see friendship more broadly than simply looking for our one BFF, the proverbial needle in the haystack—the one person you think you're waiting for to make your life more meaningful and supported.

WE NEED MORE THAN ONE BFF

Brandi, one of my neighbor friends from childhood, saw my Facebook post about a recent TV interview I'd done on women's friendships. Watching it reminded her of a time when we were kids and she had been brought to tears by something I did. In her memory we had all been coloring at the table when I announced that I wanted to read aloud something I had written for school. Apparently I had written a story about my best friend—and to her surprise, and pain, it hadn't been about her. I don't remember the incident, but she still does, very clearly.

It was in her home two houses down that I'd first heard the songs of Michael Jackson's "I'm Bad" blaring from her big brothers' radio, it was in my basement where a group of us neighborhood kids all played truth-or-dare, which included her little brother having to pull his pants down, and it was that same little brother that we married to my little sister in an elaborate wedding complete with raw spaghetti noodles covered in butter and brown sugar for the reception. (Yes, it was as inedible as you would imagine it to be.) Despite the plethora of special shared memories, I hadn't named her as my best friend.

Hearing her share that long-ago memory reminded me of my own hurtful moment in the third grade coatroom during recess. My best friend, Amy K.—who always saved a swing for me at recess—announced that she was now going to be best friends with Kristin H. instead of me. I couldn't be consoled. I was convinced my life was over.

I Want to Feel Chosen

We do eventually grow up, but the drama around feeling chosen, or not, never quite goes away, does it?

Elizabeth Gilbert, in her book *Committed: A Skeptic Makes Peace with Marriage,* lists the losses associated with marriage for women: married women are more likely to suffer from depression, die younger, accumulate less wealth, earn reduced pay, experience more health problems, and thrive less in their careers than those who are unmarried. She then points to the fifty percent divorce rates and asks the question: why is it that we get so consumed with marriage when it doesn't appear to be all that good for us?

Her ponderings include the theory that we all just want to feel chosen. Picked. Wanted. Loved. A wedding allows us to publicly say, "Someone thinks I'm amazing." A wedding tells us that we are the one. The only one. The chosen one. And that feels good. (Although my friend Daneen points out that the demands of motherhood made her more sympathetic to the idea that a few more wives/mothers in our homes to share the workload might not be a terrible idea!)

But Being Chosen Doesn't Have to Be Exclusive

I wish as a little girl I had been taught to value the importance of having several different friends. That we didn't have to be exclusive to feel special. That my worth wasn't tied to one girl and who she wanted to play with at recess. That I felt more accepted when I decided to choose others. That the term "best friend" didn't refer to a number but to how well we treated each other.

To my sweet childhood friend Brandi: please know you were at the center of some of my best childhood memories. You were definitely a best friend . . . I was simply too immature to know I could bequeath the title on more than one.

As adults we don't want any less to feel chosen, but most of us now know that just because we're chosen, doesn't mean others cannot be. And, even more important than someone else choosing me, is my ability to choose myself, believing in my worth and value. That security allows my BFF's to have other BFF's without me feeling jealous, knowing their other friendships don't make what we share any less valuable. In fact, I know that our friendship will be healthier and stronger if she's getting some needs met by others, because I can't be all things to her. And I definitely don't want her to feel lonely. I want her to be loved by as many people as possible!

Because I call her a friend, I will cheer for her when she finds new friends. Friends who have kids the age of hers. Or friends who know what it's like to be single again in their fifties. Or friends who can afford to go to fancy spas with her. Or friends who get excited about her political or spiritual passions. Or friends who can make her belly-laugh. Or friends who live close enough to go on a spontaneous walk with her. Or friends who know firsthand how scary it is for her to be starting her own business. Or friends who stimulate her imagination, creativity, and curiosity. Because I can't do all those things. Even if I could, she's still better off with a circle of support, with more than just me waving my pom-poms for her.

Best is a quality, not a quantity. If we say something is best, we're not saying that we have to dislike everything else in order to like this thing. Best means that something, or someone, has reached a level of excellence, trust, appreciation. It doesn't mean that nothing else can. Like a mother with multiple kids, we can hold love for several friends without loving any of them less. We are human beings capable of loving many.

ASSESSING OUR CIRCLES: FOUR DIFFERENT "NEW" FRIENDS

The goal is to have the right balance in our life to support us in all of the ways that we need. When we feel disconnection, it is frequently because one Circle of friends isn't being fostered in ways that feel meaningful.

The Friendship Continuum can be unbalanced in four common ways. Do you relate to any of these?

Right-Side Low: Need Deeper Friends

When you write the names of all your friends along the Continuum you may find that the Circles on the Left Side—in your Contact & Common Circles—contain almost all your friends, leaving the Right Side—your Community and Committed Circles—looking empty. This imbalance means you haven't yet invested in the few that you want to transform into deeper friends.

Maybe your business requires you to network, your kids' busy social calendars keep you on the go, or you're single and feel pressure to always be out and about. We would never consider ourselves to be women who need more friends! Truth be told, we have a hard time keeping in touch with the ones we already know and seem to keep meeting.

Some of us are phenomenal networkers and can easily consider anyone a potential friend. It's a great gift! These women always know what events are going on, seem to be on everyone's invitation list, and would consider their lives full of good friends. They are never without someone to call.

The downside of this inflated Left Side can be that we are at greater risk of not ever feeling really known. Everyone seems to know us, but they all see just a fraction of who we are, with few of them being close enough to really know our story, our fears, our insecurities, and our daily life in the quiet moments. We feel the twinges of loneliness because we're not really sure they know us. We recognize that simply knowing people and labeling them friends doesn't create intimacy.

It may be that you feel popular, but unsure which friends to call to just come hang out with you when you want to be vulnerable or low-key. It may look like you have lots of people to invite out for brunch, but you don't feel safe asking any one of them to loan you their car for an afternoon,

No matter how many people we know, most of us long to have a couple of friends that are really there for us. The desire to have a relationship that isn't always based on an activity or an event is something to honor.

This was the situation that Dannah and Vania found themselves in several years ago. They were both popular and had tons of friends, but they lacked closeness with a select few.

I shared Vania's and Dannah's stories because I love that they both needed the same end result, but the obstacles to getting there were different. For Dannah, a social bee, her challenge was to carve out regular time to be with the same people, even if it meant not saying yes to meeting new people. That's a sacrifice some women don't make for the friendships they say are important to them.

For Vania, someone who withdraws more easily, is introverted, and after the breakup didn't feel like being social, her challenge was the opposite: forcing herself to make plans and going through with them even when she felt awkward, uncomfortable, or tired. Furthermore, when she started her next relationship, she would have to do it differently, choosing to stay present in the lives of her friends even when tempted to lose herself in romance. That's also a sacrifice some women don't make for the friendships they say are important to them.

Both of them had to figure out who they wanted to invest time and energy into in order to foster greater trust and commitment.

*Either Side Low: Need **More** Friends*

Perhaps you have one or two close friends on the Right Side and a handful of Contact Friends, but the rest of your Circles are more or less empty. Some people try to convince me that all they need is that one friend, but this belief that if you have a best friend you don't need to be friend-making is dangerous.

As I said earlier, while that one BFF may be terrific and feel eternal, the truth is that all those other empty circles make us incredibly vulnerable. Your best friend could move away, have a baby, need to care for an aging parent, or get a new job and be less available to you. Her own seasons of life may take her away from you when you least expect it.

If you don't have other friends in place, then you can quickly feel betrayed and isolated. You might blame her when it's really your own responsibility to build a wider circle to support the myriad of needs your life is sure to hold.

Even if you could guarantee me that you and your BFF will never, ever not be friends, I'd still argue that not only is your life enriched by having a variety of other intimate confidantes, but it also helps relieve the pressure on your BFF to have to be your only lifeline. I cheer for my friends who take responsibility for building a circle around them that includes others. Imagine if you had a health crisis—having several friends able to give to you in different ways will be more meaningful to you and less burdensome to any one of them.

Remember, "best" often refers to quality, not just to a quantity of one. For example, Google the word and you'll see things like "The Ten Best Cities to Live In," "The Five Best iPhone Apps this Year," "The Best Movies Ever." I give you permission to have a handful of best friends, building up your own list of "My Five Best Friends."

Those of us who prefer spending time with our one or two Committed Friends are gifted at spending quality time with one person, going through the ups and downs of life together, and loving each other well. We know we're good friend material. We know how to stay in touch, how to sense when she needs to be cheered up, and when she just needs to vent. These are comfortable relationships that matter to us.

However, we have to own the fact that we need to foster more of them. The tricky part, of course, is in not comparing every new friend with our closest friends in this Circle. It's easy to forget that it takes a lot of time and intentionality to move people into the Committed Circle. If you begin inviting people in now, a year from now you'll have many additional potential close friends.

Our desire to expand the Committed Circle does not suggest a lack about any of our current friends, only that we love them enough to not ever expect everything from them. For our health, and theirs, we are willing to welcome a few more in.

Middle Circle Imbalance: Need Current *Friends*

An imbalance in our Confirmed Friends Circle can go two ways—it can be either a circle that we ignore, or one that is overinflated.

Let's start with the latter. When you list your friends along the Continuum and acknowledge that a large number of them land in the middle, women you felt closer to in the past than you do currently, this may leave a hunger for more current connections.

Because our shared past deeply connects us still, we have a hard time admitting we may need more than we're currently experiencing with these women. Karen, Krista, Liz, Kerry, and J'Leen held my heart after a traumatic divorce, as I went through the ups and downs of dating again, and when I celebrated my eventual second wedding. When I was new to San Francisco, I was like a stubborn preteen girl, with crossed arms, stomping my little foot, refusing to play with anyone except the friends I already trusted and loved. With a pouty face I pronounced (to myself), "I don't want new friends."

And who can blame us when we do this? We have depth, intimacy, and history with these women. This is the goal of friendship and we have achieved it. So any new friend I try to meet is compared against the winning ticket. Naturally, a coffee date with a new friend, in contrast to a proven friend, will leave me unimpressed as we awkwardly try to find our common ground. So of course we are tempted to say these friends from our past are enough. We're too tired to start all over with others when we already have the women who would do anything for us. I could call one of them tomorrow, say I needed her here, and she'd be on the next flight. So there.

The problem is that even though I know she'd be on the next flight if, say, I had to have an emergency appendectomy, I'd feel silly asking her to fly out for an afternoon of shopping. We know we can call our Confirmed Friends for anything, but we end up reserving them for life's biggies: births, divorces, dream jobs, moves, the scary diagnosis.

But life only has so many biggies in it. And we're still left with all the seemingly mundane moments that don't seem important enough to warrant the phone tag and eventual one-hour phone call. But that's not to say we don't still want to share them with someone.

Eventually, I reached a point where I wanted to make new memories with friends, rather than simply reporting my life events or reliving the past with those I used to be close to. I needed present friends. I needed local friends. I needed new friends. I uncrossed my defiant little arms and mentally changed my pouty expression that said, "Prove you're as good as they are," and replaced it with a hopeful smile that said, "Let's make something new."

Obviously I didn't expect my new contacts to replace the amazing friends who lived in my old home city. But I realized that if I didn't start meeting some Contact Friends, I would never have local, face-to-face friendships that felt easy and comfortable. Sometimes the greatest intimacy isn't knowing who you could call, it's actually having someone you do call.

The solution to an overinflated Confirmed Friends Circle isn't that we need to weed out friends so much as that we need to be committed to growing new friends. We can't use their love as an excuse to not invite in more women who can care for other parts of us. We have proven we know how to foster meaningful friendships. Now, we are called to do it again.

The opposite problem is realizing that your Confirmed Friends Circle is empty. Sure you have some fabulous past friends, but the idea of calling them feels more awkward than enjoyable since you've lost touch with them through the years. Perhaps you've moved a lot or gone through some major life change where you simply "started over" and didn't look back. For whatever reason, you have walked away from friendships, from people who knew you well.

And while starting over can feel justified, it can leave a hole that all the current fabulous friends in the world can't fill. For everything you can tell them, they didn't live through it with you. They can't validate how far you've come, laugh with you at who you used to be, or remind you that there was another way of seeing that experience. There is an intimacy that comes from history. Even awkward history. Even painful history.

Better than having a friend who thinks I walk on water is having a friend who knows I don't, and loves me anyway. Many of us are afraid to reconnect with people from our past. They represent a time in our lives we'd rather forget or remind us of who we used to be. But that's not all bad. There is an intimacy available in this circle that can't come from anywhere else. To be in relationship with those who knew us when we were in that dumb relationship, twice our current weight, unable to pay rent two months in a row, or had frizzy hair at summer camp—these friends from our past can be some of our most meaningful friendships.

Our ego will usually try to convince us that we're fine without all of them. And without knowing your circumstances, I won't tell you you're wrong. What I will say is that some of us don't need to make new friends as much as we need to create peace where we've been. We are being called to forgive ourselves, and others, so that we can live more fully in the present by removing the fear and shame from our past.

Some of you may feel no shame or fear from your past; you've simply told yourself that you're just not a person who keeps in touch. So you've drifted away after every move or change. You proudly brushed the dust from your shoes, stuck your chin out courageously, and just kept making new friends.

On the one hand, I say kudos to you for the skills you've developed in the making friends department. On the other hand, I challenge you to consider growing skills in the maintaining friends department. A nearly empty Confirmed Friends Circle can lead to a huge sense of disconnection.

Right-Side Full: Need Specific Friends

Many of us have a wide variety of friends, including some close ones, but frequently after a life change we can find ourselves looking for someone who understands our specific experience.

This hunger to find friends who are "like me" happens frequently: after a breakup or a health diagnosis, when we start a new business or develop a newfound interest or hobby. We hunger to be with people who "get" us.

But just sharing an interest isn't always enough. We also want our friends' details to be similar to ours. It's not enough that we're both single and dating; we want to know if you like going to clubs or hanging out at wine bars. It's not enough that we both run our own business; we want to know if you're facing similar challenges and striving for comparable goals. It's not enough that we're both moms; we want you to have two kids the same ages as ours, be a stay-at-home mom like us, and have a similar parenting style.

Clearly, it's unrealistic to expect your BFF to meet all these needs. There are just too many options on the menu of life! We cannot all go through every life change at the same time, in the same way.

It's not that we stop hanging out with our friends who are in different stages; but we do need to add to our Common Circle a few people who can connect with us in this new experience.

This was the experience of my friend Daneen when she was the only one of her current friends to have a baby. She was part of the same weekly girls group that I attended, so certainly we all felt a huge commitment to journey with her through the change she was experiencing. But no matter how much we cheered for her, there are too many things that non-moms can't relate to or understand. We were inadequate—not in the amount of love and commitment we were ready to give, but in our similarity of experience.

This new need often catches those who experience it off-guard, and they can feel guilt or disappointment if they don't identify the type of desire they feel.

The natural human response to these times is to be frustrated with our current friends for not understanding what we're going through. Our lives feel so important, so huge and consuming. Whatever change we're going through feels big. It can be painful to sense that our friends don't resonate with our current experience as much as we do. They're still all married while you're newly divorced—how can they understand? They make twice as much as you—how can they understand? They're still all working while you're newly retired—how can they understand? They all moved to the suburbs—how can they understand? They're still all employed while you're sending out résumés—how can they understand?

Without meaning to, we can start feeling a bit resentful. It's our heart's way of saying that we want to be understood. The mistake is when we project it onto them as though it's their fault for being in a different place, at a different time. Then we feel guilty for expecting so much.

This is a moment that helps us articulate that it may mean, no matter how many friends you have right now, you need some specific ones that totally understand what you're going through. And you'll be healthier and happier for recognizing that need and opening yourself up to new friends.

Making new friends doesn't mean that you should replace the friends who are meaningful in other areas. Daneen joined mom's clubs and appreciated seeing other understanding, sleep-deprived eyes and hearing tips on how to ease a baby's gaseous stomach. But while they bonded over motherhood, if she had expected them to be like her Committed Friends, she'd have been sorely disappointed. To dismiss Common Friends because they don't act like Committed Friends is shortsighted. Relish the purpose these friends have. Eventually one of those mom friends might become one of Daneen's Committed Friends, but that transition won't be instant.

Common Friends and Committed Friends simply serve different purposes.

If the need to have friends who share a specific commonality resonates with you, you need to foster Common Friends.

COLLECTING MY CIRCLES

In the book *Consequential Strangers,* co-written by a journalist and an academic, the authors highlight that one of the marked changes between our world today and that of a couple of decades ago is that while "we were once connected through institutions, we are now linked as individuals."

Perhaps it's true that we once were all part of a "dense network" where everyone in an institution (e.g., church community, civic organization, small town, union) knew each other, but now it's clearer than ever that we are each developing our own unique collection of Circles. As the authors of *Consequential Strangers* point out, "We are not living the Greatest Generation's lifestyle. We don't work for one company; we don't limit ourselves to one career, one religion, nor even one family. Most of us traffic in a variety of worlds—family, work, organizations, volunteer groups, spiritual gatherings, web communities—and in each realm, interact with a different assortment of people."

I feel a bit torn about this reality. I can wish we all belonged to one big happy tribe of friends, much like the family depicted at Thanksgiving dinner in Norman Rockwell's famous painting *Freedom from Want*. There is a romantic and idealized vision of us all creating our perfect shared tribe that I don't want to let go of. Yet I also realize that just wanting it doesn't mean it's realistic. Even if we could hypothetically create it, we can't maintain it. People move, people change—the revolving door doesn't stop.

I grew up in a religious denomination with that tribe-like quality: anyone I met invariably knew someone else I knew. So I imagine there are still pockets where we can belong to one group with life revolving around that sense of everyone belonging to the same collective group. But even in that kind of a culture, I watched many people have to suppress parts of themselves that they sensed might risk exclusion. So even belonging doesn't always mean feeling accepted.

Today it's just as likely that my closest friend, my sister, and my mother all have a conglomerate of individual friends and acquaintances that I don't even know, and may never meet. In fact, there's now only a fifty percent probability that any two of our friends knows each other. We are no longer all one tribe.

We need more than the elusive best friend we think we're looking for. We're creating our own tribe from here and there, and our needs are more varied than we probably know.

Though, as we'll see in the next chapter, we all need Frientimacy.

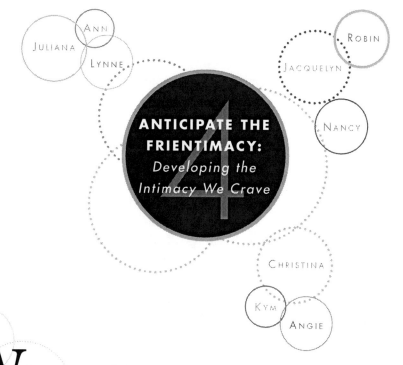

ANTICIPATE THE
FRIENTIMACY:
*Developing the
Intimacy We Crave*

JULIANA ANN LYNNE ROBIN JACQUELYN NANCY CHRISTINA KYM ANGIE

W hen a group of close girlfriends and I all lived within driving distance of each other in Southern California, we met weekly at my house for over a year. We all live in different cities now, but every spring we still fly to a chosen destination for our Annual Girlfriend Get-Together.

This group of women walked the road with me after my divorce— witnessing my tears as I recovered from rejection, reminding me of my commitment to self-forgiveness, and refusing to let me give in to my fear that no one would ever love me again. And I strived to do the same for them in the heart monitors of their lives that inevitably always holds both ups and downs.

While we make an effort to have a group conference call two or three times a year and connect sporadically on our group Facebook page in between our annual weekends, we still have to spend considerable time catching each other up on what has occurred since our last conversation. The gift of intimacy between platonic friends is that we have a comfort level that lets us be immediately honest and pick up where we left off. This is a benefit of time put in, love proven, deep knowledge of one another. There is nothing like being seen by friends we love, who love us back. I call this experience "Frientimacy."

Frientimacy is defined as the state and expression of being close, familiar, and affectionate in a non-romantic relationship, as it is when I am with these women. But what does that really mean?

FRIENTIMACY DEFINED

One might expect a chapter on the closest of friends to be filled with stories of women whose bonds inspire. The examples would be of women who served their friends heroically through bouts of cancer, of women who wouldn't have made it through divorces without a BFF to lean on, and of women who kept in touch over the decades through multiple marriages, children, and careers. We eat those stories up. They're like catnip to all of us who crave healthy relationships. We're used to all these aphorisms that get re-tweeted and poems that get forwarded saying things like, "Friendship is a single soul living in two bodies," or "A friend is one who doubles your joy and divides your grief."

I'm struck by how often we all say we want BFF's—Committed Friends—and yet how little we seem to understand what that means. We romanticize the stories, almost more than we do in romance.

When we're dating we often talk about how no one is perfect. We know that we'll go through countless breakups and disappointments. We acknowledge that conflict is part of a healthy relationship. After we're married we talk about how hard we have to work at it. We know that the person we love the most can also be the one who annoys us the most. The same person who gives us roses one day can leave his dirty clothes on the floor the next. An entire industry exists around marriage counseling, ways to deal with disagreements, and personal growth resources for helping us become better partners.

But when it comes to female friendship, it's almost like we think we'll always agree with each other, automatically know the perfect things to say, never be offended by the actions of the other, and always feel supported.

This chapter, a celebration of Committed Friends and Frientimacy, is not about clichés, poems, laughter, and friendship bracelets. It is decidedly not about the stuff that friendship legends are based upon. While those feelings and friendships are inspiring, it is the other side of Frientimacy that is most instructive, and least celebrated.

Marriage *can* be about waking up next to your best friend, planning your dream life together, and having passionate sex every night. But if that's all people expected, they'd be in for some big disappointment.

The truth is that the person we fight with the most is probably the one we live with. The closer we are to each other, the more likely we'll bump into each other once in a while. With commitment comes responsibility, decisions, schedules, bills, and chores. In the same way, Frientimacy invites us into real-ness.

We don't get there without awkwardness, hurt feelings, and pain. Those things are part of life, and if you want the quintessential friend who is "always there for you," then that means showing up for each other when you're at your worst. Which also happens to be when you're the messiest, the most needy, and the least impressive.

We can't have one without the other. Frientimacy holds both.

And we wouldn't want it any other way. Those responsibilities, decisions, and messy parts also bond us, grow us, and increase our trust in each other. They are not to be avoided, but rather to be embraced. Besides, what we label "bad" often becomes the best gift of our lives, and what we quickly label "good" can end up not serving us down the road. We aren't always the best judges of what will serve our lives most effectively. If we go through life avoiding everything that doesn't feel easy and comfortable, we risk never experiencing Frientimacy.

Easy isn't the goal. Having strong, healthy, meaningful friendships is—even if that means there are awkward and difficult moments along the way.

FRIENTIMACY DEVELOPED

We can only trust our future because we've weathered our past. Our Frientimacy wasn't instant. It's out of consistent intimacy that we have fostered this Frientimacy.

A decade ago my friends and I were mostly strangers to each other. I invited a few women I had only recently met to commit to a weekly group in my apartment. Some invited someone else. And over time, with one leaving here and another joining there, we had a group that was consistent. We didn't all necessarily feel like we would be friends with each individual in the group if it weren't for the collective time, but we knew the value of going deeper with other women, so we kept coming.

What we celebrate now has taken effort. It has taken commitment— far more than most women are willing to put in. Most of us think that if we get together once a month with a new friend a friendship will blossom. And I'd say once a month is enough to keep liking each other, but probably not enough to build sufficient history so that when our lives change (and they will), we have enough history behind us to stay connected through it. Once a week for one year gave us a gift we can enjoy the rest of our lives, if we keep fostering it.

We did not "discover" our friendship; none of us could have predicted that we'd end up with this level of commitment. Rather, we chose to develop the potential.

THE FIVE STAGES OF FRIENTIMACY

When it comes to marriage, we know that there is a lot of territory between being interested in someone and marrying him. "Going on a date" is different than "dating" which is still different than "dating exclusively." And just like romantic dating, friendship develops in stages.

But with female friendship we lack non-romantic language to articulate those stages. It takes time to develop a level of comfort that's mutual and implicitly understood. We may think that becoming friends should happen quickly, maybe with a couple of conversations.

When members of GirlFriendCircles.com, the women's friendship matching site I founded, get frustrated during the friend-making process, it is typically around the gap in expectations between what they want and what they find: they want deep friendships that are comfortable and require little energy, but what they find are strangers that require getting to know. And so they are tempted to give up, sighing in frustration that they aren't meeting their best friends.

We neglect the evidence in our memory banks that most of our friendships were developed over consistent time together (i.e., at work, in school, at weekly gatherings).

In romance, some couples elope after knowing each other for two weeks; and others date for ten years before getting married; but on average, it takes one or two years from meeting to marriage. In friendship, it's more or less the same. There will always be exceptions due to personality, life timing, willingness, and so on. But we'd be wise to set our expectations for a journey. It might take a year—or more—to find one or two people we can really call Committed Friends.

I'll be unpacking the stages of friendship in more detail later in this chapter and in the second part of the book. For now, here's a summary:

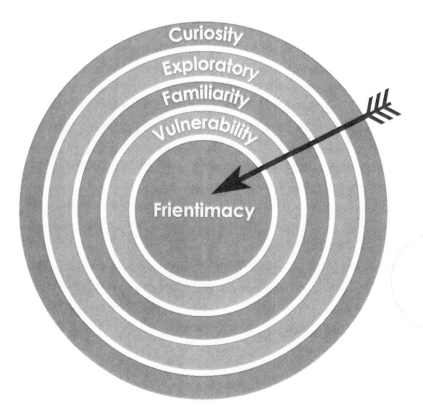

1. Curiosity

This is where every friendship begins. There has to be something that attracts us to a person, gives us a sense of willingness to talk, and increases our desire to learn more about them. These feelings don't have to be conscious or even obvious to us, but at this stage we have to have reason to lean in, even a little, if the stranger we're meeting is going to have a chance of becoming a friend. We're going to unpack this more in Chapter 5 as we look at how to meet new people—inviting more of them into our Left Side and appreciating the vast value they have in our lives.

2. Exploration

Every potential friendship requires that the potential friends spend time together. Sometimes that happens automatically (at a play group, a choir rehearsal, yoga class, or work), but often we'll have to initiate it and pursue it. For it doesn't matter how much attraction we may feel in that first stage, if we don't show up for time together, it will never become a friendship. This stage requires initiation. Repeatedly. It means arranging lunch this week, and making a phone call next week.

Fear can crop up at this stage— fear that the "potential friend" might not be receptive. Fear can mingle with doubt—uncertainty about whether this person has the qualities we hope she has. This stage can hold some silent gaps when we allow our busyness to let too much time pass before we reach out again. It can be met with disappointment when we e-mail but don't get a response and we're left wondering if we should follow up or not.

Exploration means just that. It means we're venturing into uncharted territory with another person. Neither of us has been here before together with the other. We don't yet know what we will become, what our time together will be filled with, or how long it will take before we feel comfortable and familiar. Remember this truth: no matter how much potential we sense, we still have to forge a way of interacting and getting to know each other.

Chapter 6 is going to unpack this concept even more as we look at how we must initiate repeatedly to explore our new and potential friendships.

3. Familiarity

This is the stage we often want as stage one. We wish we could experience this comfort level with someone upon first meeting them, forgetting that it takes time to build.

What psychologists call the "familiarity principle" or the "mere-exposure effect" applies to paintings, fashion styles, new languages, and people. (This explains why I'm always about a year behind clothing trends; it takes multiple exposures to transform me from the eye-rolling skeptic to the converted purchaser.) In studies of interpersonal attraction, the more often we see someone, the more pleasing and likable that person appears to be. It's the principle upon which advertising operates. We tend to like people more the more we see them.

Here's a simple example: I think of times when I've met someone casually at an event. No fireworks. Nothing memorable. No big deal. Fast-forward to another event, when I walk into a room full of strangers, if I see that person I met before, chances are good that I will feel what psychologist Edward Titchener described as the "glow of warmth" that we feel when we're near something familiar. I will most likely gravitate to her, thinking I like her more than I did when we last met.

For developing relationships to what we call familiarity, I find that it takes most women six to eight times meeting with someone before they reach this stage. Of course how quickly this happens depends on what we're doing and how we're sharing, but at some point we reach an ease in our togetherness. It might be when we're okay just hanging out spontaneously together without it taking two weeks to schedule; a sense that we are beginning to be able to predict how our potential friend will respond to different life events; an excitement in reaching out with an invitation, trusting that she will be glad we extended it.

Chapter 7 teaches how to maximize these times together with consistent positivity as we build this familiarity.

4. Vulnerability

This stage starts and overlaps with some of the previous stages, as we begin to share our histories and increase our trust with one another through our storytelling.

We must be authentic through all the stages, being willing to be seen in both our glory and our insecurities. But we shouldn't walk around vomiting our emotional stories on new friends. Many women make the mistake of thinking that just because they share something deep and raw they should now be super close. Unfortunately, if the commitment is not yet there, the relationship can actually feel quite awkward and shaky, holding too much emotion too early as a result of such divulgence.

In the first couple of stages we should not expect friends to prove themselves and be there for us in extreme ways. The friend we crave who will "always be there" for us is the result of commitment and vulnerability that grow over time. If a friend of yours doesn't seem to be there for you in the ways you think she should be, it doesn't mean she's not a good person; it might just be that the friendship you have developed with her isn't far enough along to warrant the commitment you crave. No two people progress toward friendship at the same rate.

However, after some consistent times together, if we're not willing to share beyond our PR image, laugh at ourselves, and express insecurities, the friendship will stall or disintegrate. Vulnerability means courageously risking the part of us that could get hurt.

As we move into this stage of vulnerability, we now earn the right to "cry on each other's shoulders." We've proven in the last three stages that we're willing to put in the time to practice the friendship dance, so in this stage we now bond in deeper ways, increasing our commitment to each other.

Figuring out how our two puzzle pieces together look different than any other friendship, we co-create a third entity, one that isn't you or me, but us. In her friendship-search book, *MWF Seeking BFF,* Rachel Bertsche describes what she calls an early indicator, when she and a new friend are stepping into this stage: "It's usually recognizing a dialogue versus two monologues. . . . Do we have an interchange of ideas, or are we both just telling our own stories?"

This subject of vulnerability is so important that I devote all of Chapter 8 to the process.

5. Frientimacy

This last stage is for those who are our BFF's—those in our Commitment Circle. And notice that I made BFF plural. Remember, best doesn't speak to quantity as much as quality. There is enough research out there to suggest we need between three and seven people in this category. No need to limit ourselves! Conversely, not everyone we interact with needs to move into this last stage.

This friendship intimacy stage is my category for the people I trust implicitly. We trust each other's boundaries, have proven ourselves to be emotionally healthy people for each other, and are willing to go out of our way for each other's benefit. We love each other. This stage takes time and energy. Lots of it. While we may see the potential and some of the benefits approximately six to twelve months into the relationship, it may take even longer to really build the required trust and intimacy.

My Southern California girlfriends are far from being a homogeneous group: some are married, some single, some divorced, some with kids, some with stepkids, some with none. It is formidable being the first or only one in a group to have kids, and equally hard to be the last or only one to not be in a relationship. And through the years many of us in our group have traded roles: the married one becomes single and the single finds her love. Often at the same time. We have to celebrate one and grieve the other.

We listen attentively as one shares that she's not sure she wants to stay married. Another just found out her husband cheated, but wants to make it work. And another just broke up with the man she thought she wanted. One is trying to decide if she wants kids. Another is due next month. Another just found out her baby isn't developing on schedule. Another isn't sure she'll find someone to marry before having children is no longer an option. And no matter how unfair it can feel, how different our issues can seem, we keep showing up for friendship, learning from each other and standing alongside each other.

There is one who is always unhappy with her weight, while another seemingly can eat whatever she wants and never put on a pound. There is someone who feels she is financially drowning, and another who could finance the whole group's trip. There is one who fears she will never fall in love, and also another who has that enviable relationship filled with apparent ease and joy. We sit with those who have what we want.

Frientimacy isn't only learning how to trust people with the parts of us that feel shame, fear, and anger; it is also about honestly expressing our worth, our ambitions, our hopes, our gratitude, and our strengths.

When these girlfriends and I get together, we choose to start our time together sharing three things to celebrate about our lives in the last year. It's always spectacular: The risks. The wins. The accomplishments. The completions. The new beginnings: the Ph.D., the new baby, the new business, the new office, the new love. The big anniversary. The lesson learned. The major purchase. The dream trip.

Being able to show up in front of friends without having to downplay our success, fake humility, apologize for getting something that we know someone else is wanting, or brush off that which makes us amazing, is paramount to our learning how to bring our best contributions to the world. If we can't practice owning our beauty—inside and outside—in front of people who love us, then how can we expect to feel comfortable showing up in this world with joy, taking greater risks, and following our convictions?

We must learn to applaud each other. A lot. Even when we're jealous. We must learn to embrace ourselves, and others, as holistic human beings who have the capacity to both screw up and to shine brightly. And sometimes do both at the same time.

It is indeed beautiful to be among friends who have history sharing both success and failure. We are six beautiful, amazing, professional, intelligent women who live life fully and are committed to truthful friendships. But our authenticity did not come naturally or easily.

Just like you, we had to start at step one in our relationships. At one point, we looked across my kitchen table at each other as strangers.

It is in the second part of this book that we break down the steps of how to get from Curiosity to Frientimacy.

I HAVE THIS THEORY THAT *FRIENDSHIP* CAN SAVE THE WORLD.

And by "friendship," I mean relationships where we are committed to practicing the best version of ourselves, while simultaneously choosing to go beyond pretenses, images, and insecurities to risk our shadow side being seen, too.

I HAVE THIS THEORY THAT FRIENDSHIP CAN *SAVE* THE WORLD.

And by "save" I mean greater happiness, less stress, healthier hearts and bodies, increased sense of personal worthiness, less rejection, fewer actions initiated by fear.

Our friendships are like gymnasiums for our souls. Gymnasiums where we can practice being the people this world needs: building up our muscle for compassion, increasing our endurance for giving, and stretching our ability to see the best in the other.

- So we can practice cheering for people even when we're jealous.
- So we can practice listening even when we think we're right.
- So we can practice empathy even when we're tempted to judge.
- So we can practice serving even when we're busy.
- So we can practice saying "I forgive you" even when we're disappointed.

All skills this world desperately needs.

I HAVE THIS THEORY THAT FRIENDSHIP CAN SAVE *THE WORLD*.

And by "the world" I mean that if we can't do this in relationship with people we love, then what hope do we have of doing this with people who live on the other side of the world from us? Who have different religions or political views? Who live lives that differ from our own morals and values?

I HAVE THIS THEORY THAT FRIENDSHIP CAN SAVE THE WORLD.

Less splintering, less judgment, less criticism, less loneliness, less fear, less pulling away, less war.

I HAVE THIS THEORY THAT FRIENDSHIP CAN SAVE THE WORLD.

More smiles, more acceptance, more love, more hope, more applause, more joy, more positivity, more belonging.

I HAVE THIS THEORY THAT FRIENDSHIP CAN SAVE THE WORLD.

Visit ShastaNelson.com to watch Shasta share this on video.

part two

FIVE STEPS TO TURNING FRIENDLY PEOPLE WE MEET INTO FRIENDS WHO MATTER

PART TWO

*Five Steps to
Turning Friendly
People We Meet
into Friends
Who Matter*

JULIANA   ANN   LYNNE   ROBIN   JACQUELYN   NANCY   CHRISTINA   KYM   ANGIE

I n the first part of this book we focused on the five Circles of Connectedness so that we might better understand which of our circles most
need our attention. In so doing, we also looked at the five Stages of a
Friendship to clarify how exactly we move people from one circle to another, from an initial curiosity to meaningful Frientimacy.

In this second part of the book, our focus will be the five steps of
friendship, which will be our action plan for how to progress our friendships from one stage to the next.

If you recognized that you already know many friendly people that
you want to advance into the more consequential and meaningful territory on the Right Side of the Continuum then you might find that your
personal call to action will be most convicting in Chapter 7—Add Positive
Consistency—in order to foster Familiarity. Whereas, if you're new to an
area and don't know many people, then you will undoubtedly find that
you need to focus all your current energy on the first step—Be Open—in
order to foster Curiosity.

With that said, most of us will find that at any given time, we are navigating multiple relationships, all in different circles. We may find that we
are navigating the first step with one potential friend, while simultaneously
nurturing another friendship through the fourth step. Our invitation,

then, is to become adept at seeing what stage any relationship is in so we can know what steps we can be taking with those whom we want to grow closer to in order to cultivate the relationship into the next experience.

Following these five steps will lead you to friendships that matter.

STAGES OF FRIENDSHIP

1. Curiosity

2. Exploratory

3. Familiarity

4. Vulnerability

5. Frientimacy

FIVE STEPS

1. Be Open.................................5

2. Initiate Consistently 6

3. Add Positivity.......................7

4. Increase Vulnerability 8

5. Practice Forgiveness................9

CHAPTER

I f I were meeting my friends today for the first time over coffee, there are only a few of them that I could've guessed would turn into the friendships that they are now. Nothing against them since I obviously adore them now, but my first impression of each of them wasn't always enough for me to know just how close I'd become to them one day. And I have good intuition!

Think about it. Name the people you feel closest to right now. Then pretend you don't already love them and know them well and imagine what you'd think of them after only one conversation.

Going down my list I'd probably talk myself out of following up with most of them for some reason or another: too insecure; different religious place than I am; talks way too much about herself and interrupts me; is from such a different background than I am; is way too into dating/motherhood/career—some stage I'm not currently in; seems too hard to get to know; comes across like a know-it-all; and the list continues. I almost feel mean saying these things, but let's face it—even our best friends aren't perfect. And I'm certainly not either. (And even if we all were impeccable, that, too, could be annoying to our friends.)

Love makes up for a host of imperfect traits. Knowing a friend's deep loyalty to me compensates for her neediness. Knowing how much she makes me laugh and puts me at ease makes up for the repeated interruptions. Knowing how solid her core is makes me care less about whether we're at the same life stage this year. Knowing that we get each other spiritually leaves me totally unconcerned about how little else we seem to have in common. Love, history, and experience have bonded us to women that we might not choose today if we didn't already know them deeply.

WHAT KIND OF AN OUTLOOK IS IMPORTANT

If there is a first step to making friends, it is being open to possibilities beyond what we can see with our limited judgments. It's recognizing that we're making judgments about someone without yet loving them, forgetting that it is love in the end that makes all the difference.

If we want to meet friendly people, we have to be one first.

Our mission at this point is to show up with compassion and consideration for those we meet, and to do it in an intentional and authentic way.

In the following chapters we will talk about how to maximize our interactions and evaluate which budding relationships we want to keep investing time and energy into. But first, we want to develop eyes to see the opportunities of connection, courage to initiate even when we feel awkward, and kindness so that each person we converse with will feel better for having met us.

We'll click instantly with some people. But to pretend we know what the future holds with those people, or why the Universe had us meet is beyond our pay grade. Rather, we want to be present with an open hand, swallow the egotistical advice that insists we need to size someone up, and approach with humility the precious experience of two people meeting each other.

Our relationships, even those on the Left Side of the Continuum, give us moments to practice being our best self, a reminder that what we choose to be to them, they will be to us. We're called to trust that we are right where we need to be in any given moment—giving attention to the person facing us that we may learn to love in new ways.

A futile way of showing up at this stage is for us to judge someone hastily as if we can determine their value to us when we've only just met. We can't. We simply don't know. That simple fact should encourage us to see the new acquaintance sitting across from us as someone more than the person we're interviewing from a specific checklist of what we think we're looking for in a friend.

We don't yet love her because we don't yet know her. The obstacles we perceive may prove to only be imagined. The differences we think divide us may become the bonds that bind us together. We just don't know yet. Too frequently, we want to expeditiously resolve whether we could see the two of us becoming close friends. If the answer is no based on some apparent flaw or difference we think we see, we then subconsciously check to see if the relationship will provide any obvious gain to our career, or any of our other endeavors (what will this person do for me or give me?). And if the answer is no again, then we lose interest.

I've witnessed mothers dismiss potential friends because the other woman didn't have children. Retired women have told me that they're not interested in meeting women who are still working. I've seen women not even try to engage in a possible friendship because of an age gap, a different marital status, or a perceived income difference. Many of those identifiers can—and do—change over time, and certainly the meaning we assign to them can expand beyond the limitations we associate with them. What we do or don't seem to have in common at the moment we meet doesn't need to matter as much as we think it does. There are countless examples of meaningful friendships between women with every difference possible.

If you have a plethora of meaningful connections in your life and think that all you need is someone in the Common Circle category, then by all means seek out other women who share one of your current experiences: other pregnant women, singles, widows, CEO's, empty-nesters, city-dwellers, followers of the same religion, or any other designations you think are important.

But when it comes to finding friends, few of us have so much love in our lives that we need to reject possibilities just because they don't fill the one opening we think we need filled. (Sometimes the Universe knows better what we need than we do!) Like those who live with sleep deprivation and think it's normal, not knowing what being well-rested feels like, I think the vast majority of us are largely disconnected and could probably benefit from adding more love in our lives from an array of people. I invite you to cast your net wider, not narrower. Don't doubt someone's potential just because you don't instantly see it.

In fact, hard data tell us that it doesn't matter which particular parts of our lives are similar to those of our friends, only that we end up finding those similarities. The Brafman brothers, who co-wrote the book *Click*, share research that reveals people bond more deeply over the *quantity* of perceived similarities than over the *quality*—the number of similarities matters more than their content.

They wrote, "Sharing a strong dislike of fast food, for example, was just as powerful a predictor of attraction as favoring the same political party." In other words, what we consider as the "big" thing we think we need to have in common isn't as effective at bonding us as having two or three "small" things in common. The Brafmans further explained, "You'd think that people who share the same religious convictions and political views, for example, would be more likely to hit it off than those who share only similar tastes in films and music . . . but it didn't matter *at all* which topics underlay the similarity—it was the degree of similarity that was important."

Although we would never limit our circle of friends to only people who share our name or birthdate, we might be limiting ourselves in a similar way if we insist we both have to be single or from the same ethnic group. If we confine our search for friends to those whose lives mirror ours, we might not take the time to be more curious with each other, which could result in not discovering that we both worked at a summer camp in college, both traveled to Zambia, or were both at the same Madonna concert tour in the 1980's—all of which could prove more bonding than finding another woman at the same life stage as we are. We're shooting ourselves in the friendship foot to fall for the myth that we know what "one thing" that person needs to possess or be in order to bond with us.

As an example, two women can belong to the same church, both vote Republican in every election, both stay at home raising their children who are the same ages, and both share the same economic status—but that doesn't guarantee a friendship. Similarly, women who are apparent opposites, and whose lives took completely different paths, can still cherish each other.

Who I Want To Be:

I want to show up in life in such a way that you feel **greeted** in my presence. Welcomed. Worthy. Accepted. That means when I see you I start with love. It means I refuse to wait until my ego can determine your value to me. Forgive me for my impulse to judge, I want to unlearn that behavior. The truth is that you are human—my sister, my brother—and that is enough. Your value is exponential and I greet the lessons you will teach me. Thank you.

I want to show up in life in such a way that you feel **abundant** in my presence. Abundant in the awareness that you are enough. More than enough, in fact. Where, for a moment, you can find refuge from your inadequacies, insecurities, fears, and judgments. For I want to see you—the part of you that is innocent, beautiful, perfect, and true. I give you my word that I will seek that in you, knowing that those who seek, find. I desire to be someone who sees your best, even when you can't.

I want to show up in life in such a way that you feel **loved** in my presence. For you are. I believe in a God that loves you. A God that asked me to do the same. I regret how frequently I do it imperfectly. Nonetheless, I will keep trying. For it's never because you're not worthy of my love; rather, it's always because my own fears get in my way of expressing it. I don't bestow upon you your lovability, I only affirm what is already there. You are lovable and loved. May I remember that truth so that you might feel it when I'm around.

I want to show up in life in such a way that you feel **gratitude** in my presence. May my words and actions remind us both that not only are you enough, but so am I. And so is this world. There is enough joy for both of us. I can promise you that when I feel lack—as I sometimes do—I will own it as my own hunger; refusing to devalue what you have, or who you are. You deserve all that is yours and I celebrate it. May I become the person who holds so much gratitude for your life that I invite you to rejoice in it, too.

I want to show up in life in such a way that you feel **encouraged** in my presence. Not just applauded, but deeply hopeful. I want to hold enough faith in the Universe that I can share it with you at any time. I want you to be able to look in my eyes and see your best self reflected back at you. May you feel supported in owning your strength, your beauty, your talent, your power, your love, your goodness. An encouragement that roots itself in a soil of knowing and branches out in vibrant action.

It doesn't matter who you are—you deserve these things from me.
- You can be someone I only walk by in the grocery store, or someone I commit my life to. Both can be equally difficult.
- You can be someone I am drawn to, or someone I feel repelled by. Either way, how I show up with kindness should not differ.
- You can be someone who has loved me well, or someone who has hurt me deeply. My interpretation of my experience with you doesn't change your worth.
- You can be famous—a celebrity I only see on TV, or someone I know intimately and personally. Your inherent goodness isn't dependent on my knowing you.

How I respond to you says more about me than it does about you. I know that. I own it. Indeed there is a gap between who I want to be for you and who I am. For that, I am sorry.

Life is not a competition where one of us holds more value than another. And no one, other than my own ego, has given me permission to go around making judgments about your merit. So when I show up, as humans often do, without being all that I want to be, forgive me. And just know it's no reflection on you.

My prayer is that I keep growing in love, becoming, expanding, inviting, welcoming. I trust that as I see my own worth more clearly, I might better show you yours.

My prayer is that the best in me honors the best in you. That I can have God-eyes to see you the way you are. The way you are intended to be loved.

May it be so.

HOW MANY WOMEN DOES IT TAKE TO FIND ONE NEW FRIEND?

Assuming that we all want more than one or two women on our Right Side, then how wide do we need to cast the net on the Left Side?

I heard a business lecture that I think has good cross-over philosophies for our friend searches. The presenter, Michael Charest from Business Growth Solutions, was teaching how to build a life coaching practice into a six-figure income business. He pointed out that since most life coaches don't go into that industry in order to be rich, but rather from a desire to be in service to others, it's not uncommon for us to find ourselves struggling to pay bills, often hoping that if we simply have good intentions and fabulous skills, people will just find us and pay us. (You might have fallen prey to a variation of this belief too: If I have a good product, people will flock to it. Or, If I'm a fun person, people will want to date me. Or, If I say exercise is important to me, I'm sure I'll do it. Or, If I articulate my beliefs clearly, people will agree with me.) For our purposes here, many of us often assume that if we want friends, they will just happen.

Charest talked about the formula he uses to calculate his desired income. If he needs X amount of money, then that means X number of clients, which means that he needs to speak twice a month to an audience of thirty people to get six of them to sign up for a free consultation. Of those six, usually four of them will actually follow through with the appointment, resulting ultimately in two new clients. With the math in front of him, he can prepare his expectations to work hard and smart for what matters to him. If public speaking isn't your thing, he explained, then figure out how much you can make from publishing newsletters, networking, advertising, referrals, etc. That process requires experimentation, intention, and perseverance—nothing automatic about any of those words!

Let's apply a similar idea to making friends. How many close friends do we want to end up with in the next year or two? To get there, how many women will we need to initially meet to find the ones that we want to meet again? And of those, how many of them are willing and open to schedule in the consistent time it will take to develop a friendship?

I think we often expect, or hope, that when we like someone she'll feel the same and our friendship will progress to the Committed Circle. So we go out looking for that one friend, dismissing other potentials. If Michael Charest went out looking for clients one-on-one, he'd fall far short of his income goals. He knows he has to start with thirty potentials to get to those two real clients.

I don't know that there's a similar formula in a friendship search (it's like asking how many dates we have to go on before we find the one we want to marry!), but the principle whispers truth to us: On the Left Side of the Continuum, go fishing with a net, not a line.

A fishing line allows us to catch only one fish at a time. We just stand there and hope. And then we either need to be okay with pretty much whatever we hook or throw it back in the water. Then we have to be ready to stand there some more, throwing our line repeatedly into a big ocean.

Rachel Bertsche, who went on fifty-two friend-dates in a year, helpfully tallied up her numbers for us at the end of her memoir, *MWF Seeking BFF*. On those dates she met fifty-nine women, thirty-five of whom she met again for a second date. (If you're doing the math with me, that's twenty-four women she never saw again, forty percent of the total.) Those thirty-five women dropped to twenty-eight after the second date.

Of the remaining twenty-eight, four moved away before the end of the year and four others didn't respond to her repeated attempts to pursue friendship, leaving her with a grand total of twenty-two women (thirty-seven percent of the net) she'd consider friends to varying degrees. After a year, none of them could be called a BFF in the way she had started off hoping. All of them, however, still held that potential for her.

Like Rachel, I believe that developing friendship is no less worthy of my time, intentionality, and greatest effort than building a business or finding someone to marry. We know that it's possible to be offered a job we didn't apply for, but it would be irresponsible to be unemployed and not go out for interviews. Likewise, occasionally a love story seems easy and magical—that they "knew it" from the moment they met—but even that lucky couple usually had to date others before they found each other. Everything in life is a process.

Knowing we can't just stand here and wait for "the one" to jump on our hook emboldens me to open up to the possibilities that are out there. It reminds me that I may need to meet several groups of women before I find those two that will develop into a "best friend." It reminds me that I can't give up after only one or two attempts. It reminds me that this isn't an instant process.

Relationships can fall under Malcolm Gladwell's 10,000-hour rule, too—that one masters something only when they have gained at least 10,000 hours of experience or practice in that particular area. In his phenomenal bestseller *Outliers,* he points out that Bill Gates got his 10,000 hours of computer experience in when he was a kid, so by the time he entered college he was ten years ahead of his contemporaries. Similarly, it is the quantity of practice hours that make the difference between those who become top musicians and those who play for a hobby. Hours of dedication matter. Time determines the results. Likewise with friendship. It takes practice and time to develop healthy relationships and become more loving and compassionate. Who we become on our search is as important as finding one perfect friend—or maybe even more so.

And, it reminds me that Charest's only gain wasn't in the two who became clients. He still got to share his message with thirty of us, be stimulated by a new crowd, sell his books in the back of the room, and practice his life work. Those are not small things!

We don't want to be so focused on getting to the one BFF that we forget how transformative the process can be or how valuable everyone else on the Left Side of life may prove to be.

SEVEN BENEFITS OF LEFT-SIDE FRIENDS

Left-Side Friends, those who are in our Contact and Common Circles, may not be the ones we easily text just to say "thinking of you" or end up calling when we just need to talk, but life is made up of far more complex needs than only Committed Friends can meet. And let's face it, while our Right-Side Friendships may be deeper, the vast majority of people we know will be those on our Left Side. These dozens of people, in varying degrees of intimacy and connection, do indeed shape us in unplumbed and discerning ways.

1. Left-Side Friends Contribute to Our Sense of Belonging.

There's a difference between just owning a home and owning a home *and* knowing some of the neighbors. Neighbors don't need to become our confidantes to help us feel more rooted, to help us feel that we belong. Even if we never ask them to feed our dog, it feels good to know we could. Whether it is on a school campus, in a particular city, in corporate headquarters, or in a café where we sit with our laptop—knowing those around us (by name or simply recognition of familiarity when we both nod in passing) confers inclusion. Left-Side Friends can help us feel recognized, which helps us feel more supported in our role, place, or interest.

2. Left-Side Friends Provide Links to What We Need.

Recent research has found that the proverbial six degrees of separation (the average number of acquaintances separating any two people in the world) is now really only 4.74. And it's even lower than that when we need a referral for a plumber in our city, a suggestion of a new restaurant to try, or the name of a possible child-care provider. If we limit our reach to only our Committed Circle of friends, the pool of options is invariably smaller, especially if what we need is outside where they live or beyond the hats they wear.

This is never more obvious than when we're looking for work. Referrals are still the number one way most of us find our next job. An aspect of this is played out on sites like LinkedIn, where apparently my 340 Connections link me to 6.5 million professionals. In real life, those numbers are smaller, but no less impactful.

All of us, at some point, will find ourselves needing information that our closest friends can't provide. We might be the first to get married and need to know where to try on gowns, or the only one to start a blog and need to talk to a few who have done it before us—our Left-Side Friends give us greater access to information and resources we can trust.

3. Left-Side Friends Stimulate Our Interests and Give Us Ideas.

All it takes is a mortgage, a job, and a family to sometimes make us feel as though our world has narrowed—like a gerbil just going from one end of a tunnel to the other. Engaging with Left-Side Friends in our volunteer work, academic or professional conferences, social networks, and at local community events can help combat that feeling and give us a sense of living a fuller life, breathing more deeply, and feeling more fulfilled (even if we are busier!). We don't have to call these friends to reap the benefits of merely seeing them when we are in those common settings; we metaphorically step out of our tunnels and play in the open space.

Our Contact and Common Friends can be a mix of ages, religions, ethnicities, and careers. They can come from different ends of the political spectrum and surprise us with stories we wouldn't otherwise hear or read. They might invite us to a conference we wouldn't have heard about, or mention a new Lady Gaga song that we make a mental note to go listen to on iTunes. A Contact Friend might carry a reusable canvas bag that inspires us to try that, too, on our next grocery shopping trip; and a Common Friend can easily entertain us with her latest travels and motivate us to add that location to our bucket list.

We don't have to be best friends with all the moms in our playdate group to be exposed to one's reasons for trying to breast-feed until her child is two years old. We don't have to be close to the other moms in the classroom to agree to help plan a fundraiser. We don't have to know all the women in the book club to give us an excuse to read and discuss storylines. We don't have to be intimate with the ladies we play bridge with to hear about a doctor's visit that informs our own health concerns.

In other words, we don't have to see someone as future best friend material in order to have her add interests, joy, stimulation, and curiosity to our lives.

4. Left-Side Friends Evoke Different Sides of Us.

Our closest friends and family are like puzzle pieces, each interlocked with our own piece, such that they know one side of us very well. Not so incidentally, we have way more sides to our puzzle piece than a handful of people can possibly know—meaning there are sides of us that can be stimulated by people who don't have a set picture of us being a certain way.

A fabulous example of this is the Red Hat Society. This club of women over the age of fifty don purple clothes and red hats as their way of embracing the aging process on their own terms. Many of us would be shocked to see our mothers dress up in the actress-like regalia, taking on the brazen diva inside as they ride Harleys, walk in parades, and turn heads in restaurants across the country. A group of seemingly diverse women our mothers may barely know can invite them to experience something that they'd never do in a classroom as a teacher or at home as a wife and mother.

Our Contact Friends coax us to go salsa dancing instead of saying "Oh, she's usually in bed by nine P.M." They readily believe us when we say we plan to start a diet, as opposed to reminding us of the last twenty diets we've started and given up. They accept us as successful professionals, because they don't know how insecure we really are. They can see us in ways we want to be seen, or ways we don't even yet see in ourselves, which allows us to expand who we are.

5. Left-Side Friends Expand Our View of Normal.

We tend to hang out with people who are most like us, especially the more diverse our environment is. Which means that it is often a handful of people who influence our definition of normal.

If, for example, our close circle of friends all chose to go back to work after their maternity leave, it's harder to hear our own heart say we want to be home for a couple of years. If everyone in our circle hates their jobs but keeps going out of a sense of responsibility, it's harder to see being an entrepreneur as a credible choice. If everyone around us sees status in the car we drive, it's harder to not take that into consideration in our next purchase. If our close friends are all divorced, that becomes a more accessible option in our mind than if they all believed divorce to be the ultimate failure.

The more diverse our Left-Side Friends are, the more options we have to genuinely hear our own voice, knowing that normal looks different on everyone.

6. Left-Side Friends Lower Our Demands on Others.

I can release my expectations that any one of my friends needs to be all things to me when I know I have a well-rounded collection of people in my life.

An abundant Left Side reminds me I have options when needed. I am not a victim that insists my spouse, my sister, my closest friends, or my children (frequently relationships that land on our Right-Side) have to fulfill my agenda for what I need. It's when I haven't been intentional to make sure that I have the abundant Left-Side Friends in place that I am most tempted to be frustrated with unmet expectations from those closest to me.

As much as we love our children, adore our spouse, feel loyal to our parents, and respect our boss—those relationships are also the ones in which we feel the most pressure, responsibility, and tension. To gossip with our hairstylist, attend our weekly Bible study group, and greet the same people at the gym every day, on the other hand, allows us to engage in meaningful ways without feelings of disappointment, stress, and complicated decisions. Those lifelines on the Left Side remind us that the world continues to revolve and engage with us even when our child is pulling away, our marriage is crumbling, our mother is ailing, or our boss is putting us down.

Developing a full Continuum of Circles of Friends honors what each one can give and who they each are. I don't need the practical one to come shopping with me and I don't need the funny one to be serious. I know which friend will help me see the other side of the story and which one will take my side no matter what. And I need both.

7. Left-Side Friends Spur Us to Act Outside Ourselves.

Even our engagement in the causes of this world that need our attention is linked to the web of relationships we have developed. I love the story of sociologist Doug McAdam, as told in *Consequential Strangers*—he spent most of his career studying the connection between our social networks and our involvement in social movements. He highlights "social proximity" as the biggest determining factor separating those who show up and those who back out. From his research he shares the example of those students who in 1964 put themselves in harm's way to participate in the Freedom Summer activities in Mississippi. In looking at the questionnaires that 959 applicants had filled out, McAdam found that the number one difference between the 720 who showed up and the 239 who didn't was how many people they knew who were also going. For those who showed up, backing out would have meant disappointing people they knew.

The more people we are exposed to, the more causes we become aware of, and the more opportunities we are given to say yes to participation. Community organizers, whose entire goal is to move people to action, know that for our interest to be sustainable it has to be linked to self-interest. Even wanting to change the world has to be linked to someone we care about, someone we want to impress, someone we know who was affected by the problem, or someone we want to help. Our contacts will largely be what inspires our involvement.

Even assuming that the reason we often engage is for the benefit, or in honor of, someone on our Right Side (i.e., a mother whose son is murdered resolves to tackle gun control policy, a daughter who loses her mother to breast cancer commits to raise awareness, a friend who comes back from Africa decides to fundraise for an orphanage), our success in those endeavors will be only as strong as our reach.

One person can indeed change the world, but the change is most often carried out through other people.

10 WAYS TO MEET NEW PEOPLE

1. Say yes. When someone invites you out, say yes. Even if that person doesn't thrill you, she can help introduce you to other people. People we know will introduce us to people they know. Go to events, parties, and gatherings with the goal of meeting new people. If you know someone who has a large social network be sure to tell her you are looking forward to meeting more people so she knows to include you in her events.

2. Pursue a hobby. Join something that stimulates an interest, whether it be a training team for a race, a hiking club to get you out more often, or a book club through the local bookstore.

3. Go to church, temple, or another personal development community. And remember that you're there to meet people, so don't put it on them to do all the work. Make sure you sit next to someone, introduce yourself, stay for a potluck, or attend one of their extra events. And go repeatedly.

4. Volunteer. Certainly finding a way to volunteer for a nonprofit or charity is a great way to find others with compassion, but even volunteering for a responsibility in any kind of group is the best way to go deeper in that community. Whether it's offering to serve on the board of your networking organization, showing up at a neighborhood association to provide input, or offering to organize the nanny-share with other moms, your increased involvement will not only provide more ways to meet new people but will also provide a role that requires you to do so, which makes it feel more comfortable.

5. Use your dog or kid! Dogs and kids provide instant icebreakers as people often want to start asking questions about the breed of the dog or the age of the child. Go to dog parks at a consistent time every day so you start meeting the same people. Go to your neighborhood kids classes, stores, and community centers where chances go up you'll meet other moms.

6. Join a womens network. Do some online research pairing "women" with words like *network, club, community, group,* and *social events* to find a local network that can provide op-portunities to meet people. Then join and promise yourself you'll start attending some of their events. (Start with Girl-FriendCircles.com to see if we can match you in your area.)

7. *Take a class.* Signing up for a language course, craft class, creative writing session, weight loss workshop, professional round table, improvisation workshop, or parenting seminar will provide you ways to connect with others in areas of your interest. But be sure to actually look for ways to introduce yourself to at least 2-3 others every time!

8. *Alumni events.* See if any of your schools or sororities have a local chapter or an annual get-together in your area. If not, you can contact the school and offer to help co-host it. They'll typically be thrilled to do the inviting and organizing. These events provide an instant commonality and can expand your local network quickly.

9. *Meet your neighbors.* Everyone likes the idea of knowing their neighbors. So be the one who helps make it happen. Whether you bake plates of cookies to take with you or sim-ply show up with a "I just wanted to introduce myself to you in case you ever needed someone to water your plants while you're on vacation"—people are flattered to connect. Maybe a neighbor you meet will help co-host a neighborhood barbe-cue or holiday meet-and-greet.

10. *Become a regular somewhere.* Whether it's your local Starbucks, a neighborhood café, or the bar down the street—start talking to people you recognize. Show up regularly for their poetry readings, live music evenings, or game nights. Get to know the owners and managers, become a local they recognize. This regularity works at gyms, community centers, restaurants, parks, community gardens, Pilates studios, farmers markets, manicure parlors, and other local places near you where people gravitate.

THE VALUE OF CONTEXT

Now let's return for a moment to me standing on Polk Street watching the women in the café laugh. (The way I picture it is like a slow-motion scene in a movie—four beautiful friends leaning in close to hear a secret, then their heads fall backward in laughter, knowing eyes looking at each other as they share some inside joke, confident in their shared bond.) I was the one who instantly felt pathetic and lonely, staring at them on the other side of the store window, wishing I were sitting there with them. Like a kid in a candy store with no money to spend, I saw what I wanted but had no access to it.

One can wish we lived in a world where we could simply walk up to each other and exchange phone numbers, but alas we do not.

However, we do live in a world where most people are craving what I call *consequential connection*, interaction that feels more significant than small talk and conversation about shallow subjects.

Therefore, our invitation is to find mutually acceptable and comfortable ways of moving toward those moments. We do that initially by starting with whatever context we share (i.e., we're both at the same party, we're both friends of Mary, we're both standing in this line, we're both in the same class).

This shared context gives us social permission to engage.

Compare my Polk Street story with the time I was sitting at Sweet Revenge, a fun little cupcake and wine bar in the West Village on a trip out to New York City. There was another group of girls whose warmth, laugh, and friendliness also impressed me.

This time, fortunately, I was at this particular venue for a ConnectingCircle, a small group event hosted by GirlFriendCircles.com for the express purpose of giving women a chance to meet each other. So, while they were all complete strangers to me, suddenly the context isn't that I'd be weird to talk to them, but I'd be weird not to. Our shared context encouraged connection.

That mutual understanding inspired us to answer questions about what we were like in high school and what vacations we were looking forward to taking this summer. It invited us to laugh and tell stories. It ensured us that when the evening was over, we could follow up with each other. So much so that now when I travel to NYC, I count Kelly—a woman I met that evening—as a friend I can call to schedule a lunch.

It wasn't so much that the women I met at Sweet Revenge were nicer than the women I saw on Polk Street, or that I was braver in one situation than the other. Rather, it was that in one case we had a context that assumed permission for us to initiate friendship. And that made all the difference.

Having context is everything because it shapes our expectations. It's what determines whether it's "socially acceptable" for us to engage with each other.

Context shapes what feels appropriate:

- It could feel inappropriate for someone to ask me how much I weigh . . . unless it was my workout buddy or personal trainer.
- It might feel weird to have someone I don't know ask me about my failures . . . unless it was in a support group where that was the point.
- It would be odd for a stranger to ask me what I thought of a certain book . . . unless I was sitting in a new book club with him.
- It's not normal to just have someone walk up to me, introduce themselves, and hand me their business card . . . unless I'm at a networking event.

The point is, we're capable of all of these conversations, but it's the context that makes them feel either appropriate or inappropriate. Having that mutual approval of certain expectations determines whether we feel safe engaging.

So as we recognize what types of friends we most want to meet, we can then make a list of places and contexts that will help us meet them. It's called shaping serendipity.

THE THREE STEPS TO SHAPING FRIENDSHIP SERENDIPITY

If serendipity is the aptitude for making desirable discoveries by accident, then trying to increase that encounter with luck would be what we call "shaping serendipity." John Hagel, one of the authors of *The Power of Pull*, speaks of shaping serendipity as a decision we can make to pull more of the people, ideas, and objects into our lives that we need (thus increasing the possibility for serendipity). Hagel highlights three levels of pull—Access, Attract, and Achieve—whose definitions I've tailored to our subject of friendship:

1. Access.

Let's start with the obvious: We know the chances of making interesting, stimulating, essential relationships are less likely when we're sitting in our living room watching TV every evening than they are when we're saying yes to strategic encounters. By showing up at something our chances have just gone up that we could make a new friend. That's called accessing serendipity!

Where we spend our time affects our choices. How scheduled or open we are affects our availability. How much we're around people impacts our options.

2. Attract.

The next level up is recognizing that some events are more likely than others to be filled with the kind of women we want to meet and could be more conducive to our purposes than others.

For example, I've found that small groups are easier for me than large networking events. Something about a small group gives permission to everyone to introduce themselves, whereas at a large mixer some of the people have to be very willing to walk around introducing themselves. Events or networks that cater to women increase my odds of meeting other women than events that are coed since we're not there to flirt or show off our husbands. Additionally, it's easier to show up to something where interaction is expected such as at an entrepreneur's network, church community, or mother's/toddler's playgroup than it is to attend something where we're all there for the concert, lecture, or workout class. I've also found that my chances for connection seem to go up if I'm either by myself or with someone else who is also committed to meeting people. Otherwise it's too easy to stand there with my friend and talk all night to her.

What we eventually want to do with our female friends can also give us information about where we have the best chances of meeting them. If we are hoping to find someone to hike with, a hiker's group ups our odds exponentially.

Joining a female friendship matching community like GirlFriend-Circles.com is obviously one of the most strategic moves we can make since we know that everyone we meet is open to new friends and wants to connect. It's hard to get better odds than that! (But then it still goes back to Step 1 where we have to show up for it to work!)

3. Achieve.

This is the step where we maximize the serendipity, pulling out the full potential of the experience. This is where we smile and make eye contact with others, lean in toward the person we're talking to in order to hear everything they're saying, ask questions that communicate our interest, assure them how happy we are to have met them, exchange our contact information, and follow up.

That is no small list. But without this third step all we're doing is networking up the wazoo, making small talk, and exhausting ourselves.

It's *how* we engage and take advantage of the opportunities that will determine our ultimate success. We could be in the ideal group of women, all engaging in meaningful conversation, but if we never follow up to repeat the experience then we haven't achieved our serendipity.

One of the most powerful ways to maximize serendipity is to care less about *impressing* those we meet and more about *loving* those we meet. Sometimes our insecurities get the best of us and we erroneously think we need others to be wowed by us. On the contrary, most people aren't drawn to people they are intimidated by as much as they are drawn to people who seem to care about them. Our odds of building friendship escalate when we show up caring more about how *they feel* than how *we look*.

Vulnerability elicits trust. One of the things John Hagel says is, "We can't invite serendipitous moments if we don't expose our needs, problems, and struggles." It's so true. It's when we risk showing our needs that solutions are most readily offered. I am going to keep hitting this point especially in an upcoming chapter devoted to the topic—it's that important.

Neuroscience describes a secret that helps make caring interaction easier for us. Our brains are filled with mirror neurons, which essentially ensure that what we give is the same as what we receive. It's why we yawn when we see someone else yawning, why we're more likely to get a smile back when we smile, and why they're going to like us more when we tell them we like them.

Spiritual sages would call this the Golden Rule—treat others as you want them to treat you. It's our maturity that allows us to see that we are more likely to feel accepted if we start off accepting her. What we give is what we will feel.

FOUR TIPS FOR INTROVERTS TO MEET PEOPLE

Many introverts feel that they are at a disadvantage when it comes to the first two steps of making friends—meeting people and initiating. While it's true that it may take more energy for you, the good news is that Steps 3-4 may come more naturally to you than they will for many extroverts. So while each of us will have some steps that produce more anxiety than others, we're all asked to do all of them. Here are four ways to reduce your stress.

1. **Copy Yourself.** Pay attention to your facial expressions and body language in moments when you feel strong and confident, and practice copying them in moments when you might feel greater stress. Studies show that knowing how to "fake it" can help us align to the feelings that are associated with those expressions. For instance—smiling does make us happier.

2. **Do It Your Way.** Just because you're at a big event doesn't mean you need to work your way around the room. Walking away having had one substantial conversation may put you

way ahead of the person who made small talk with ten people. Look for another introvert standing along the edges and
make your way over! Or tag along with an extroverted personality who can help break the ice, making sure you end
up asking questions and engaging after the extrovert moves
along. Be at peace with meeting fewer people, because you
know you'll make each conversation count. Or try to attend
only small, less overstimulating events—dinner parties, dis-
cussion groups, and small book clubs.

3. Restore Yourself. If you're saying yes to an event this evening, try to schedule a quiet hour beforehand to fill up your
energy tank. Or promise yourself a reward of reading a good
book after the event. Tell yourself you only need to go to x
number of events a month—then go to them and don't feel
guilty for saying no to the others. Make sure you are responsible for your recovery time—doing enough quiet things in
life that recharge your batteries so you can afford to lose some
energy meeting people here and there. And remember that
every stranger you meet now may soon be a confidante who
can be a part of adding joy and ease to your life one day!

4. Join Others. If you don't feel comfortable initiating, inviting, and reaching out to others, then acknowledge that it may
be easier for you to build friendships by joining groups that
are already meeting. Sign up for classes, join associations, and
say yes to invitations.

THREE EASY BEGINNING POINTS FOR ESTABLISHING INTRODUCTIONS

If we are new to an area and want to meet Left-Side Friends, or if we
recognize that we have a very small circle and want to broaden our connections, then here are three of the easiest areas to begin with:

1. Places We Already Frequent

Geography is one of the most important indicators for who will become our new friends. And we're not just talking about both living in the same city, though that helps. Nicholas A. Christakis and James H. Fowler, co-authors of *Connected: The Surprising Power of Social Networks and How They Shape Our Lives,* make a compelling case for the impact our nearby friends have on our well-being. Happiness, and also unhappiness, is contagious. So a friend who lives less than a mile away and is happy increases the probability that we will be happy by twenty-five percent. Even the mood of our next-door neighbor influences us.

The Brafman brothers cite a project in their book *Click* where the researcher looked for patterns in a police academy class to try to determine why any two cadets were more likely to connect. It turned out that it had nothing to do with age, religious affiliation, marital status, ethnic status, or hobbies, but could be predicted solely on their last name: their classes had alphabetical assigned seating, and ninety percent of the cadets had ended up forging their closest friendships with the person they sat beside.

Studies on college campuses and workplaces prove over and over that no factor will prove as influential as the shortest distance between us. Where your office is located in comparison to mine, whether our dorm rooms are next to each other, or whether we end up sitting beside each other at a conference—proximity will be the greatest determining influence as to whether we become friends.

Make a list of the places you frequent: home, café, grocery store, gym, children's school, favorite restaurant. Next, make an effort to build some rapport with those you regularly see at these locations.

In other words, you have social permission to ring the doorbell of people in your neighborhood or apartment building. Is it still awkward? Of course, but we value connection more than we value avoiding awkwardness.

One of my successful neighbor meeting stories came up in conversation once when I was sitting with Krissy, Carmen, and LeeAnn, who all lived in my condo building in downtown Seattle. LeeAnn thanked me for having the guts to go knock on all their doors to meet them, but not without teasing me with how surprised she had been to open the door to a stranger with cookies. They had all lived there for years, never meeting each other, until I went up and down the hall of the eighteenth floor. It wasn't that they didn't want to know each other before I initiated the contact, and it also wasn't as if everyone I met became a close friend, and I can't deny looking a little weird ringing their doorbells and saying hi. But feeling momentarily stupid and insecure is a small price to pay for the friendships I have with these women now!

So maybe we should go ring those doorbells now and say, "Hi! I've lived next to you for two years and I regret that I have yet to make it over here to introduce myself . . . my name is Shasta." If it's only a five-minute conversation this time—that's okay. Or maybe you go the next step and say "Maybe sometime this month you and your family would like to come over for dessert?" And neighbors extend far beyond one door on each side. If we live in an apartment building the majority of us view everyone in the building as a neighbor; and in single-dwelling homes we extend the definition to easily include the entire block.

Wherever we do business, like a local grocery store, we can choose the line with the same cashier every time. Make eye contact and smile. As we gain familiarity we can ask questions like "How long have you worked here?" or, "Are you getting off today in time to enjoy the weather?" No-brainers. Easy connections. Remember the goal isn't that these people need to become our Right-Side Friends, but that we're acknowledging that being connected to someone, even loosely, increases our joy on that errand. And we never know if one day we'll be volunteering on some project that needs grocery donations . . . won't it feel good to know we're connected to someone who can introduce us to her manager?

Do the same at a favorite restaurant. It feels so good to walk in the door and be recognized or greeted by name! When Greg asks me where I want to go out to eat I, more often than not, choose Sushi on North Beach. I do love their vegetarian sushi plate, but not as much as I love being recognized as regulars by the wait staff.

The quality of the service we receive will likely increase wherever we have a connection, but also our sense of belonging is intrinsically linked to these contacts, and they must be developed.

Proximity is at its best when there is a shared experience going on around us. Walk into any bar during a football game and you'd be forgiven for thinking that everyone knows each other the way they are high-fiving strangers and buying rounds for the table beside them. Once, on a bus, all of us passengers started talking to each other after some obnoxious teenagers departed, expressing how awkward it felt and how unsure we all were at how to best react. Whether it's at a concert, in front of a shared TV during the news, or alongside a parade route—there is a bond we feel with those who share the moments with us. Even if they are initially strangers to us.

By virtue of sitting next to each other on the subway or both waiting beside each other for our kids' school to let out, we have more excuses to make small talk because we're beside each other. Had that group of women in the café been sitting beside me, I would have had more social license to have at least commented to them how much fun they all looked like they were having. Proximity, be it sitting at tables next to each other in a café, sitting on a plane beside each other, or riding our office elevator together, invites us to acknowledge each other. Move closer to people—a few feet makes a world of a difference!

It's largely up to your personality and the actual context in which you two are near each other whether the conversation sticks to compliments—"Love your purse!"—and weather—"Sure is cold out there today!"—or can move into actual introductions. I told you the story of Judy in Chapter 3—what started as genuine appreciation (or more aptly, coveting) of her red leather bag as we both stood in line to register for the writers conference was able to be turned into a bit more when we followed each other in to the main session and sat together. (Incidentally, since then my husband and I have shared many dinners with her and her boyfriend, including a weekend with them at his ranch. And this upcoming year, we'll be co-officiating their wedding. All because I drooled over her sense of fashion while standing insecurely in line.)

You can also brainstorm a list of places where you're likely to end up beside people that interest you. Attending the church potluck will ensure you have opportunity to sit beside someone where it's normal to engage in conversation. Volunteering for a nonprofit charity will put you shoulder to shoulder with others passionate about the same cause. Attending a GirlFriendCircles.com ConnectingCircle will put you at a table with women who value meeting new friends. Joining a writing class will put you next to someone else who's ready to put words to paper. Signing up for a local and intimate personal renewal retreat can put you in an environment that is conducive to connecting with others who value self-awareness and life discovery.

2. People We Already Know

Research shows that we love to connect people to other people, ideas, movies, restaurants, and new products. But we don't do it in a vacuum—we are selective with whom we pass along information in proportion to the degree that we think that other person is interested. If a friend wants us to help promote her business or event, we ponder who we think would be interested—we don't just send a mass e-mail to everyone. The takeaway from this is that we need to tell our network what types of friends we're looking to meet so they know how to best connect us.

Here are ways this can play out: If you're moving to a new city next month, post on Facebook: "I'm moving to St. Louis next month—I welcome any and all introductions to any of your friends who live there!" If you're looking to meet more creative types, post: "Anyone recommend any bloggers I should follow who focus on crafts and the arts?" If you're looking to meet possible job leads, post: "I'm going to make someone very happy when they hire me as a web designer . . . any chance any of you know who that future employer might be?"

We are not without people in our life—help them help us meet more people.

With any recommendation or introduction comes a powerful shared context. To be able to contact someone through her blog, her Facebook profile, or via e-mail with a sentence that names the person who referred us gives us instant reason to be connecting.

3. Profession We Already Have

I define profession very, very broadly—more like our life work in this world—which can certainly include our career, our side project, the book we want to write, the workshops we hope will increase our understanding, the classes that will challenge us, or the any other countless endeavors that capture our interest. Make a list and start strategizing about how you can create or join the contexts where you'll meet friends in those areas.

As a new entrepreneur, I started signing up for technology conferences, small business classes, and after-hours networking events—all giving me the opportunity to meet Contact Friends. Before long I realized that, for me, what would be more significant would be to journey with other entrepreneurs in a more consistent and devoted way. I ended up reaching out to two women I admire—Ayesha and Christine—to see if they would create a monthly group of female entrepreneurs with me. They both said yes and extended the invitations to women they knew. Now I meet monthly with a group of ten women who wow me—women who will largely stay as Common Friends, though I'd be honored to build deeper friendships with any of them. Other options include finding a group on meetup.com or doing a Google search for networks and associations in your industry.

What's important in all these settings is to let go of the need for it to look a certain way or produce a specific outcome. Having eyes to see people as potential friends means that we'll be opening ourselves to many more introductions. Some conversations may simply be a moment of small talk that will only add value in that moment, while others will pan out in ways we cannot yet even begin to fathom.

And we cannot know the final outcome up front. Nor do we need to know it now when we're meeting them.

HOW TO HOST AN INTERESTING PEOPLE PARTY

Focus: An Interesting People Party is a fun excuse to invite near-strangers to sit around your dinner table and get to know each other. By offering the invitation, we are affirming that we find them interesting and would like to get to know them more. Simply invite 2-3 people and request each of them to bring someone else along to create a unique dinner party experience that always results in synergy.

Invite: When I see someone I want to invite I say something like, "This may sound a bit crazy, but next week I'm hosting what I call an Interesting People Party where I basically invite

2-3 people that I'd like to get to know more, invite them to each bring a guest, and we all enjoy dinner and conversation with other new and interesting people. Any chance you're up for the adventure? You can bring anyone you want with you!"

It can be someone from work, someone who lives next door, and someone you met at an event—just as long as they don't all know each other. I always go with my gut and simply invite those I see that week. I've never had anyone turn me down—people have always been honored, flattered, intrigued, and excited to attend.

Ideas:
- Don't take it too seriously—hold it with an open hand, trusting that who needs to be there will be there. Your joy and comfort will be contagious. Be light with it. Laugh at the novelty.
- When people arrive, introduce the one you invited to everyone by telling people them how you met that person and what you found interesting, and then invite them to introduce the person they brought in the same way. "I met Samantha on the bus last week, I just randomly decided to invite her because I loved her skirt and thought 'anyone who can pull that skirt off has to be interesting!'"
- When everyone is seated, I always welcome them, applaud them for their bravery in coming, and offer up a toast to a night filled with joy and connection (and I hold the belief that this will transpire).
- At the dinner table, start by inviting everyone to answer a sharing question such as "Introduce yourself and tell us three things about you that you think are interesting."
- The conversation has always flowed in ways that are dynamic and thrilling. If you feel more comfortable having 1-2 more sharing questions on hand in case you need to keep the conversation going, here are a few ideas: "What is one of the most interesting places you've been—it can

be country, a building, an experience?" or "What is one part of your job that you still find interesting?" or "Can you tell us about a recent book you read or movie you watched that you found interesting?" Or fill a jar with similar questions and have everyone draw one question to answer!

INITIATE CONSISTENTLY:
Every Friendship Needs Momentum

think it's her turn to initiate. Did she mean it when she said, "We should do this again sometime"? Why didn't she respond to my e-mail? She said she'd get back to me after her trip and never did. . . . Maybe she doesn't like me. Maybe she has all the friends she needs. Maybe she just doesn't have time. Maybe . . . Maybe . . . Maybe . . .

And here is where most potential friendships die.

Nothing bad happened—no betrayal, angry breakup, or massive shifting apart. It just simply never got off the ground. We can't land in Friendship City if we never take off.

Momentum. The lack of it can kill a relationship quickly.

A romantic relationship would never get off the ground if two people went out for a date, then ended the evening saying, "That was fun . . . we should do it again next month."

When it comes to love, we clear our calendar for every possibility. Yet with friendship, it somehow seems normal to only see each other every couple of weeks or months. We schedule *her* several weeks out, even if for *him* we'd make time two days later. (The irony is that friends have a higher likelihood of actually being in our life longer than most of the men we date.) Oddly enough, if a guy were interested enough to see us next week again, we'd be flattered. But we're scared to give that same gift to a platonic friend, lest we appear desperate.

With romantic dating, we know how to flirt and show interest, wanting to be wanted, even if we're not yet sure we want them. With friend dating, however, we all too often initially show up with a reserve that says, "Prove first that you're worth my time, meeting my checklist of similarities." We put up our guard *until* they appear valuable to us. Then, assuming they pass their "interview" and are accepted for consideration for our friendship vacancy, we repeat the subtle standoff again. This time we use our reserve as an excuse to justify waiting for them to initiate our next time together.

And if they mirror the same wait-and-watch attitude, then momentum rarely happens. We feel judged because we're judging.

I feel for us in this situation. I really do. In romance, we want to be pursued. In job interviews, it's up to the HR team to make the offer. But in friendship, there isn't a clear conductor of this symphony, a leader in the dance. We're just two women who probably could both use more support in our lives, but if we both sit back and hope the other reaches out, then I'm afraid that we'll end up with a country of disconnected, depressed, lonely women. (Please tell me we're not there yet!)

So we're going to initiate. Yes, we are. Again. And again.

Because we're the ones reading this book, the responsibility falls on us.

REASONS WE DON'T INITIATE

To initiate means to set something into motion, to originate, or to propose a new idea or piece of knowledge. A basic law of relational physics is that nothing gets set into motion without some force acting on it to get it going.

Two women can meet each other, mutually adore each other, feel like they were twins lost at birth, and yet never become friends without repetitive initiation. It's true.

So it might serve us to examine why we want friends but don't always keep the ball rolling. Here are the five most common reasons women tell me that they don't initiate more:

1. A lack of time

2. Uncertainty as to whether the feeling was mutual

3. No instant attraction

4. Hope that the other would initiate
5. Just too tired

We can quickly see why friend-making at school or work feels so much easier. Those consistent settings eliminate most of our excuses. We have to make time to work; we're there whether we're tired or not; and we keep getting to know our peers whether we felt instant chemistry or not, whether it is mutual or not, and sometimes even despite no one taking the initiative. That's why we become friends with people that we'd probably never give the chance elsewhere! At work we end up bonding with people that we'd have dismissed as "too different" (she's too old, too preppy, too adventurous, too dramatic) had we just sat across from them on a friend-date.

Undoubtedly there are people with whom no amount of working beside each other is going to make a friendship. But the factors of consistently seeing each other, swapping day-to-day stories, sharing bonds of office gripes and politics, and teaming up on projects are like fertilizer in the rockiest of soils.

In one of my workplaces, there were seven of us who became Common Friends. In some cases they knew more about me than my Right-Side Friends—they saw me limp to work on a Monday after running a marathon, noticed when I formed a new Starbucks iced coffee addiction in the early afternoons, and experienced me in leadership roles in ways my closest friends outside of work may never see. Because I never invited any one of them into my life separately, creating a structure for our friendship outside of our shared work, when that job ended, those Common Friends became Contact Friends—people I could call but won't unless I have a specific reason.

At a previous job, while I had camaraderie with the whole team, the two of us who were female hit it off. We shared lunches together, secrets about our romances, and a few movie nights here and there. Interestingly, we probably wouldn't have ever given each other the time of day had we not worked together, for as much as I admire her, our lives were very different. She was married to a doctor with unlimited funds, whereas I was divorced and waitressing on the side to make extra money! And did I mention our age gap? She had two adult daughters not that much younger than I was! But working together gave us a place and bought us the time to learn just how much we could add to each other's lives. For the year I worked there, I'd say Tami was in my Committed Circle, and had I stayed in that geographical area, she would definitely have been a friend who I would have kept no matter where each of us worked.

Nearly thirty percent of us end up establishing a best friend at work. And those of us who do have at least three friends at work are ninety-six percent more likely to be satisfied with our lives.

But what about the eight percent of us who are unemployed, the twelve percent of us who are retired, the eleven percent of us who are self-employed (all changing numbers, but you get the idea), and the countless percentages of us who work 1) in companies where for whatever reason (size, culture, competition) friendships don't easily develop, 2) in male-dominated fields where our options are fewer, 3) in positions where most of our work is done alone in a lab or in telecommuting roles, 4) in temporary or travel-heavy positions where consistent time with the same people is impossible, or 5) in management positions where friendships could be inappropriate or challenging? Add to these the metastasizing numbers of us who don't want to mix our work and personal lives, or who simply don't like who we're working with, and our options for friend-finding at work can seem bleak.

Which brings us back to those five excuses we offer to explain why it's so challenging to transform these friendly people we've met into friends who matter: claiming lack of time, uncertainty if the feeling was mutual, no instant attraction, hope that they would initiate, and being just too tired. There are two major categories that I think they all fall under: insecurity and priority.

Yes, we are short on time, with many responsibilities begging for our attention. And, yes we are tired, under-slept, and low on extra energy. At the root of both of those, though, is a lack of priority. There are many activities we do and choices we make under the same conditions. Likewise, wondering if the feeling was mutual, hoping they'll initiate, or dismissing the possibilities because we can't yet see them can all have insecurity at their root. Those are statements we tend to make when we don't want to risk rejection or disappointment.

Let's address our insecurities first.

FACING OUR INSECURITY TO INITIATE

Our voice of insecurity can probably talk us out of just about any potential friendship! Either there is something we're already judging about them, or we tell ourselves, "I bet she has all the friends she needs since she grew up around here," or "She's too busy—if it's going to take her three weeks to schedule me in, then that's not what I'm looking for." We have a part of us masquerading as the voice of reason that insists we reject others before they have a chance to reject us. (As though her being busy or having other friends is really a personal rejection of us anyhow!)

One of my newest friends from the last year (whom I first met on Twitter!), Dr. Michelle Gannon, is one of those psychologists you wish you could send everyone in your life to talk with. She and I try to pull off lunch about every other month. Sitting outside in a café in Sausalito, across the Golden Gate Bridge from San Francisco, she shared with me that while Attachment Theory is often discussed in the realm of infancy and child care, she has recently been discussing it with her clients as a way for them to see how they primarily interact in their adult relationships. I leaned in and listened.

"There are four main styles of attachment: secure, anxious-preoccupied, dismissive-avoidant, and fearful-avoidant," she pointed out. "Basically we all have a primary behavioral pattern that we tend to follow—it can be different for us in romance than it is in friendships or other relationships, but if we watch ourselves, we'll begin to see which one is our default blueprint in those settings."

I leaned in a bit more as she explained that anything assisting us in observing patterns for how we might be engaging, or not, can guide us to do the personal work to become healthier. (The wisdom she holds about human relationships is one of the things I love about her.) Here's what I learned from her about these styles:

Securely attached adults tend to have positive views of themselves and their relationships, even new ones. They feel comfortable with both intimacy and independence. For our purposes, we could expect a securely attached adult to reach out to someone else, with the unspoken assumption that the other person will be happy to hear from them. If they don't hear back, they try anew, guessing that the e-mail they sent must have gone to a spam folder, or the recipient was just so busy that they need a reminder to respond. It wouldn't occur to them to just give up, take it personally, or shun that person. In an ideal world, this is where we would all be living from, as much of the time as possible.

Anxious-preoccupied adults seek high levels of intimacy, approval, and responsiveness from those around them, becoming overly dependent. They tend to be less trusting; have less positive views about themselves, their partners, or their friends; and may exhibit high levels of emotional expressiveness, worry, and impulsivity in their relationships. Surely we've all been here before at times—I know after my divorce I tended to operate from this place, seeking validation and assuming that if people didn't respond to me, or even reach out to me, then it meant they were probably disappointed with or mad at me. When this mindset is our default, we tend to take things personally. If a new friend doesn't invite us to a party, we assume that she must not like us, brushing aside other possible explanations.

Dismissive-avoidant adults desire a high level of independence, often appearing to avoid attachment altogether. They view themselves as self-sufficient, invulnerable to attachment feelings, and not needing close relationships. They tend to suppress their feelings, dealing with rejection by distancing themselves. These are the individuals who talk themselves out of caring about their relationships. If a securely attached person assumes the e-mail went to spam, and the anxiously attached person assumes the other person received the e-mail but didn't value her enough to write back, then the dismissively attached person concludes, "It doesn't really matter. I didn't like her that much anyway." Instead of feeling a sense of rejection, the dismissively attached adult pushes it onto the other, shrugs her shoulders, and moves on.

Fearful-avoidant adults have mixed feelings about close relationships, both desiring and feeling uncomfortable with emotional closeness. They tend to mistrust their friends and view themselves as unworthy. Like dismissive-avoidant adults, fearful-avoidant adults tend to seek less intimacy, suppressing their feelings.

Obviously entire books have been written on this subject, but it's worth examining briefly here so we can realize that just because we have a tendency to believe something about ourselves based on the actions, or inactions, of another, doesn't mean it's true.

Unlike aging, which happens to us whether we want it or not, maturity comes when invited. Wisdom comes when we hold the possibility that there might be a better way to approach life. It comes when we humbly recognize that just because we think something is true doesn't make it so. It comes when we know our own worth enough to not see everything as a reaction to us.

I've been on both sides of secure attachment in recent months and I can genuinely say how glad I am that no one gave up along the way.

Even those whose lives appear full, busy, and brimming with all the friends they need can be worth pursuing. One of my newest friends, Christine, runs an entire social community called A Band of Wives, hosts legions of events, speaks on countless panels, and networks with people most of us couldn't reach without going through numerous gatekeepers. But despite all that intimidating me, something about her irreverent say-it-like-it-is-fiercely-passionate-and-yet-perfectly-laid-back personality drew me in immediately. We had an amazing lunch where we bonded over our shared passion for women's issues and our recognition that we were both married to amazing men with a few years on us. We hugged each other goodbye, swearing we'd do it again soon. I reached out to her via e-mail several times to try to transform the "We have to get together sometime!" statements into realized dates on the calendar. I'm sure I sent at least three e-mails that were never returned that fall. And once when an e-mail was returned, the response had no commitment or clarity, just another "we need to get to together sometime." Um, yes please!

While there is fear of being the one who is more interested than the other appears to be (and certainly I had proof that she was one busy woman who probably didn't have obvious vacancies in her friendship circle) somehow I was able to not take it personally (I am maturing!) and I chalked it up to her either being super busy or behind on e-mail. But because of that I almost didn't invite her to participate in the new monthly business group I started. It was easy for me to conjecture that she didn't seem to have the need or the time.

I'm so glad I didn't make that decision for her! She instantly said yes without reservation. We are both swamped with life details, with neither of us feeling a gaping hole in our lives for more people. But while we may not need each other as Committed Friends right now, we will soon become Common Friends as we interact monthly in this business group. There is a chance that a year from now, some bonding event will happen where we could become Community Friends because we've put in the time together, or she may stay as a Common Friend and energize me there. Either way I'm glad I didn't give up, as this is one woman who inspires me.

I think of another networking contact who continued to write me on Facebook with invitations to go grab coffee with her. I haven't scheduled it, not because I don't like her, but because I really do have a life full of people right now. Nevertheless, to her credit, she has written enough times that I can't keep putting it off with ambivalence. I either need to say, "This is never going to happen" (and why would I? I like her!) or, "How about next Wednesday?" Wouldn't it be ironic if a year from now she was one of my favorite regular coffee dates? Kudos go to her for not taking my delay personally. And, I'm truly looking forward to our friend-date!

Many of us will recognize ourselves in the default patterns listed above. But we needn't stay there. We can schedule the counseling, do the personal work, and adopt the mantra, "I am determined to see things differently." And then we can bravely reach out again, knowing that their response, or lack of it, doesn't reflect our value.

If you initiated last time and you had a great time out—do it again! If you wrote her and haven't heard back—write her again! If this is a gift you can give, then give it freely and generously. The world needs way more people willing to give energy to initiating relationships.

I WILL INITIATE

Initiating does not have to be fifty/fifty in a mutual relationship. We certainly want to develop relationships where both people are giving, but we all give in different ways. My husband and I share the housework, but that doesn't mean we each vacuum half the house and then switch. It means Greg washes all the dishes and I track our finances. Mutual contribution can take on many different forms.

Maybe the gift we give to relationships is enough initiation to get the plane off the ground.

In a new potential friendship, it is too early to discern whether they can love us well based on whether or not they initiate evenly with us right now. We don't want to attach more meaning to their behavior than is possibly there. My default position may be to take someone's perceived negligence as personal but that's giving too much energy to a situation that undoubtedly isn't about me.

Some people don't initiate because they are introverts, shy, or fearful of imposing. Those aren't to be used as excuses for them to not practice reaching out, but it would be our loss if we didn't get to know them or assumed they wouldn't be irresistible friends to us at some point.

I think of Eydie, a beautiful woman twenty-five years older than I am who has become a sage in my life. Her deep heart, nonjudgmental spirituality, and profound wisdom are hard to find in this world. But had she not been related to my husband, I don't know that I would have kept calling, kept initiating, kept inviting. She's a classic introvert, a woman who has to consciously force herself to leave the house to engage with people. When I'm with her, I shake my head in dismay at the thought that I might not ever have known her and been blessed by her had we not become close. She doesn't force her way in, but I so value what she offers that I've simply accepted that I probably must be the one to keep initiating.

Introverts often have profound things to offer to a friendship, amazing people skills, listening hearts, and wise souls—the loss would be ours if we refused to step into the role of initiator.

What introverts, non-initiators, shy people, withdrawers, or those who are merely inexperienced at reaching out need to hear, though, is that just because it doesn't come naturally doesn't mean we shouldn't practice it. (Conversely, the stereotypical extrovert who never stops talking and has to be the center of attention must practice listening, asking questions, and biting her tongue.) All of us are called to growth. Knowing how we're wired is important so that we can see our patterns and begin to catch ourselves in our default tracks, but that's not an excuse for shrugging it off—it's a call to learn new ways of loving.

A relationship needs initiation. We may as well accept the role.

So if the disease is good intentions that never get scheduled into our lives, then the cure is to figure out how to easily start scheduling potential friends into our calendars. An easy way to do that is to follow up the phrase "Let's get together sometime," with a tangible offer of times that would work on your end. For example, *"I can almost always steal away for an hour for lunch on Tuesdays and Wednesdays. I love going to brunch on*

Sunday mornings, or I was thinking of going to a movie this weekend if you want to join me and get drinks afterward." That makes it easy for the other person to help make it happen.

Always, always follow up "sometime" with several options, the more exact in dates and times the better. It takes less energy for the recipient to check their calendar for specific times than it does to put it on them to offer up options.

Another simple strategy is to never leave one date without setting the next. This saves you both from meaningless e-mail exchanges, delays, and unnecessary stress. It's much easier to commit when you both have your calendars in front of you at the same time. One of my favorite lines is, *"It has been so good to see you again. Are you up for putting our next get-together in our calendars so I can plan around it?"* This communicates value, priority, and responsibility.

Who in your life holds potential for more meaningful connection if you actually took that hope and turned it into a scheduled time?

FACING OUR MISUNDERSTANDING OF PRIORITY

Now let's tackle some of the excuses we make—like being too tired or not having enough time—for pursuing friendships.

Priority is an overused word that we mistakenly think means something that's important to us. In actuality, the word means "superiority in rank or position." Someone or something with priority has "the right to precede others in order, rank, privilege, etc.; precedence." This implies, of course, that something else has to be ranked behind it.

The Power of Following Through on Our Priorities

Whenever Marcia Weider, the founder of Dream University, dismissed her workshop attendees for a break, she made us all pledge to return to the conference room at the appointed time, not one second late. She asked us to all set our watches to the clock in the room, telling us how important it was to her that we not walk in after she had begun talking.

Two hundred adults nearly tripped over each other in their attempts to avoid humiliation by walking in late.

I assumed her reasons were practical: no wasted time, no distractions, no one misses anything. But toward the end of the workshop she disclosed that the reason she makes such a big deal about punctuality is that people who show up late (or not at all) lose trust in themselves because they've broken an agreement that they themselves had set. "By signing up for the workshop," she said, "we told ourselves it was a priority. To treat it in any other way would segment our intentions."

She observed that those individuals who commit to attend any event but then are tardy end up wounding their ability to trust themselves. They develop a picture of themselves, usually subconscious, that says, "I can commit, but I can always get out of it."

How, then, can they be expected to trust themselves when they take on a new diet, decide to start writing their book, or pursue a career goal if their history has shown them that they don't live up to their "little" agreements? By giving themselves an out on their promises, they inevitably also give themselves an out on their dreams. They get in the habit of undermining themselves. They lack alignment when they make a decision, for some part of them keeps whispering, "I don't have to do it just because I said I would."

You can only imagine how that indictment flared up a few people who had justified their tardiness over the years with "I lead a really busy life," "I live spontaneously," "It's just who I am," or "Emergencies come up." But she stood her ground regarding tardiness and loss of self-trust.

One of the most significant ways, then, of increasing our self-trust is starting to show up on time to things we commit to attending, proving to ourselves that we can, in fact, trust our own word. We then get to experience a "win" in our life—the accomplishment of following through, and a sense that we can trust ourselves to do what we say is important to us.

For the sake of our relationships, but also for our own personal integrity, we need to be people who do what we say we're going to do.

DEVELOPING TRUST IN OURSELVES

I think about that a lot with GirlFriendCircles.com, the community of women who are committing to gatherings and events to meet potential friends. I cringe when I hear that someone had to wait over thirty minutes before the others showed up, several women canceled their attendance at a ConnectingCircle the day before—or worse, someone simply didn't show up.

At first I just feel so awful for the person who was stood up, who was inconvenienced, and didn't get the chance to foster a new friendship. I feel badly that someone had so little respect for the time she carved out to meet them.

But then, I feel worse for the person who convinced herself that it was okay to not show up, because she just wounded her ability to trust that she can make the friends that she says matter to her. She was willing to sign up and pay the membership dues because she values the idea of good friends, but she isn't backing up her commitment with the action that will actually create them. Whether she felt that something more important or fun came along, or felt too insecure or overwhelmed, or simply thought, "Oh I'll go to one next week instead," she has deepened the pattern in her life that prevents her from fostering the friendships she hungers.

The girl who showed up may feel embarrassed or frustrated, but she has proven to herself that she is willing to be present at what she says is important in her life. I believe that energy will serve her well. She is building her self-trust, putting her stake in the ground, and reminding herself of what she's willing to risk for what she values. She will leave stronger.

Compare that story to one I heard last week from a member of GirlFriendCircles where five of the six women showed up to meet each other for their first time at a local wine bar. Their sharing was only interrupted by the realization that hours had already passed; the late time had gone unnoticed due to all the stories and laughter. Someone in this group of women gave the gift of initiation by asking the others if they would like to turn that evening into a bi-weekly event. Following the chorus of "yes's" they dubbed themselves the Red-and-White women in honor of their chosen drinks and committed to meeting each other again "two weeks from tonight." In this case, the one woman who didn't show—for whatever justified reason she had—has missed out on a ritual that will create long-lasting friendships. These five women are committing to the time it takes to build relationships.

When we say we "don't have time" to foster friendship, what are we really saying? Or when we sigh and say, "I'm just too tired to go talk to strangers," or "I just forgot to follow up . . . and now too much time has passed to reach out," what is our brain supposed to make of that? We're sending mixed messages to ourselves.

Our brain hears us saying two different things: that it is both important and not really important at all. To live in alignment, with congruency, we'd be wise to either say it is in fact important to us to foster new friends and be clear how we want to prove that to ourselves (no matter how awkward it feels, how tired we are, or what other distracting event comes along), or admit to ourselves, "It really isn't that important to me. It is not a priority," and be willing to accept the consequences of this choice as they play out in our health, happiness, and fulfillment.

Priority means choosing something over something else. That means it will always involve a "no" to something else, be it sleep, tucking your children in that night, productivity on a project, or a TV show. It's impossible to prioritize friendship and not sacrifice something else.

Accordingly, every Tuesday night that I'm in town, I go to Girls Night, where five of us gather in rotating homes for supper. I don't ever ask myself on Tuesday afternoons if I want to go. Some nights, I fear, I'd vote against attending if I raised the question. I find when I'm sad or stressed that I am more prone to want to cancel plans, withdraw, be alone, or simply vegetate in front of the TV. Typically when we feel depressed or have low energy, our desire to interact wanes. Sometimes all I want to do is spend an evening curled up on the couch with my husband, a man who easily wins my title for bestest friend.

So I choose to set a rule with myself that I don't connect with people based on my moods, but rather based on my values.

Anyone who has had any success with regular exercise knows the need for that rule! If I only went running when I was looking forward to it then I probably wouldn't make it out there all too often.

Consequently, for the sake of my health, my happiness, the things I value, and the life I want, I will connect. I just go. It's scheduled into my life the same way I wake up and go to work, brush my teeth, meditate and pray, watch *Private Practice* on Thursday nights, eat pizza on Saturday nights, show up in spiritual community every weekend, and check my e-mail. We routinize those things that are significant to us, those things that matter. And friendship is one of them for me.

What would be one thing you could do to prove to yourself that establishing compelling friendships is a priority to you beyond just words and wants? What could be your theoretical "stake in the ground" that reminds you you're willing to invest in the desire?

WE CANNOT PRIORITIZE BFF'S WITHOUT PRIORITIZING NEW FF'S

Showing up for my Tuesday night friends isn't always without sacrifice just because I know they are fabulous. You might be thinking to yourself, "Well, if I had those kinds of friends then I'd prioritize them, too." But here's the truth: I had to show up and be there when I said I would be before I knew what made these women fabulous.

That's the reality that we all have to swallow—we cannot get to that always-be-there-for-you friendship that we crave without the scheduling-you-in-even-though-I-barely-know-you phase. We fantasize having someone drop everything for us, forgetting that to get to that point we have to be willing to at least drop our TV show tonight (which really means just watching it on DVR, right?) so that we can go have an awkward date with someone we barely know.

It's easy to justify booking her one month out because we don't know her well and so feel little urgency to connect. We feel excused in canceling our attendance from a small group because we don't yet know their names or feel personal responsibility to them. We rationalize that postponing isn't that big a deal because we aren't sure it will really be worth the time anyhow.

All of that postponing, canceling, and treating each other like we don't really care can make the dream of a friend who would do anything for us a little more challenging to realize. Friendships don't start there.

We earn the right to cry on each other's shoulders by proving that we can schedule and show up to dinner when we said we would, even when we don't yet know each other. She may be our future BFF, and we'd be remiss if we didn't start our relationship with a precedent of mutual respect, priority, and trust.

If not for the person we barely yet know, then for our own commitment to be someone who proves that friendships, in general, are important to us—we have to show up when we commit.

INITIATION MUST BE REPETITIVE

And then we have to do it again.

Most of us are meeting people on our Left Side. And most of us know how to be a good friend with those who are on our Right Side. It is when we initiate consistently that we begin to see how we can transform the friendly people that we meet into the friendships that matter.

We don't become friends without consistency. Repetition. Regularity.

Just as only one time at the gym just leaves us more achy than strong, friendship only progresses with consistency.

Our goal isn't just to go around life making small talk in the cashier line, passing out business cards in networking meetings, attending cocktail parties, and patting ourselves on the back for setting up a lunch here and there. Rather, our goal is to have the weight-bearing beams of our lives buttressed by people that matter. And to get there, we must forge on in the building of strong relationships beyond having a wide net of possibilities.

As teenagers we spent about a third of our time with our friends. As adults it drops to about ten percent. We don't have a schedule anymore where we all have to be at school every day for seven hours with a whole bunch of people who are our exact age, in the same life stage, all trying to be like each other, impressed by the same teenybopper stars, playing together at recess, and sharing the same cool words and trends. Inviting friends over after school circumvented boredom. Finding neighborhood kids to join in the game of tag was the only solution when mom said, "You need to go outside and play." Signing up for classes and leagues to ensure we were "well-rounded" provided easy ways of meeting new friends. If my mom would have let me, I could have talked on the phone for hours in the evening, having nothing else to do that was of interest. Friends were everything.

When we look back at our lives in grade school, high school, and college, it seems that real friendships didn't require effort and work. But as we've already discussed, it wasn't friendship that just happened naturally—it was consistency that did. Without doing anything beyond showing up for classes, we saw the same people over and over, resulting in shared experiences that produced a bond.

When I think back to my friends, it's the moments we lived day-in and day-out that are seared more readily into my memory bank. It's not a single day of basketball practice that I remember, but the conglomeration of all of them that makes me smile. I can picture playing in the cattails of Puma Park with my neighbor Brandi and my sister, Kerry, because we always rode our bikes there and explored. I recall the pride of doing flips off the vertical ladder at recess because Amy K. and I practiced on those nearly three recesses a day for at least three years. I still have a warm place in my heart for a memory where Michelle, Teggin, Wendy, and I sat on the same barrels in high school that we had played chase in while in elementary school. It wasn't one game of chase that made the memory; rather it was a childhood filled with the game that memorializes it. It wasn't only one afternoon that Wendy and I cooked up and ate way too much Kraft macaroni and cheese while my mom was at work . . . the ritual still comforts me to this day because of the conversations we shared while downing it regularly during my junior year.

We may recall the time we went bungee jumping with one friend, had to hitchhike with another, or splurged for a weekend in Hawaii with yet another. But more than the individual standout memories will be the moments that we repeated.

Putting in the time matters. Should we not have those full-time work or school schedules that push us toward people we like, then our task is to figure out how to develop consistency in new ways.

This is a big truth to swallow for those of us with busy schedules, spontaneous moods, and lots of priorities. It doesn't mean we have to connect every day; it simply means we have to consistently keep connecting. The possibility of a friendship has to matter enough to us that we are willing to give it consistency to see if it can grow.

FIVE TIME-SAVING TIPS FOR OUR FRIENDSHIPS

Book it: Make a standing appointment with your nearest and dearest. Say every Tuesday night. Or the first Sunday of the month. Or get really creative and buy yourselves a season subscription to a theater, orchestra, or sports team. That way there aren't multiple e-mails back and forth to figure out what works. You've got the slot; stick to it.

Piggyback it: Figure out what you need to get done, what your dear friend needs to get done, and do it together, be it a pedicure, shopping for undies, or a trip to the gym.

Bond it: When you do make time to be together, don't dawdle around on the surface; take it deeper. Ask questions that matter. Don't just get updates on the kids, but go deeper and find out how she's feeling about her parenting. Use the time to actually bond, not just be together.

Make it multiples: See a few friends at the same time. Get together in groups of anywhere from three to six close friends. It takes less time to share stuff once than to call each of those friends and retell the same story. And that way you get four unique responses at once. This generous approach helps more of you reconnect—and if a pressing deadline or last-minute obligation forces one person to cancel, the rest still get to bond.

Pare it: The challenge for some women is that their network of friends is so vast, they feel they can't possibly keep up with everyone. Pick a handful of women who are going to be your priority—the ones who will get the best of you. You don't have to be friends with everyone—that strategy risks you not really feeling close to anyone. Prioritize. Give the most time to the ones who matter most and who feed you the most.

CONSISTENCY IS REQUIRED

Consistency is so important that it shows up as the first required quality in my favorite definition of friendship. Dr. Paul Dobransky, a board-certified psychiatrist and the sex-and-dating columnist for *Maxim Fitness* magazine, asserts that "friendship is consistent, mutual, shared positive emotions." His definition is not warm and fuzzy, fun and flowery, or clever and memorable. It is, quite simply, a formula.

Dobransky's Friendship Formula:
C + M + S + PE = Friendship

As with any math equation, if we remove one of the four entities—consistency, mutuality, sharing, or positive emotion—then we don't have a friendship! By Dr. Dobransky's definition, friendship isn't defined by what qualities we like in a person, how similar we are, or what we do together—all the things we often focus on—but rather it's based on whether all four crucial elements are being exhibited in the relationship.

He believes so much in his definition that in his book *The Power of Female Friendship,* he says, "When a friendship is failing, one or more of these four criteria is missing. When a friendship lasts and is durable, happy, and organically blossoming . . . all four of these are well maintained."

This formula therefore can help us *make* new friendships, intentionally *grow* friendships, *repair* friendships that aren't working, and even *end* the friendships that have run their course.

When our friendships start on the Left Side, our goal is to begin putting as many of these four qualities into place as possible. For no friendship can make it over to the Right Side without them. We can have amazing energy and really like each other on the Left Side, but if we can't get something scheduled consistently, if we postpone or reschedule too much, or if we simply fall victim to the "we should definitely get together sometime," a friendship it will not become. We cannot move someone from the Left Side of the Connectedness Continuum to the Right Side without consistent time together. Period.

But consistency is only the first non-negotiable.

The second non-negotiable quality is mutuality, which speaks primarily to the fact that both people need to view that relationship as a friendship for it to truly serve that function. Over time, there needs to be the belief that both people see this friendship as meaningful and nourishing to both of them. You can feel close to someone—your coach, your pastor, your parent, your therapist, your boss—and that doesn't negate the significance that person can play in your life; but if it's not mutual, then it's not a friendship, it's something else.

I want to clarify this one a bit more because it doesn't speak of specific actions being mutual—i.e., Who initiates more? Who does more nice things for the other? Who does most of the talking?—but rather of the importance for both people to eventually view it as a friendship, not a job description, a role, or an obligation. I talk more about the give and take in relationships in Chapter 10 since a misunderstanding of it is a threat to many relationships.

The third element—sharing—speaks primarily to what is discussed and shared. Are the conversations staying vague? Or are they deep but only in one area? For a friendship to grow, sharing, wide and deep, must be occurring on both sides. To cross into the Right Side of the Connectedness Continuum, both people in the friendship must be sharing beyond the area that brought them together. The next chapter in this book is about vulnerability, and there I will unpack this concept of healthy sharing in more detail.

Lastly, if we don't have positive emotions together, we don't have a friendship. If you always leave their presence feeling worse about yourself and life, drained, and full of more negative emotion whether it be guilt, anger, or pity—this is not a friendship. You can stay in the relationship because you want to be of service, because it's your ministry, because they need you, because you're related, because you have extra to give, or any other reason you're committed to staying present—but call it what it is— it's not a healthy friendship.

Basically, a friendship is about two people raising each other's emotional energy levels and helping foster positive feelings. There has to be more positive energy than negative energy between us. Chapter 8, which is devoted to vulnerability and healthy sharing, explains how to appropriately grow this quality in our relationships.

IDENTIFYING MY OPTIONS: WHO ARE MY POTENTIAL FRIENDS ON THE LEFT SIDE?

Before the next chapter, though, let's look at your Circles of Connectedness and identify where a little initiative on your part might be best invested. You don't have to commit to all the ideas right now, but take a few moments to brainstorm your options.

Do you already know people in your social network with whom, if given the time and opportunity, you could foster deeper connectedness? Write their names down. Or do you need to meet new people and start fresh? What are the resources you have that can provide you with opportunities to meet those individuals? Is there a group of people you already know about (through a friend, a religious community, a nonprofit, a project) that if you showed up for regularly could potentially become your community? Keep writing names down.

Who has exchanged the "we should get together sometime" with you that you can now cash in? Who do you know in your Common Friends Circle with whom you could brainstorm ways to initiate connection beyond that area of commonality? Maybe you could invite a colleague to a barbecue? Or invite some of your clients to start a book club with you? Or invite a mom to bring her family over for a Sunday afternoon? Or invite the friend-of-the-friend to do something with you alone so you can build your own relationship with her? Also put on this list anyone you have some track record with so far, even if you're not yet certain there's friendship potential. For example, put the wife of your husband's college roommate that you only know from double-dating a few times a year, the other mother from your daughter's class that you talk to occasionally in the parking lot, the girl you sweat next to in your spinning class, the work colleague from your last job that you liked when you worked there, and the high school friend that lives nearby but you haven't seen in a year since you're not convinced there's enough there to try to rekindle.

If only one or two names come up as potential friends then it's Chapters 5 and 6 that you may need to focus on the most right now: meeting more Left-Side Friends by casting a wider net and following up with a few of them in your effort to lean in and explore the possibilities.

Making a list of all the potential friends helps gives us the vision in the month ahead to see possibilities when they are approaching. We are going to keep casting our friendship net wide, welcoming more people into our Circles. Most of us have met many people that we don't yet feel close enough to initiate. But that's the whole point! That's why we must.

If you tell me that you want to foster more meaningful friendships, then my response back to you will always be: tell me who you have scheduled in the upcoming two weeks and I'll tell you if you're on your way to stronger friendships.

TEN TIPS FOR STARTING FRIENDSHIPS

*1. **Own the Opportunity:*** Value friendship enough to do something about it! Be proud of yourself.

*2. **Use Your Resources:*** Offer to help someone local host a dinner party with their friends. E-mail your friends from across the country and ask them if they know any fun women in your area they can connect you with since you're new! Look through your friends' local friends on Facebook and introduce yourself. Follow locals on Twitter and see what events they're inviting people to attend.

*3. **Practice Friendliness:*** Even if you're shy, you simply have to decide what places feel authentic for you to be practicing friendliness: association meetings, lectures, networking events, the dog park, church, poetry readings, cafes, classes, and so on.

*4. **Affirm Her:*** No need to talk about the weather! Start conversations with the things you noticed about her: her hair, her outfit, her confidence, her laugh. We like people who like us.

*5. **Ask:*** Just making small talk with someone in the locker room after yoga is hardly the same as making a friend. As you meet women that you want to get to know better, you have to take the friendly chat to the next level. Try this: "Want to get a drink after class sometime next week?"

6. Be Specific About Your Availability: The disease of "we should get together sometime" can ruin the best of potential BFF's. Instead, try, "I'm usually available for happy hour most nights or for Sunday morning brunches. What works best for you?"

7. Ask Personal Questions: By personal, I don't mean private, but make sure conversation is about the two of you. Don't risk an entire evening wasted on celebrity gossip, the latest movies, and hairstyles-gone-bad. These subjects feel temporarily bonding, but you haven't shared yourselves with one another. Ask her why she appreciates where she works, what she looks forward to becoming, what she loves to do in your new city, or what her highlights have been in the last few months.

8. Share the Positive: It's a proven fact that we want friends to improve our happiness and health, not to bring us down. We haven't yet earned that right to cry on each other's shoulders. For now we will be warm, positive, and open-minded—someone she wants to spend more time with.

9. Follow Up: If it were a new romantic relationship, we'd be less than thrilled if he didn't call for a week after our first date. Give the same respect to the women you connect with by writing an e-mail or text of thanks, expressing interest in getting to know her better.

10. Follow Up Again: If it were for work or romance, we'd suggest the very next opening on our calendar when we could pull off another rendezvous! Why delay for friendship? Let's just say it takes 6-10 times of connecting with someone before we feel "close" to them. Why spread those out over a year if you can make a friend in two months of weekly get-togethers? Momentum helps the bond—keep getting together as frequently as possible.

ADD
POSITIVITY:
Bringing Joy to Our
Friendships

7

JULIANA · ANN · LYNNE · JACQUELYN · ROBIN · NANCY · CHRISTINA · KYM · ANGIE

N o one wakes up one day saying, "I want to make new friends because I need more people to take care of, more people whining and
complaining in my life, and a few more people who have unmet needs that
overwhelm me."

No, the truth is that we seek out friendship because we want to feel
more love, increased happiness, and increased hope. We crave positivity.

But we don't always know what positivity should look like in a
friendship.

When my mom was visiting last summer, she told a story about me
from junior high—one of those random snapshot memories that revealed
just how strong my people-pleaser tendency was at a young age. Apparently, I had insisted, with a tear-streaked face, that I couldn't go to school
"Because everyone expects me to be the happy one who cheers them up.
And I simply can't today."

Unfortunately, it's not just people-pleasers that can fall for the trap of
misunderstood positivity. Some misconceptions about certain theologies
or worldviews can create an unease around anything perceived to be negative; be it Christians who think that faith means never doubting, Buddhists
who want to pretend to not care or suffer over something they desire, or
followers of the Law of Attraction who believe they might not get what they

want if they don't claim affirmation the right way. Some of us are simply uncomfortable with anything that hurts, squirming whenever the conversation goes negative or getting nervous if someone sheds a tear, perhaps because we have unhealed pain in our own lives or grew up with unhealthy modeling of showing emotions and reacting to pain. And some of us have our identity wrapped up in being the giver, cheerleader, encourager, and problem-solver—like we're a corporate brand that believes its own ads.

Positivity isn't about denying our needs, thinking only positive mantras, or trying to plaster smiles on everyone's faces.

WHAT DOES POSITIVITY MEAN?

As girlfriends we often say that we know who our real friends are when they stick around through the bad times. We believe that it's our duty to be present through life's heartbreaks and disappointments. We often don't even feel close to someone until we've survived some yuck together. Crisis unites us. Secrets bond us. Tears connect us.

The good news is that no one who studies positivity in the field of positive psychology is promoting full-time happiness. In fact, psychologists define high emotional intelligence as actually being able to feel the full range of feelings, identify and express them in healthy ways, and know how to return to contentment. It's not in avoiding fear, sadness, and anger that we experience positivity, but in the midst of them.

When we express our feelings honestly, it tells others we will *accept* them when they do too. When I was in eighth grade, I thought that making people feel better was the loving thing to do. I made the mistake of thinking sadness wasn't good—that we need to avoid it. We don't. Sadness isn't bad; it's a real feeling that gives us important information. By refusing to show up with my tear-stained face, in essence, I was saying to my friends that sad wasn't an acceptable way to feel—which is hardly a statement of love.

Positivity doesn't mean never complaining, or being constantly cheerful, or acting as if our lives are great when they aren't. Certainly no one wants to be around someone who is constantly complaining, criticizing, pouting, whining, or acting as if life is never good enough. But that's different than being willing to share our honest dislikes, stressors, and frustrations. Positivity doesn't preclude being honest—pretending that we like everyone, every idea, and everything.

In fact, sharing frustrations is one way we bond with people. A *New York Magazine* article titled "Hating the Same Things: Why Shared Dislikes Make Fast Friends" makes the point that "Everyone, after all, can say kind things. And everyone does. This is how we supposedly make friends: by being nice. But by going negative—thereby breaking a general rule of first impressions—you signal that you instinctively trust this new person, because you suspect he or she might feel the same way."

The article references research by Jennifer Bosson of the University of South Florida, who confirms that people feel closer when they discover a shared dislike than when they discover a shared like. Whether it is the colleague that rubs us both the wrong way, a food neither of us can stand, or a complaint we both share about a particular company, we bond with people who understand our pain.

This phenomenon probably accounts for the jokes about women getting together just to complain about their husbands and their children. We're not sharing those frustrations because we want our families to look bad or even because we need advice or help. We're probably intuitively sharing the frustrations as our way of bonding and ensuring others that we're safe and trustworthy. To respond to someone else's frustration with platitudes, blank stares, or statements about silver linings or thinking only positive thoughts guarantees that the one sharing will feel an imbalance in vulnerability.

The Chinese philosophy of Taoism reminds us that things that seem contrary are interconnected. That which seems dark has light in it, and exists only in relation to its opposite. What strikes me is our tendency as humans to put pain in one category, as though it's all simply to be avoided, if possible. We act like we forget that in the middle of joy is some pain, and in the middle of pain is some joy. Life is a mixture of ups and downs. There are grievances, real stresses, and hard choices we have to make. Tears slide down our face in both pain and in elation. We aren't served in pretending otherwise.

Positivity includes us all being as honest as we can about our reality, holding it with gentleness, and engaging in the real process of moving to an authentic place of greater wisdom and healing.

HOW DO WE ADD CONSISTENT POSITIVITY?

So now that we're crystal clear that positivity isn't about pouring syrup on a relationship, blowing smoke up each other's skirts, laughing our heads off all the time, and acting as if life is hunky-dory, let's look at how to co-create it in our new relationships.

While friendship legends are built on "being there" in the tough times, that is not the job description of new friends. That is an intimacy that we build toward, and the road there is paved by being someone that others feel better for having been around. Rather than trying to vomit our own pain on people looking for friends, our call as new friends is to enjoy each other as much as we can.

Boosting their happiness strengthens not only the friendship, but also our own outlook on life. Research shows that it's more significant to our overall happiness to learn how to add positivity to our lives than it is to spend all our energy trying to eliminate negativity or heartache. There are a lot of stressors and frustrations that we can't erase, avoid, or fix. Our time is better spent being intentional about how to add more joy to our lives and to our relationships.

Barbara Fredrickson, a leading researcher in the study of the impact of positive emotions and author of *Positivity: Groundbreaking Research Reveals How to Embrace the Hidden Strength of Positive Emotions, Overcome Negativity, and Thrive,* says, "Negative emotions are necessary for us to flourish, and positive emotions are by nature subtle and fleeting; the secret is not to deny their transience but to find ways to increase their quantity. Rather than trying to eliminate negativity, we must balance negative feelings with positive ones."

It helps sometimes to think of positivity as putting "money in the bank" so that when a withdrawal in the relationship happens (and it always does at various times), there is a stockpile of positive emotions available to both people. That stockpile is made up of the frequent experience of pleasant emotions, such as joy, hope, gratitude, interest, serenity, pride, amusement, love, inspiration, and awe.

And unlike with a bank balance where a dollar in means we can take a dollar out, Fredrickson's book on positivity asserts that the benefits of positivity occur when the ratio of positive-to-negative emotions is at least three-to-one, (more ideally five-to-one). In other words, since we know there will always be stressors in our relationships and lives, we must strive to put in three times the amount of positivity. Using the bank balance analogy, the exchange rate is three dollars in positive currency to have one dollar available on the balance sheet.

In newer relationships we sometimes choose to offer a temporary loan from the bank of friendship if we lack the shared history to have built up the stockpile. But as any financial advisor would caution, we never want to loan out what we can't afford to lose, so we don't want to overextend ourselves in ways that will leave us feeling resentful or used. A relationship cannot be strengthened in the red. Positivity, even in small gestures, is needed to create reciprocation that feeds both people.

When people increase their daily experience of positive emotions, they find more meaning, effectiveness, and purpose in life. Not only are our relationships with others improved, but we also experience greater personal health, reporting fewer aches and pains, headaches, and other physical symptoms. We sleep better, make wiser decisions, problem-solve with greater hope, and savor life more fully.

Fortunately, what matters is the ratio of positive-to-negative emotions over time, not the intensity of those emotions right now. We can engage in small acts of kindness that move us all past the 3-to-1 tipping point.

5 WAYS TO BRING MORE POSITIVITY TO OUR NEW RELATIONSHIPS

1. Affirm Her

Women are complimenters. We give approximately two-thirds of all the compliments in this world and receive three-quarters of them.

We compliment each other somewhere between five to ten times more often than men exchange verbal support, and we also receive more compliments from other women than we do from men. Furthermore, we are quick to add intensifiers such as "really," "very," "always," and "love." And we mean it.

Deborah Tannen, a leading voice on the differences in gender communication, says that men tend to compliment as a way of making evaluative judgments, whereas women do it to build rapport, to create connections, and to strengthen affiliations. We may subconsciously know it strengthens bonds between us, but that doesn't make it less genuine. For why would we ever want to bond with someone that we are unsure likes us? No! To be affirmed makes us feel more accepted.

Compliments boost our self-esteem instantly. The praise can fall in the category of our appearance, ability or performance, possessions, or personality—any of them reinforcing that we have good taste, that we have made a good decision, or that people approve of or admire us. We can love her shirt, be impressed by her comments on the panel, admire her kitchen, or appreciate that she makes us laugh.

Our affirmations are crucial to friendships, for when we think of women being "here" for us, it's often less about them doing something tangible, and more about them speaking their support to us. Telling us we're not crazy, not overreacting, not worthless, or not asking for too much. Compliments reaffirm the identity we want to hold, remind us what we have to offer, fuel our self-image, and outvote the inner critical voice we hear in our heads. Even in new relationships, it's important to remember that telling someone what we admire about them is the way we say, "I like you."

Monica Strobel, in her book, *The Compliment Quotient,* notes that "a simple compliment embodies and transmits many fundamental qualities, including generosity, gratitude, appreciation, esteem, hope, and more, wrapped up in an all-in-one, pay-it-forward comment." Compliments are powerful positivity boosters—all those outcomes mirror the feelings we're trying to boost with our intentional focus on positivity.

Words of Affirmation is in fact one of the five love languages identi-fied by Gary Chapman in his now-classic book *The Five Love Languages,* in which he describes how we all give and receive our love in different ways. Knowing about this love language, even if our personal love language is one of the other four—Quality Time, Acts of Service, Physical Touch, or Receiving Gifts—we still need to learn this popular language since chances are high that many of our friends rely on hearing these affirming words to know they are accepted.

If it doesn't come naturally to you, here are a couple tips I'd offer up. First, it's important to remember this is a very valid and appropriate way to communicate. In fact it's as valid and appropriate as any of the other love languages, including whatever your personal preferred language is, so you can be generous without feeling like you're sucking up, stating the obvious, or feeding someone's low self-esteem. Love is love, and affirming words are a powerful way to communicate it.

Second, be as specific as you can when affirming. While I wouldn't refuse a friend's "You're amazing!" it would definitely mean more if I knew what prompted it. Following compliments with words like "because" or "such as" are ways of heightening the sincerity of the message. "Love your shirt" is improved with "because the color is so cheerful," or "because the cut is so flattering."

And third, wait to see if the compliment was received, because if not it can be repeated. For, as much as we all love compliments, we're still not very practiced at receiving them. Our fear of being seen as arrogant or proud often leaves us dismissing or brushing off what others give to us. So if my recipient begins to make excuses or starts to devalue herself, I gently and sincerely say it again. Often, with a good friend, I can interrupt her misgivings with a smile and give instructions, "All you have to say is thank you." My goal isn't just to throw compliments around as much as it is to make sure they are caught.

Affirmations about someone's appearance are some of the easiest and fastest ways to give compliments to women we don't yet know, but it's important as we make our connections and foster our friendships to get in the habit of going beyond what can be physically seen. Women, especially, have been raised with an imbalance of value placed on our appearance and the need to win people over with our looks.

While our bodies are a part of us, we show a lot of respect when we cheer for each other over tough decisions made, risks taken, responses chosen, abilities exercised, achievements earned, good-byes said, peace held, sacrifices offered, purchases saved for, ideas presented, skills mastered, self-discipline revealed, love embraced, subjects learned, and perseverance demonstrated.

HOW TO HOST A GIRLFRIEND GRATITUDE PARTY

Focus: The focus of the evening is a time to love on a handful of friends. First decide how you most want to do that: If you love cooking, plan an elaborate menu that excites you. If you love crafting, then keep the menu simple and spend your time on making nameplates and table décor. If you're a musician, perform a song for them. Have fun creating a memorable evening in ways that best express you.

Invite: Invite only the number of women that fit around your kitchen table or can sit comfortably in your living room. It's a fabulous way to introduce your friends if they don't know each other yet. Or, if you only have one or two close friends in your area, then invite them to each bring a girlfriend who they appreciate and turn it into an evening of meeting new friends!

Gratitude Ideas: Incorporate some variations of the following ideas throughout your evening. They may not all feel natural to you, but the impact that gratitude has is worth any awkwardness.

- After sitting down to the dinner, introduce each friend with a toast to what you love about her.

- Include a handwritten note at each place setting about that person—either invite them to read it out loud or seal it in an envelope as a take-home gift.

- For a blessing for the meal, invite each woman to go around the circle and share one thing they feel grateful for in their lives.

- During dinner invite everyone to share a "high/low" which means expressing gratitude for one thing that was a highlight/celebration in the last year and find gratitude in one thing that was hard/difficult. This question ensures an evening with authentic conversation and joy.

- On some occasions, before the start of dinner, I have everyone list out 30 things they are thankful for. (The length of the list ensures that we get the obvious ones listed and still have to think hard about all the other aspects of life we appreciate.) During dinner, invite people to share parts of their lists and some of their observations.

- Find a reading or poem about gratitude, contentment, or living in the moment to share at the end.

These parties have proven incredibly meaningful to the guests who have been around my table, but also end up being a hugely grounding activity for me every time. Even during the years when I was hurting from job loss or reeling from my divorce, it was a way to give back and express my appreciation for the people who surrounded me.

We offer hope, love, acceptance, generosity, and joy to people when we tell them we have found something we appreciate about them. In pain and crisis, a card in the mail that says "I admire the courage you're showing" is a gift of positivity. In times of celebration and achievement, a public Facebook post that says "I'm so proud of you for launching your new blog" is a gift of positivity. There need be no shortage of supply in the ways we find to speak one another's value to each other.

2. Ask Meaningful Questions

It's estimated that we use around 16,000 words a day to connect with people. Depending on how fast you talk, that's around two hours of daily conversation, most likely spread out in bits and pieces. If you had to make a little pie chart of your linguistic content, what is it that you spend your time discussing? What percentage of your words is about the weather and other surface subjects and what percentage is about the things that really matter to you?

A couple of years ago the University of Michigan released a study suggesting that when we participate in "girl talk," the hormone progesterone increases, which elevates mood, decreases stress, leads to improved health, and makes us more willing to "promote the well-being of another person" (*Los Angeles Times:* "A Scientific Take on Female Friendship"). Who among us doesn't want those results? In other words, we become healthier and happier by sharing subjects of emotional connectedness with each other (as opposed to neutral conversations).

In addition, the women in the study were paired up with partners at random, proving that the results have more to do with *what* we talk about than *who* we talk about it with! This is fabulous news for our new friendships—we get the payoff even if we're connecting with Left-Side Friends!

Most of us probably have no idea how we actually use our personal quota of daily words, but a psychologist at the University of Arizona, Matthias Mehl, also provided evidence that our conversations consisting of substantive material rather than small talk are linked to happiness. Mehl placed lapel microphones on a sampling of students and recorded thirty-second snippets every 12.5 minutes, and he found that overall about a third of our conversations would be considered "substantive." His research, published in the *Psychological Science* journal, shows that about 17.9 percent of our conversations are considered "small talk," which was defined as banal and uninvolved conversation, compared to the thirty-five percent of substantive talk that required personal involvement, sharing, and processing. The remaining words fell into neither category, such as practical information or requests like, "Can you please take out the trash?"

Mehl's interest was also in how the chosen subjects correlate to our happiness. The early research is showing that those who ranked themselves happiest seem to have almost twice the number and frequency of substantive conversations and engage in only a third of the small talk compared to their peers who were the least happy. In other words, the happiest person in the study interacted in substantive conversations in nearly every other conversation (45.9 percent), and the unhappiest person engaged in a meaningful way in only one out of every five interactions (21.8 percent).

"We found this so interesting, because it could have gone the other way—it could have been, 'Don't worry, be happy'—as long as you surf on the shallow level of life you're happy, and if you go into the existential depths you'll be unhappy," Dr. Mehl said. "Together, the present findings demonstrate that the happy life is social rather than solitary, and conversationally deep rather than superficial."

As a pastor and life coach who's had the benefit of interacting in a large number of substantive conversations, I have reached the same conclusion that there is a correlation between subject matter and fulfillment. I have found repeatedly that even people who consider themselves shy or less experienced with deeper conversations crave them. I have watched people feel stronger after sharing something that matters. I have witnessed clients make more empowered decisions after having the opportunity to talk about the substance of their lives. While we might think that substantial conversations would take more energy or cause more stress, I actually think that most of us feel more drained after a night of small talk at a party than after interacting over an involved subject.

This is why I designed the ConnectingCircle feature of GirlFriend-Circles to have a Sharing Question format. The structure of the evening provides a format to share in more meaningful ways: each person picks a question from a provided list and everyone has a chance to answer it. While most of us fidget a bit before sharing, we actually really do want to be heard, known, and validated. We do appreciate having the opportunity to talk about ourselves. We yearn for friendship as a place to share about ourselves—not just the weather, a recap of a recent movie, or a funny story about our kids.

This means both asking more personal questions that elicit stories and offering up our own stories—stories being the key word.

Do we *really* care what school she went to or where she grew up or how many siblings she has? To the extent that those facts provide context and ways to better understand each other, we do care, but those are things we list on public profiles that can actually do little to bond us with the person. What brings us together are the stories *about* why she chose that school, what she loved and hated about her hometown, and her favorite memories with her sisters when they were growing up. When we're with new people, we can accelerate our chances of bonding by prioritizing stories over information.

My husband and I have made a practice this year of inviting our "San Francisco family" over to our home on Friday nights. There are six to eight awesome friends and relatives that have a standing invitation every week. I make a pot of soup, they bring the bread and cheese, salad, and drink; together we create a family dinner of friends. We all have a shared level of intimacy due to the regularity with which we all see each other, but there's still a marked difference in our conversation between the first half of the night and the second.

There's always a spirit of love and connection in the room as we sit around and tell stories from our week, but there's a remarkable shift in our evening when I say, "Okay, tonight's sharing question is . . ." In this setting my goal is to offer a question that gives the space to each person to share something substantial of their choosing about the last week since we've all been together: "Tell us something that really matters to you right now," or "What is one thing bringing you joy and one thing bringing you stress?"

With that permission to reveal, we change from talking *about* life, movies, events, school, work, and kids to talking about those things in relationship to *us*. Most of us aren't likely to interrupt a dinner party to tell everyone how stressed we are, what we're scared of, what we're proud of, or what we're feeling bad about this week. But that's not to say we don't want to tell those things. We do. We want to be heard in a safe place. It feels good. Stories undoubtedly increase our positivity.

Sample Questions for Increasing Happiness & Bonding

- After a movie: "So what was your favorite part and why?" or "Was there any part of the story or any of the characters you resonated with?"
- At a birthday dinner: Ask the birthday guest, "So what were the highlights of your last year?" or, "If you had to give a name to your 46th year, what would you call it and why?" Or ask the other guests (if everyone fits around the table) to all share one thing they appreciate about the birthday girl!
- When we're out shopping: "Did your mom shop a lot when you were little? What were her shopping habits? What is one of your earliest memories of shopping?"
- When having dinner with friends: "It's so easy to talk with

everyone, but before we go, I'd love to just have everyone go around the table and share with us one thing going on in their lives that really matters to them right now."

- At lunch with a colleague: "So what attracted you to the job you have now? What aspects of it do you like?"

Go to http://girlfriendcircles.com/staticSharingQuestions.aspx for a list of additional Sharing Questions.

3. Validate Feelings

"Your feelings make sense. Not only do I hear you, but I understand why you feel the way you do. You are not bad or wrong or crazy for feeling the way you do."

We bring positivity to the relationship when we choose to empathize with each other because validating feelings creates safety, trust, and acceptance. What cheers us up when we're depressed isn't someone telling us to be happy and look on the bright side, but rather someone accepting us right where we are. When we counter someone's feelings by trying to be more positive, it can be a subtle way of invalidating that person's feelings, making them feel judged or shamed for what they feel. And when someone doesn't feel heard or witnessed, they tend to either stuff it all inside in embarrassment or false bravado, or simply get louder and stronger in their expressions of anger, fear, or sadness. Neither response leaves them feeling more hopeful.

Culturally we have picked up subtle messages that maturity means never getting angry, healthy means never feeling depressed, and bravery means not feeling fear. As friends, we can give each other the space to just feel what we feel.

No one validates feelings better than my husband, Greg. Empathy oozes out of him. People are drawn to him for his ability to understand what they're feeling without casting judgment. Sometimes when he needs the favor returned, he has to say to me "Shas, I don't need you to point out the silver lining right now; is it okay if I just want to be sad for a bit?" Kudos to him for asking me for it, bummer that I can't always do it automatically!

Validating someone's feelings doesn't mean we agree with them; it means we've heard them, we understand how someone could feel that, and we accept them right where they are. And by accepting their feeling we're not saying that we'd handle it exactly the same way or that we can't possibly picture a better way to respond—only that we understand the feeling. And who among us doesn't know what it feels like to be stung by rejection, bitten by anger, or bullied by fear? Even if their problem doesn't feel *that* big to us, most people aren't asking us to talk them out of how they're feeling, as much as they are asking us to give them our permission to be right where they are now. When they process that feeling, they will then be able to go to the next step toward returning to contentment and peace.

Greg and I have friends who bought a fixer-upper house and have spent the last three years making improvements. When we have visited them, I have made the mistake of minimizing the woman's feelings by responding to her statements of "Ugh, this is never going to be done" and "Every time I look around I see three more things that need to be fixed" with statements that felt like encouragement to me: "It's beautiful just the way it is even if you did nothing else!" and "Look how far you've come!" But in thinking about it, while I was sincere, she wasn't fishing for compliments as much as she was simply trying to express her exhaustion and fear. Positivity in that situation would have been to let her know I heard her feelings. Had I said, "I can only imagine how exhausting that must be to have a never-ending to-do list," then our conversation would have given her room to be heard, resulting in more peace and eventual positivity.

One of the best ways to validate feelings is to practice reflective listening. As listeners we must identify the primary feelings our friend is expressing and then reflect back that understanding with an empathetic tone. This lets them know they've been heard and we're not trying to judge, minimize, or discount feelings, give advice, or start telling our own stories to steal the spotlight.

Any time we can offer a variation of the words "Me too," or "That sucks," we're saying to that person that what they're feeling has been heard.

4. Create Memories

If positivity is made up of joy, hope, gratitude, interest, serenity, pride, amusement, love, inspiration, and awe, then any experience when those reactions are anticipated should be the kind of events we want to invite others to do with us to create new memories together.

Make a list of the things you love doing and seeing—what types of concerts move you? Which museums inspire you? Which outdoor activities excite or awe you? What subjects stimulate or interest you? What experiences provoke your gratitude or serenity? What practices do you regularly choose for self-care? What adventures do you want to try once? Know what makes you happy and resolve to extend invitations to various new friends to accompany you.

A point from Gretchen Rubin's book *The Happiness Project* that I often quote is her analysis of the three different categories of fun. She describes *relaxing fun* as that which requires the least amount of scheduling, preparation, or skill—such as watching TV; *accommodating fun* as that which requires a fair bit of effort and organizing—such as taking the kids to the park or planning a date night; and *challenging fun* as that which is the most demanding due to the potential frustration, required energy, and hard work or practice—such as learning golf, planning a family vacation, or landscaping the backyard.

And wouldn't you know that, over the long-term, the things that require the most energy are also the ones that produce the most happiness? Challenging and accommodating fun are most likely to produce the strongest relational bonds and give us a sense of achievement and mastery. It's a paradox in life that the things that give us the most energy—like exercise and relationships—are also the things that require the most energy up front. It will always be easier to watch re-runs of *Friends* or *Sex and the City* than to go foster our own circle of friends. But we're not looking for easy, are we? We're looking for happiness, joy, and meaning.

Bonds are built on this stuff. Shared memories are glue because they become one more thing we have in common. And every time we increase our sense of commonality, we increase our sense of satisfaction in a relationship. Even someone who we think we have nothing in common with can become someone we feel close to when we climb Mt. Rainer together, perform in a flash mob beside each other, or collaborate for the annual fundraiser as co-chairs.

We want to look for ways to invite new friends into new experiences with us. Yes, it may be easier to meet at a theater for a movie, but it won't bond us as much as going bowling for the first time in ten years, deciding to go camping together, or training for a race together. Another idea is to give each other the privilege of planning one afternoon where we both do whatever the other one has planned.

Looking for unique or creative ways to spend time together is one of the prerequisites for accelerating Left-Side Friends (who share one commonality such as book club, PTA, or work) to the Right Side. Our goal is to experience each other in new ways, not just because it boosts our happiness but also because the more glue we have between us, the longer we'll last when the one area we initially had in common comes to an end.

5. Add laughter

One of the easiest ways to add positivity to our friendships is to bring our sense of humor to our shared moments.

I think I'm funny. But my sweet husband, who never speaks poorly of anyone, might make a case that trash talk during games, sarcasm at the expense of others, and making fun of each other in embarrassing moments isn't really all that funny. Well, in my childhood home, that was what we had.

But I admit that if I had all my friends list the top ten qualities they admire about me, I'd be surprised if a single one of them listed humor. I'm not the one who remembers jokes like my sister, Kerry; does crazy and daring antics that get everyone riled up like Valerie; tells stories reminiscent of a stand-up comic like J'Leen; or laughs at herself in such a warm and comfortable way that she welcomes everyone else to join her in self-mocking like Kari. I do eye-rolls at slapstick comedy, rarely find bathroom humor worthy of the effort, and never know what movie line someone is quoting with their pop-culture prowess. But that's not to say I don't love to laugh. We all do.

I may not be the funniest one in the bunch, but I know I still contribute to laughter. There are many ways to instill moments with silliness, smiles, and laughs. And we're all called to participate in those moments and be generous with our laughter.

One study showed that merely holding a pleasant expression on our face lifts our mood. The researchers asked half the subjects to hold a pen in their teeth, which forced an approximate smile, while the other half held the pen in their lips, which forced a slight pout. During a series of jokes, the people with the pen in their teeth ranked the jokes as funnier! Starting with a smile increased their laughter. Sometimes just showing up willing to laugh, with a smile on our face, is all that is needed for us to participate in the humor around us.

I remember going to the L.A. County Fair with four girlfriends one September. I can't recall a single ride we went on, any show we watched, or anything else really, other than going into a hat store and getting pictures taken of all of us with goofy hats on. One of these pictures is framed in my living room. One of my favorite memories with my Seattle friends was a night where we each donned a wig to wear at our chosen restaurant. It was hilarious how differently we all acted as we took on our various personas for the evening.

Sometimes the best way I know to foster laughter is to simply provide the space for it. On my dining room wall is painted the saying, "Sit long, talk much, laugh often." I know how to throw a pasta dish together, put out piles of plates, light a fire in the fireplace, and call it a party. While studying at seminary, I used to host girls nights over at my apartment every month with some of the wives of my fellow classmates. There's nothing like assigning a color theme to a potluck to ensure lots of photos of a table full of red food, laughter as we consume dyed-red mashed potatoes, and oohs and aahs over the creative beet-red risotto. Name a color—it can be done! To this day I smile thinking of those times shared with Michelle, Amy, Kim, Elysabeth, and others.

An incredibly bonding form of laughter is inside jokes—I use the word "jokes" loosely. Simply recalling memories in the present moment can subconsciously remind us that we have moments that no one else knows. And secrets bond us. With Valerie all I have to do is ask her if she wants to hitchhike and we'll both recall the night in Italy where we thought we might die in the backseat of a drunk's car. What wasn't funny then now becomes our badge of honor, giving us a sense of being courageous, adventurous, and crazy. With Martt, when talking about any new date she goes on, all she has to do with her closest friends is say, "Well he hasn't given me any Tin-Tin books," and we will all recall the man who did, sigh in relief that this one appears different, and then bust into laughter informed by the shared prior secret.

Inside jokes don't even have to be memories as much as recognition that we both belong to the same group. One mom saying to the other how well-rested she is will bring wistful laugher and guffaws as the two bond over the irony of the statement, reminding themselves that there is someone else in the world who feels just as sleep-deprived. We can do this if we both share a religious background, a culture heritage, an age group, or a life stage. Making a joke that not *everyone* would get bonds us in a club of understanding. Commenting on our bonds, our shared experiences, the moments we survived, our inside knowledge, and our private conversations heightens our feeling of connection.

Laughing out loud releases endorphins and oxytocin, naturally occurring chemicals that relieve stress and increase our feelings of well-being and belonging. Oxytocin also facilitates a greater sense of trust, which is obviously important in the establishment and fostering of any relationship. Laughing together floods our bodies with these feel-good chemicals, making it easier for us to think that the other person won't take life too seriously, is less judgmental, is fun to be around, will lower our stress, and bring us joy.

Rachel Bertsche, in her journey to find a new BFF, said, "If I had to pick a single indicator of whether a friendship will take off after the first date, how many times I laughed in a given meeting would be it."

MORE IDEAS FOR BOOSTING POSITIVITY WITH FRIENDS

- *Take photos!* Happiness research shows that people who remember happy memories are likelier to experience happiness in the present. Be the friend that captures the memories and e-mails out copies and frames special ones for gifts.

- *Create rituals.* Maybe it's debriefing the week over Friday evening happy hour every week, maybe it's making apple sauce every fall together, or maybe it's meeting at the same restaurant every time you celebrate something. Sometimes you may decide ahead of time, "Let's make this something we do every month!" and other times maybe it's only when you look back that you will see what habits were created. A gift to a friendship is to notice the opportunities and help ritualize them. To write and say, "Hey, are you up for choosing a TV show this

fall that we watch together?" or, "Going away for that weekend was so fun, we should do it every year together," is a gift
of appreciation and priority.

- ***Honor anniversaries.*** Make a note in your calendar of when
  and where you meet people so that upon a one-year anniversary you can write and say "It has been a pleasure getting to
  know you this last year!" Be conscientious after her miscar-
  riage so you can send a card on the day the baby would have
  been due. Mark the date of her father's death so you can call
  her one year later and check in on her. Record the day of her
  first day at work so you can invite her out for drinks after she
  completes her 90-day performance review.

- ***Text, text, and text.*** This is a fast and easy way to bring a
  greater sense of access to each other in a way that doesn't
  require much time or energy in your busy schedules. The
  ability to say, "Just saw someone running and it reminded
  me of your upcoming race . . . sure am proud of you!" or,
  "Just walked by the café where we met last time and it reminded me I miss you. Let's do it again!" boosts our feelings
  of closeness and give us that sense of being in touch. (Just
  make sure they have a phone plan that includes texting!)

GOOD MOMENTS MAKE A FRIENDSHIP

All of my relationships have included misunderstandings, jealousies,
hurt feelings, and unmet expectations at one time or another. The negative emotions have undoubtedly been there.

But I can attest that the positivity and joy have far outweighed any
fight or disappointment. So much so, that when I think of them, it's a feeling of complete love that is felt and recalled.

If you name my friend Daneen, I'll think of drinking tea with her in
her studio apartment. Mention Christina and my brain will feel stimulated with all the books and ideas she has exposed me to, and my heart
will feel full because of her unwavering belief in me. With Ayesha's name

I'll think of being entrepreneurs together—supporting and cheering each other on. If I picture Beth I'll immediately think of small group nights at her house in our youth, with meaningful conversation and idealism. Karen makes me think of exercising and eating egg-white omelets, as she always impresses me with her dedication to health. Mention Sher and I'll think about feeling heard and validated, as she's a friend who asks questions, listens, and encourages. Name Jennifer and I'll think of our shared activism—she's another woman who will jump into any far-fetched dream with her whole heart and body. With LeeAnn it is weekend brunches around Seattle that will pop into my head. And just the mention of Krista will leave me with a feeling of calm wisdom.

Those aren't the kinds of memories that can be developed over one meal together. And while we've also been there for each other through some stressful times, those aren't the moments that pop into my head when I think of my friends. Rather, it is because we have repeated positivity so much that the collective memories of all the good times have been seared into my consciousness.

Good moments are what make a friendship. Moments like sneaking off the school campus during third grade recess to go buy Fireballs with Amy K. and Heidi at the nearby candy store. Or watching my first R-rated movie with Aimee R., Jennifer, and Kristin. (It's hard now to believe that Eddie Murphy's *Coming to America* would be scandalous!) Or performing in the high school talent show to "Ain't No Mountain High Enough" with Aimee S., Heather, Vanessa, and Wendy—thinking we were so cool with our song-and-dance routine! Or feeling all grown up when Heather got her driver's license and drove a carload of us to see *Wild Hearts Can't Be Broken*.

Those are the moments we crave repeating. We want to laugh, not just offer our shoulders for tears. We want to create memories, not just exchange updates. We want to have fun, not just be needed by one more person. We want joy. That is why we seek out friends.

We can't forget this truth. To ignore it means that we risk only showing up in our friendships when we need them. To remember what friendship can truly be means to show up consistently and always look for ways to bring more positivity to their lives, and to our own.

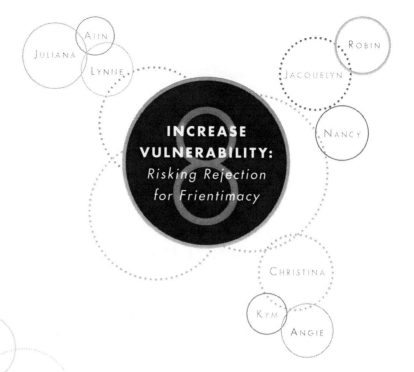

INCREASE
VULNERABILITY:
*Risking Rejection
for Frientimacy*

JULIANA
ALIN
LYNNE
JACQUELYN
ROBIN
NANCY
CHRISTINA
KYM
ANGIE

I n this chapter I am going to share some of the yuckiest parts of my life with hopes that we can learn what vulnerability is, why it's important, and how we can best engage in it within our relationships. While the end result of vulnerability is healthy friendships, before we talk about how we practice outward interactions it's crucial to talk about where it comes from: within. All the tips, rules, and steps of Frientimacy have to come from an authentic place of self-acceptance. So that's where we must begin.

There is probably no better way to start a chapter on vulnerability than simply to step into it myself. Some of the hardest parts of my life to admit to others are the events surrounding my first marriage and subsequent divorce. We don't wake up one morning and think to ourselves, "I want to mess up my life and disappoint someone today," and yet we inevitably do just that at various times in our lives. For me it was falling in love with another man besides my husband. Not something I aspired to do, but nonetheless I soon found myself living out of alignment with my own value system. No judgment you feel toward me could match the judgment I placed on myself.

Certainly when we're not happy with ourselves we aren't going to be too keen on sharing who we are with others. Geesh, *I* didn't approve of what I was feeling! I had no doubt that everyone I knew would feel the same way. So my shame caused me to hide that part of my life from those I loved. I didn't want to disappoint others or admit anything that would risk their anger, judgment, or pity. I put on a happy face, put my best foot forward, said what people wanted to hear, and tried to be likable—ignoring that I had a shadow side that I hoped would just go away.

This story from my life is a particularly dramatic rendition of how most of us are tempted to try to show up in life: impress people with the best of us and hide the worst of us.

The irony of a learning experience such as the path I chose is that to tell people the truth would mean risking their possible rejection, but to hide it didn't result in me feeling accepted either. I could never receive the respect of others during that time because my little inner critic whispered, "It's because they don't know. If they did, they wouldn't like you." It was a losing proposition.

Shame is the fear of disconnection, the doubts about whether we're worthy of love, and the suspicion that we are never quite enough, therefore we might never quite belong.

And trying to belong has much broader ramifications than just living with some dark secret like I was. Usually it also plays out when we go to networking events and assume everyone else knows each other, attend conferences and feel overwhelmed by the talent around us, or meet strangers and wonder if they like us or not. Our ultimate hunger is to be accepted, to feel as though we are good enough. But we go through much of life seeing walls—which are really pretend and which we've put up ourselves—that tempt us to think we're on the outside. We think we don't look the right way, have the right amount of money, hold the right degree, know the right people, or live the right lifestyle to belong.

Most of our actions, whether we admit it or not, are in reaction to that desire to feel connected. Nearly every conversation we hold traces back to the issue of belonging. It's staggering how much we hurt ourselves, and others, to try to obtain it.

I know firsthand the damage that can be wrought when trying to fill the need for love and approval. What followed my divorce was a year of emotions and reactions that would take another book to fill—rejection, tears, insights, growth, darkness, fear, loneliness, shame, forgiveness, recovery, honesty, acceptance, and congruency.

What we ultimately crave is someone who knows everything about us and still loves us. We hunger for that belonging. It's also what we ultimately fear—someone who knows everything about us. Because the risk is obviously that not everyone will love us after they know.

With the action of sharing vulnerability comes all our baggage around rejection. Which is to be expected since, in its classic definition, vulnerability is the place where we're willing to get, or susceptible to getting, hurt.

WHAT DOES VULNERABILITY MEAN?

Dr. Dobransky, in his friendship formula, uses the word "sharing" to describe what I am calling vulnerability. Similarly, psychologists, university professors, and long-time researchers of non-romantic relationships Debra Oswald and Eddie Clark call it *self-disclosure*. By any name, vulnerability is the action we take to *uncover* or *reveal* ourselves, despite the risks, to make sure we're not just hanging out with people, but actually getting to know each other.

We often think we're engaging in vulnerability when we tell someone about the skeleton in our closet. But there's more to it than just the vomiting of pain and details from our shadow lives. Vulnerability isn't just about giving information to someone; rather it's about being present as we are doing so. It's not just about gauging when it's the right time to tell something, but it's also about knowing who we are when we do reveal ourselves.

If you're not one of the millions of people who have already watched Brene Brown's TED talk on the subject of vulnerability, I highly suggest you become one of them. A social work research professor who has spent the past ten years studying vulnerability, courage, authenticity, and shame, she highlights the necessity of the journey.

In her countless interviews with people who shared their vulnerability she saw a clear difference between how some people shared versus how others did. Identifying the difference as "those with a strong sense of love and belonging, a sense of their worthiness" compared to those "who are always wondering if they're good enough," she said there was only one variable separating these two groups. The contrast between those who had a strong sense of love and belonging and those who had to really struggle for it came down to one thing: believing they were worthy of love and be-longing. "That's it," she said. "They simply believe they're worthy."

From there she began to study all the interviews, looking for themes and patterns in her data of those she began to call the "whole-hearted" ones, those who were clearly imperfect and willing to express that, while still believing they were worthy of being loved.

Her research led her to four commonalities among them:

1. The *courage* to tell the story of who they were with their whole heart, including what they labeled bad.

2. The ability to have *compassion* toward themselves and others "be-cause as it turns out we can't practice compassion with other people if we can't treat ourselves kindly."

3. They had *connection,* which could only really happen when they were "willing to let go of who they thought they should be to be who they were."

4. And the last commonality was how they viewed their *vulnerability,* which was different from those who had shared theirs with a sense of shame. These individuals "fully embraced vulnerability. They believed that what made them vulnerable made them beautiful. They didn't talk about vulnerability being comfortable, nor did they really talk about it being excruciating . . . they just talked about it as being necessary."

Vulnerability is absolutely necessary.

To make friends, we have to love them. But to truly love them, we first have to love ourselves.

And unfortunately this very difficult work of self-acceptance can't be faked. Telling a vulnerable story can be easier than truly feeling one's own worth in the midst of the telling. Vulnerability is less about an external action you take and more about the internal work you do that lets you be motivated by love instead of fear.

OUR GREATEST FEAR: REJECTION

I attended a lecture by Rabbi Harold Kushner, who's probably most well known for his bestseller *When Bad Things Happen to Good People,* but whose subject that evening was his recent book, *Conquering Fear: Living Boldly in an Uncertain World.*

The introduction caught my attention: he said that the number of people who have died of fear caused by 9/11 and the idea of terrorism after the fact (anxiety-produced complications and deaths) is higher than the number of people whose deaths were caused by the actual events of that day. Pause for that to sink in.

And, interestingly, even terrorism is not our greatest fear. Nor is the economic recession. Nor is it the reality of aging or the thought of some-day dying. It's not even the fear of public speaking. We hear a lot about all of these things. The media is consumed with these subjects.

But, truth be told, greater than all the deaths that have been attributed to the fear and stress of terrorism, the most paralyzing fear we experience is . . . rejection. Rejection. It sounds so innocent and little at first, but then as you say the word, you start to feel the pit in your stomach as you real-ize how much you want to be accepted. After all, we wouldn't be afraid of standing in front of a crowd if admiration were the guaranteed response. It's the possibility of rejection—looking stupid, not being received well, not doing our best—that causes our palms to sweat and our mouths to go dry.

Rejection is at the root of all those other fears. Even death, by and large, comes from a fear that our lives didn't matter, that we didn't do enough, that we'll be forgotten—all stemming from a fear of rejection.

Sitting in that auditorium, listening to Rabbi Kushner, his observa-tion resonated with me. How many of my life choices are impacted by that fear of "them" rejecting me, of me not being deemed "enough" by someone? Anything we're doing to try to win approval—to prove we're valuable by someone else's measurements—speaks to us trying to avoid rejection. Whether it's doing something to try to get someone to like me, or not doing something to avoid someone not liking me—in both cases I am trying to avoid rejection. Whether it's not trying for the promotion, the new job, the business idea development or the sale for risk of failure, or pursuing them only to try to gain approval, I am trying to protect myself. Think about how many of our beauty decisions, our efforts to lose or gain weight, and the clothes we buy are about trying to cover up this fear. Or, what about the times I act uninterested when I really am interested, or act interested when I'm really not? So much of our lives are influenced by the desire to be accepted or the desire to avoid rejection.

I came home from that lecture thinking about how important GirlFriendCircles.com can be in this world—an opportunity for people to connect, build a sense of belonging, and surround themselves with friends that remind them that they're accepted.

But I also thought about how hard it can be to actually take steps to create that community if our greatest fear is rejection. It's a double-edged sword. We feel lonely and crave connectedness and yet can't pursue it because we fear no one will actually like us. And so we stay lonely. We hunger for acceptance, but avoid giving people the opportunity to fully accept us.

In our GirlFriendCircles community, there are thousands of women who have signed up, paid their dues, and yet have not attended their first ConnectingCircle, where they can literally meet friends at a local wine bar or café. For some it comes down to scheduling, but for many it comes down to fear. They wanted new friends enough to sign up, but when it comes down to actually putting themselves out there, the discomfort is too great. And so they just put it off.

Sometimes we assume someone is going to reject us because we're different, and so we self-reject and blame them. This happens all the time. We assume since none of them have kids and we do that they wouldn't want to be our friend. Or because she's older than we are, she'll probably think we're too young. Or she's more stylish, has more money, seems more popular, looks like she doesn't care about her looks enough, or appears to care about them too much. Because we judge, we feel judged.

We live in a world where voices are constantly telling us, "Prove you're valuable, relevant, beautiful, good enough, worth something to me . . . and then you will earn the love you desire." As though we're worthless until we do something spectacular. As though we're unlovable unless we can demonstrate that someone has chosen us. As though we are guilty until proven innocent.

Our response to this pressure usually manifests itself in stepping into one of two traps of extremes: self-rejection or arrogance. Arrogance is really just another form of self-rejection because it reveals that we are avoiding seeing ourselves for who we really are. They're both expressions of someone not living from their center.

Henri Nouwen, a deep spiritual teacher, says, "I know too well that beneath my arrogance there lies much self-doubt . . . Whether I am inflated or deflated, I lose touch with my truth and distort my vision of reality." Therefore, self-rejection, in either form, is the greatest enemy we face because it makes us unable to hear our own voice. Our own value. Our own being.

Self-rejection contradicts the truth that we have at our core: that we have intrinsic worth apart from any job, relationship, goal, cosmetic procedure, or bank balance. Self-rejection keeps us running to the next thing, looking for that sense of acceptance, always restless, never content. Self-rejection prevents us from being rooted, from living from a place of being centered, of being strong, of standing in our own strength.

HOW TO GO FROM FEAR TO FRIENTIMACY

For those of us who want Frientimacy—close and meaningful intimacy with friends—we will have to risk experiencing our fear in order to experience our goal. Like any gambler worth his money, we know that the higher the risk, the higher the potential reward. And we keep our eyes on that reward, for it is in those healthy friendships that we gain the love we crave, practice the compassion we're called to, and grow into the potential we hold within us.

Also, like any good gambler, we know that risks need to be weighed and trust built. To that end, here is how we can increase our vulnerability in the most meaningful of ways:

Vulnerability Must Start from a Place of Self-Love

Self-love is the act that will root us, ground us, and empower us to experience real self-acceptance. As my friend Christine Arylo, the Self-Love Queen, says in her book *Madly in Love with ME: The Daring Adventure of Becoming Your Own Best Friend,* "Loving yourself is not something you do instead of loving others. Loving yourself is the prerequisite to loving others. In order to give love to others, you must have love to give. How can you give what you do not have? You cannot. Just as you cannot lend money you don't have, you cannot give unconditional love if you don't first feel unconditional love for yourself." We must learn to love ourselves—which is different than narcissism, conceit, vanity, or selfishness. Rather, self-acceptance roots us, honors us, and empowers us.

In Mandarin Chinese there are two different words for *selfish*. One conveys the grabbing, grasping, and clinging of things one wants (which can come from self-rejection or arrogance). The other definition conveys caring, preparing, resourcing, and providing for what we want—more like self-care. That's a really powerful difference. We wouldn't want to avoid the latter in our attempt to avoid the former.

Caring for ourselves includes two deeply vulnerable actions. It requires us to accept that which we call our shadow and that which we call our light.

It means embracing both what I wish I could change and what I am proud of. It means forgiving my mistakes and stepping into my goodness. It includes the yin and yang of life, the good and the bad. We can't have one without the other. We don't need to pretend otherwise.

It wasn't that falling in love with someone else had transitioned me from a good girl to a bad girl. It was that finally I messed up big enough to see for myself that I could be both impressive and messy. I hadn't been perfect before, but most of my junk prior to my divorce was more socially acceptable, more "normal." Now I came face to face with the fact that I could love a person so deeply and also hurt that person in devastating ways.

In accepting both sides of me, I felt myself align. My core became strong. Refusing to bury my shame in some closet ensured that those years that hurt the worst would also be the most growing, enlightening, and wisdom-building years of my life. Disowning it would have divided me. Embracing it helped me mine the goodness that was there in the midst of the pain.

Here's how our self-love plays out in our relationships: I can honor people for their inherent worth. Our goodness is not a teeter-totter where if one person goes up, another has to go down. They can be great and so can I. They can be less than perfect and so can I. I can let go of always trying to decide if I am better or worse than they are. I can stop measuring. Stop judging. If I know my value, then I don't need to devalue someone else to make me feel better. I don't need to be connected to any one person to feel like I am more important. I can step into relationships and love those people because I am able to love myself. I can be proud of them without it making me feel bad. I can celebrate them because I know how to celebrate myself.

Marianne Williamson, in her book *A Return to Love*, says, "In every relationship, in every moment, we teach either love or fear. 'To teach is to demonstrate.' As we demonstrate love towards others, we learn that we are lovable and we learn how to love more deeply. As we demonstrate fear or negativity, we learn self-condemnation and we learn to feel more frightened of life. We will always learn what we have chosen to teach."

Fear is contagious. It's impossible to reject others without feeling rejected ourselves. And the converse is true too: we can't love ourselves without also giving love to others.

Vulnerability Should Grow with Commitment

While our first time together as new friends may include just a reference to a bad relationship, a tough childhood, or some health challenges, at some point in our continued get-togethers we should find ourselves willing to reveal more as the continued commitment creates increased safety.

We all talk about different things with varying degrees of comfortable-ness. Because of the variety of temperaments, strengths, and wounds among people, we can't assume that everyone will share or not share at the same speed as we do. And we don't need them to match us. Nonetheless, a friendship does require stories, jokes, revelations, and secrets. We do feel more bonded to someone when we realize they are telling us something they don't tell everyone. Part of a meaningful friendship is building up that trust.

We can minimize the risk of vulnerability by increasing our self-disclosure as mutual commitment to the relationship grows. I developed the Frientimacy Triangle to help showcase the fact that the intimacy we crave must be fostered incrementally:

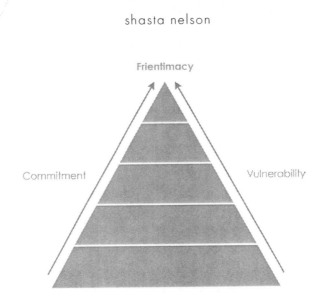

Frientimacy Triangle

In a nutshell, we start at the base of the triangle with every person we meet. If a healthy committed relationship is what we desire, then we must move up the triangle by increasing both our commitment and our vulnerability at the same rate. As our ability to be vulnerable grows, so should our commitment to that person. And vice versa: as our commitment (defined, in part, by our level of engagement and willingness to protect the relationship) grows, so should our intimacy. If we accelerate one side too fast, our triangle becomes lopsided and the relationship does not reach the pinnacle.

Acknowledge how much time it takes to build a healthy friendship where both sides of our triangle are growing stronger. Simply whispering a secret doesn't do it; nor can we just meet over coffee and pinky-promise ourselves into a significant friendship. But we can keep doing both of those things and, over time and with continued energy, find that we have co-created a friendship that matters.

The highest level of commitment I can make to someone is, "I am committed to receiving your vulnerability and giving you mine." And I don't make that commitment lightly. For I know that as life changes—divorces, moves, children, retirement—many of my friendships lower on the triangle won't make the transition. That doesn't make them less important or devalue what they offer each party for the time we share. But it's not realistic that I will consistently share deeply with every person I meet and like. Commitment grows, and is earned, as is the trust that will invite us to be vulnerable.

A BFF, then, should be a person we feel committed to and can be honest with, which could take months and years to reach. None of us should be walking around committing ourselves to strangers, no matter how charming, fun, and engaging they are. Nor should we be sharing with them beyond what is appropriate at our current commitment level.

For at least a year after my divorce I felt this need to come right out and tell people the worst about me. Because I had lost relationships from the fallout of the breakup and experienced such wide-scale rejection in reaction to what I had done, I shared too much from a place of feeling unworthy of people's acceptance and a desire to test them early in the relationship. I figured I'd rather have them reject me up front, before I invested too much care, than risk their finding out later and deciding then that I wasn't good enough for them.

Prior to my confession I hadn't told a soul about my divided heart. After the divorce, I made up for it and talked to everyone and anyone. Neither option was real vulnerability. Both responses evidence a lopsided triangle. Pre-divorce, I hurt some of my closest friends' feelings when they found out I hadn't told them this huge secret I was carrying around. In other words, my level of vulnerability didn't reflect the commitment we had made to each other. I was scared to admit the truth about myself to them. But post-divorce, it was inappropriate for me to share this drama with people I barely knew. In these instances my commitment to these people didn't match the private revelations I was sharing. I lacked equilibrium in both cases.

For the sake of illustration, let me give you some examples of how the vulnerability of gradual self-revelation might develop in each of the five different Circles of Connectedness as we grow in our friendships. Let's say the subject I want to share is discomfort with my weight.

With Contact Friends, in the right setting, I might say, "This year I am committed to losing twenty pounds!" That is vulnerable indeed, as it reveals dissatisfaction with how things currently are and sets up a goal, which we know means risking not achieving it. The value in sharing this with select Contact Friends in an appropriate context (say we're eating out with them, or the conversation turns to New Year's resolutions) is that we've opened ourselves up to resources—she might have a sister who loved a particular program she can suggest, she might have an unused two-week guest pass to her gym for us to try, or she might just order a salad with us in solidarity with the menu we're trying to follow. But notice we're not getting into our emotions, our childhood, or the unhappy marriage that we might be blaming for the pounds.

With Common Friends, if they are already in our weight-loss group, for example, then our vulnerability definitely increases. Here, with others who know the journey and share their own experiences, we can be far more vulnerable about which part of the day is hardest to resist certain foods and what exercises we're enjoying. Here we reveal more, about our process, the details, and the events surrounding the subject, than we would with someone who didn't have a similar level of interest in, or experience or knowledge of, the content.

With Confirmed Friends, we may not open up at all right away since we don't talk to them regularly. But when we do see one of them this spring or catch up next month, we know we're talking to people who remember us prior to our weight gain or perhaps who recall how we've dieted in the past, with either success or failure. With these friends who have history with us, it is appropriate to open up about what makes this time feel different or how much more energy we're feeling as we add more miles to our walking route. It's awesome to receive validation from them, hear their applause, and be reminded that they have loved us at many different weights—while happy for us, they love us no matter what the scale says. These are friends who can remind us of all the other things we've accomplished, boosting us with belief in our own goals.

With Community Friends who see us regularly, they should not only know how important this goal is to us, but also how we're doing along the way. These are the friendships that matter enough to us that we can risk being honest with our feelings and needs. This category includes some friends who might have their own stories around the subject, and we feel close enough to them that if they show any sabotaging behavior, we can gently say to them, "Thanks for trying to tell me you don't think I need to lose weight, but I want to and I need your support." One of them may be walking around the lake with us regularly to help us stay motivated, another might ask us how we're feeling about the program we chose, another might be the one who wants to go shopping with us when we reach the next size down.

With Committed Friends, we will risk saying out loud the things we sometimes think, but are too scared to admit. These are the women we show ourselves to with as little of a filter as possible. We will have the guts to say, "Sometimes I've hated myself," or process with them why the weight release matters so much to us. With these selected women who have earned our trust, we will be able to tell them how uncomfortable we are when we feel people are judging us for our size, or how deeply thrilled we are that we stayed on course even when we doubted ourselves.

While I use the Circles as an example, they illustrate how we talk about a subject with authenticity to varying degrees depending on the type of relationship. This is about recognizing that there are stages in between saying nothing and saying everything. It's about honoring that our Left-Side Friends don't have the commitment and intimacy with us yet to be treated like Right-Side Friends; and conversely, that we will have a hard time developing Right-Side Friends if we never share the fears, insecurities, and feelings that go with the stories. There are appropriate levels of vulnerability that increase as we practice trust and build commitment in our relationships.

Our new friends need to earn the right to hear our heart. We will practice being together as Left-Side Friends, sharing appropriately, so that by the time they become Right-Side Friends, we trust them more fully. We have given in stages so that by the time we're sharing whatever parts of us feel the most vulnerable, it really doesn't feel like the greatest risk ever. We trust them with what we're about to say.

Vulnerability Always Leads to Acceptance of Others

When we accept ourselves, it becomes a gift that we can give more freely to others.

Not with pride, I admit that when I first meet a person, I tend to start evaluating him or her. Sometimes it's with appreciation for her fabulous choice of boots, other times it's with some question as to whether she really thinks that hairstyle is flattering on her. Either way, my brain is quickly going beyond data collection and giving meaning to what I see. Much of life requires us to make quick judgments and snap decisions—we simply can't take an hour to pick which jam we want in the grocery aisle. So deciding to not judge someone is akin to asking someone's brain to stop working.

What I have found more helpful is to say in my head, "I accept you," whenever I meet people. I like to think that saying it over and over in my head will reveal acceptance in my eyes when I am introduced; but even if it's not visible, I know I am showing up with a different heart. Once my brain hears that I've already accepted her, it will still collect data, but now it's in the form of looking for evidence to support my decision rather than trying to make the decision.

And this reminds me right up front that she's good enough as she is. Acceptance doesn't mean that everyone is perfect and that we'll be best friends with everyone we meet. It does mean that we have given them the best start ever by seeing them and welcoming them with love before they have proven a thing. Acknowledging that people don't have to earn the right to be treated well fosters generosity of spirit.

Being vulnerable means we tell our brains that we are there to get to know her, not judge her. We are there to be two humans facing each other for an hour, complex, with both amazing qualities and traits we'll find odd—but we're willing to see her the way we hope she's willing to see us.

We have become far too heavy with the need to earn acceptance, forgetting that whatever we withhold from another, we withhold from ourselves.

Vulnerability Acknowledges Complexity

When we accept that even in our complexity we have intrinsic value, then we can embrace both our fabulousness and our insecurities. It means we are willing to go to both places, which really are the same place: honesty. It means we know we're more than just one-dimensional characters in a TV show, and we accept that there is more to us than any one script could ever capture.

What does this look like when making new friends? It looks like letting go of having an agenda to be seen a certain way—the Ideal Mother, Consummate Housewife, Perfect Christian, Superwoman, or Wonder Boss—and instead showing up just as we are. Which means we'll be both big and amazing, but also insecure and tired.

This means we'll model being comfortable with others' brightness by showing our own: "One of the things I love about myself is how I can shift the energy of a room, and let me tell you, you would have gotten a kick out of watching me today at work as I helped move everyone from awkward to laughter in thirty seconds."

And it also means we aren't afraid of our own shadow—or theirs. So we can also say things like "Ugh! After losing my husband to cancer last year I found myself wallowing in self-pity . . . I've grown so far past that place, but sometimes I still feel those thoughts of despair and sadness. I know I'll keep healing, but along the way the scab still hurts."

Vulnerability means that when we walk into a room, we resist the urge to try to only impress. This is so hard for me, as I mistakenly think that people will like me more if I wow them. When I think like this I am forgetting that most people like others they can relate to, not others who intimidate them or put on airs. When I try to show a potential new friend how amazing I am, I set the tone for her now to try to wow me, too, which leads to a conversation about who takes the best vacations, is in the healthiest marriage, has the easiest children, or gets to retire earliest. We may walk away feeling like we won some points, but we probably didn't become friends. Chances are greater that we both walked away feeling more inadequate about own lives and more judgmental about the other person. Instead, a conscious decision to show up gently means we choose friends rather than fans, peers rather than an audience.

Just as our number one goal shouldn't be to wow others, it also means we shouldn't undersell ourselves. It doesn't mean we downplay, self-deprecate, or compete for the worst sob story. Vulnerability isn't a race to pull skeletons out of our closets and get into a competition of who has the worst marriage, the most horrible boss, or the flabbiest thighs. I am reminded of the scene in *Notting Hill* where Julia Roberts' character wants to compete for the last brownie, but to win it she has to convince everyone that her life as a celebrity sucks more than that of the woman confined to a wheelchair.

Vulnerability isn't about trying to elicit pity or using our pain to garner attention. Nor is it about trying to sell someone our ego's version of our identity. Vulnerability starts from a place that acknowledges we are more complex than simply being sad or happy, good or bad, superstar or loser. Vulnerability is all of the above.

Vulnerability Is More Than Just Words

While many of the examples of vulnerability have to do with the stories we choose to tell each other, I want to also point out that gifts of vulnerability extend far beyond information shared. Sometimes the hardest way to show up with vulnerability is in offering ourselves or receiving someone else in new ways.

With Contact Friends we don't know well, we offer vulnerability by being the one who extends the invitation to meet up for drinks after work. If we've never spent time together in that way, just putting out the invitation can feel risky. Without that gift of vulnerability, it's hard to see the relationship growing.

Any time we grow the relationship into new territory (i.e., the first time we text, call on a weekend, get together without our husbands who introduced us, or connect with no business excuse) it will feel vulnerable. With any growth comes some risk, since there is always a sense of the unknown attached to the new behavior. We all develop patterns with each other, and whether it's broaching a new subject, extending an invitation, or calling them out of the blue for the first time, we become more practiced being vulnerable with each other.

One of the most bonding ways of connecting with new friends is to experience something new and unusual together. So while it may feel weird to ask her to accompany us on a tour of a cemetery, to join us at a hole-in-the wall restaurant, or to go snowshoeing through a random park, we can know that the rewards go up in direct proportion to the risk!

Vulnerability also includes practicing ways of giving and receiving affection. Like us, our friends are craving more love in this world. Giving platonic affection can include verbal affirmation, the giving of a gift, words sent in a card, and favors offered. It also includes healthy touch, as so many of us are touch-starved, sometimes being touched only by our family, or no one at all. I remember going through my divorce and just feeling so lonely, so untouched, like barriers had been put up between me and the world. Hugs are healing and empowering. Hands placed gently on shoulders, legs, or arms send a thousand words. Nearly every photo of people who love each other shows them leaning in, touching, arms around each other. The gift we give when we're willing to reach out is saying to someone that they are noticed and loved.

VULNERABILITY FROM A BROKEN PLACE

While it's always ideal to show up in new relationships having already done the work of self-acceptance, rarely do we live in that ideal. Frequently it's *because* of some crisis that we recognize our need for more meaningful friendships. In other words, it's often when we're hurting that we're most motivated to connect. From a place of perceived emptiness in our lives (i.e., our spouse died, we lost our job, our boyfriend dumped us, our kids moved out) we find ourselves hoping to fill the void. It can almost feel impossible in these situations of identity crisis, fear, emptiness, and transition to show up with self-love and positivity.

Here are four tips I hold out to those of us who are called to be vulnerable in the friend-making process while in the midst of pain and personal imbalance.

1. Hire the Support You Need

It is difficult to invest money when we feel like our lives are in chaos, but hiring a therapist or coach is money well spent. If money is scarce, there are plenty of counselors and guides who work on sliding scales, facilitate groups, or teach grief workshops where you can find more affordable support. Whatever your financial situation, your new friends should not be placed in the role of counselor. Even if they lend a listening ear, when it comes to getting together again with you, they may hesitate. They have enough in their own lives to bring them exhaustion and stress—they are reaching out to make new friends with hopes of bringing joy to their lives, not to hear more problems.

As Left-Side Friends, you have not earned the right to make emotional withdrawals from your friendship's bank account. Honor where you are in the friend-making process. At this time you need to be making deposits in the relationship, giving to the degree that you are able. You do not want a relationship that isn't built on mutuality and shared respect. Go back and look at the five stages of friendship in Chapter 4—the first step is curiosity. You want new friends to leave your presence wanting more, not less. You want them to lean in by choice, not because your need grabs them by the collar and pulls them into your drama.

So bring whatever specialists you need into your life to help you be able to show up to your new friends with some level of positivity and centeredness. Our new friends are not our therapists or life coaches.

2. Share Enough to Feel Honest

There is a difference between not vomiting your exhausting nightmare on someone and showing up with a fake happy face. No one is asking you to pretend or lie.

On the contrary, your honesty will give a gift to your new friends, letting them know you are willing and able to go beyond the surface subjects. And chances are good that they are meeting you with their own drama, too, so your honesty tells them it's okay they aren't feeling full of ideal self-acceptance either. There is beauty in your courage to be honest.

But this is where the Frientimacy Triangle reminds us that there are stages to how much we share, that our vulnerability should move incrementally up the triangle as our commitment to each other does also. And that takes repeated time together to develop.

3. Share the Spotlight Intentionally

This one is hard when it feels like no one else's life can compare to what you're experiencing. Yes, your life is falling apart and, no, it can't compare to them talking about what trip they're getting ready to go on this weekend. But such is life.

Remember that much of the reason you're reaching out is because you want to experience more than what is in your own head, and being reminded that life goes on is part of that process. While you are the lead character in the play that is your life, they have an entire stage for the story of their lives, as well. We're learning how to show up side by side—both lead actors in our own lives, but called to share the stage when we're together.

People like people who are interested in them. Practice giving what you hope they will one day reciprocate. Ask questions, cheer for them, choose to be happy for their happiness, and make sure that you don't dismiss their drama as less-than just because yours feels bigger. We're not competing with each other! Give them space to share their life, no matter how unimportant or frivolous their stories may feel to you at the time.

I remember once hearing about a little boy who was sobbing uncon trollably after losing his two quarters, resulting in his being unable to buy his desired candy bar. The storyteller told us that as parents and caregivers we aren't to dismiss the loss as "it's just fifty cents!" but rather to imagine how it would feel for us to lose our entire bank account balance right before we went to make a big purchase. We are called to hear their crisis as something we can relate to and see it as significant to them, even if it seems small or insignificant to us.

When I was going through my divorce, some of my friends expressed discomfort and guilt at sharing their woes that they felt were too small compared to the ashes of my life. And, indeed, it's not always fun to hear a friend express frustration that her husband came home late last night when I'd have given anything just to have a husband. But pain doesn't work that way—she isn't being asked to love her life just because I hate mine, nor would I want her to hate hers just to relate to me. She is allowed to still feel frustration, pain, and confusion, and also joy, hope, and bliss. And we must tell her that we can handle both ends of her emotional spectrum.

For certainly her life still matters and she will still want to share it. If not with us, then it will be with someone else, causing us to miss out on opportunities to bond and share. We must repeatedly validate the significance of her life and give her permission to feel whatever she feels, without comparison.

4. Practice Positivity

We talked in great detail about positivity in the last chapter, but I bring it up here again because it's intrinsically one of the most important things we need to cultivate when our lives feel anything but positive. One of the hardest spiritual disciplines to practice in the midst of crisis and brokenness is fostering joy and gratitude. But I believe that it's that very act that can save us.

I promised myself during my healing that I would find something to be grateful for every day for a year. It wasn't always easy to point to abundance in my own life that year. Sometimes it was simply gratitude for what I saw in the lives of others that allowed me to keep that promise. Thank God for the good things that happened around me that I could celebrate.

But while training your heart to find things to appreciate is one of the most restorative acts in the world, it also can be one of the hardest. Our ego will feel jealous of others' good fortune, and we will resent that their lives contain gifts that seem more obvious than ours. But it's all a lie.

In truth, who are we to think we're the best judge to determine what is a good gift versus a bad gift? Who's to say that her getting that promotion is good while us losing our job is bad? Maybe my job loss will lead me to explore venues I never would have otherwise. Who's to say that her getting married is good and my getting a divorce is bad? Maybe my divorce will foster a compassion for others in pain that I would not have known otherwise. Who's to say that her having enough money to start her business is good and me no longer having enough to live on my own is bad? With maturity I can acknowledge that from some of the more painful parts of my life, events that felt like losses at the time, came some of the most beautiful changes in my life.

We don't need to set ourselves up as judges. We just need to get through this crisis in the most loving and life-enhancing way possible. Yes we hurt, but it's possible that one day we will look back on this event as rich and life-changing in positive ways. We don't need to know yet exactly how, we just need to hold the possibility.

Which means practicing gratitude. For your life and for hers. It means forcing ourselves to cheer for her even if we're crying for ourselves. It means telling her how proud of her we are even if we don't yet trust ourselves. It means complimenting her on her new haircut even if we haven't showered in a few days.

It's noticing her life and staying hopeful for it. Misery might like company, but we also like people who offer glimpses of the potential to rise above the misery someday. We will use our anger or sadness to better our own lives, not to devalue hers.

Create practices in your life that will encourage your gratitude, be it listing three things a day you are thankful for or starting and ending every day with saying a blessing.

VALUING FRIENTIMACY MORE THAN FEAR

My favorite definition of courage is from a paraplegic beatnik poet who is hardly known for anything other than this quote. Writing under a pseudonym, Ambrose Redmoon wrote an article exhorting those who thought they could fight injustice without physical sacrifice. In the five-page thesis are these words: "Courage is not the absence of fear, but rather the judgment that something else is more important than the fear." We sacrifice and risk for that which we care about.

Heroes don't jump into icy water to save someone because they feel no fear, but because they value the life they are trying to save as greater than their hesitation. We don't sign up for online dating because we're fearless; we do it because we dream about having someone love us and partner with us. We don't get pregnant because we've finally erased all doubts about labor and child rearing; we do it because we are excited about making a family.

Vulnerability in friendship is not without risk, but as we weigh the dream of Frientimacy against the fear, we will find a courage that propels us toward being loved, being vulnerable, being seen.

My friends and clients will vouch that I often say, "Everything has a price tag." And it does. And that's not necessarily bad. Some things are worth the higher price. We could buy a used, beat-up car that will get us from point A to point B (and hope those points aren't too far away from each other!) for $3,000 or we could buy the top-of-the-line safety-car-of-the-year for $40,000. And there are many price points in between.

Paying a higher price isn't bad. It just means we value what we're getting for that price. Sometimes the highest priced item is the right one to buy.

Frientimacy is where we experience that place of being known and accepted. Vulnerability is a currency that helps us buy it. Every relationship has a price tag but we don't need to fear the cost if we value the purchase we're making.

In the opening chapter, I talked about how important it is to admit we want and need friends. For it's only in feeding the dream that we can starve the fears. We have to see the potential and decide it's worth the fear. We have to take the risk of being vulnerable—vulnerable enough to put ourselves out there physically and emotionally, because while we don't want to be hurt, we know we must risk it to be loved.

When Greg, my current husband, stated his vows to me on our wedding day, he quoted a few lines from Billy Joel's song "And So It Goes." The lyrics speak to how little we can sometimes say and still feel too exposed, but that the far greater loss would be to lose someone because of our inability to let them in. His voice cracked with knowing the pain possible, and the hope desired, when he quoted:

> *"So I would choose to be with you*
>
> *That's if the choice were mine to make*
>
> *But you can make decisions too*
>
> *And you can have this heart to break."*

It's nearly impossible to become an adult and not have been disappointed or hurt by the actions of others. And the reverse is just as true: though we don't like to think about having hurt others, we are not always aware of what expectations we didn't live up to.

But we are human, after all. We know mistakes, pain, and fear.

Vulnerability means we know the cost and choose the relationship anyway. Which is really another way of saying we know ourselves, and not only do we want to be seen and known by others, but we're willing to be.

JULIANA
ANN
LYNNE
ROBIN
JACQUELYN
NANCY

PRACTICE FORGIVENESS:
It's the Lesson of Relationships

Ａll friendships rise and fall with the repeated call to forgiveness.
We can do perfectly the first four steps of friendship—be open, initiate consistently, add positivity, and increase vulnerability—that we have discussed in the last four chapters, and still not have long-lasting and meaningful friendships for lack of going through this required step of practicing forgiveness. Our ability to practice forgiveness will determine, more than any other factor, whether we can co-create healthy, long-term, and mature friendships.

I'll go one step further and say that our ability to repeatedly forgive will not only determine our relational health, but also our personal health. I'm learning more about me, what is important to me, what triggers me, what rubs me, what I want to work on, what I need to grieve, and where I might want to shift the light of evaluation from her to me. My choice to let someone else off the hook also makes it a habit I can offer to myself.

The Greek word for "forgiveness" means to set free—like the freeing of a slave. The slave being freed, however, actually refers to us. Freedom isn't a gift we give to someone else as much as it is a gift we give to ourselves.

FORGIVENESS IS FOR OUR SAKE

Forgiveness Is for More Than Wrongdoing

Beyond the common issues we all struggle with on the subject of forgiveness such as understanding what it is, what it isn't, what it really does, and how to do it, is the fact that with most friendships we don't readily admit it's needed as often as it is.

Sure, we know we need to forgive her if she flirted with our husband, made a negative comment about our kids, or stole money from us, but how often is the cause of our angst that clear?

One of the biggest mistakes our culture has made around the subject of forgiveness is in linking it exclusively to wrongdoing.

Not for a second do I want to undermine the grave abuses that have been done against us, minimize how much wounding has occurred, or discount how impossible forgiveness feels in some situations. Sometimes we may have a friend betray us or blatantly hurt us and, for our own sake, we'll need to forgive her. But for the purpose of this book, one on starting and maintaining healthy friendships, I think we're better served by hearing the call to forgive others and ourselves not just for the devil's biggies but also for all the times when people in our lives just didn't do what we thought was best.

Most frequently forgiveness isn't only about whether *they* are guilty or not, rather it's about the meaning *we* give to their actions—the conclusions we come to, the assumptions we make.

What hurts most friendships is a growing resentment—often unconscious—that comes from our subtle blame, jealousy, judgment, nonreciprocation, and neglect. In the next chapter I'm going to speak directly about each of these five common threats to friendship, but before we get to the practical ways of responding to these perceived wedges in our relationships, this chapter delves into the forgiving nature that all actions must be rooted in.

Friendships of all kinds—from before we're Contact Friends all the way to developing into Committed or Confirmed Friends—require forgiveness. Lots of it. Repeatedly. We are going to be disappointed often. To admit that truth up front helps shape healthy expectations.

A couple years ago my sister told me that her family was moving from

Oakland, California—a mere twenty-minute drive from me—to Tampa, Florida. Immense sadness was my first feeling, as tears sprang to my eyes just thinking about the loss of hanging out with her regularly and having my niece and nephew nearby. If there was a prosecuting attorney in my head accusing her of impacting our relationship and taking experiences and people away from me that I loved, I was just as quick to give voice to the defending attorney who insisted that my sister and her husband had every right to make whatever choice they need to for their family. I knew it wasn't personal. I knew it was hard on them, too. I knew that I needed to support her. I knew she needed me. I felt conflicted—both mad at her for leaving me, but guilty for feeling it. I love her to death. Never would I have consciously thought, "She needs to apologize to me." Not a chance.

But that doesn't mean I didn't need to forgive her.

After all, it was me who needed to come to peace with her decision.

And to do that I had to be open to taking the time to acknowledge where I was and what I was feeling.

Wherever we judge, we have an invitation to forgive.

We may roll our eyes when she spends $2700 on a purse, feel jealous that she loses weight so effortlessly, judge her for going back to him again, and take offense at the unsolicited advice she offers us. We may bear grudges for all the times she's late, for not calling when she said she would, for acting like her kids are better than ours, and for getting too busy with her own life. We may get annoyed that she's rigidly following some new self-improvement theory that has her drawing new boundaries, baffled that she's taking the family to Disney World when we know she's in debt, intimidated that she always throws elaborate birthday parties that we can't top, and dismayed that her new health kick means she's no fun to eat out with anymore. We may find ourselves threatened when we sense our relationship changing because she was offered a higher paying job, fell in love when we still wanted her to be our single sidekick, initiated a divorce when they were our couple-friends, or announced she was retiring long before we'll be ready.

If we're extroverted then we may feel exhausted that we always have to initiate; and if we're introverted then we may feel exhausted by how she has a story to tell about every thought in her head. If we're scheduled and organized we may be disheartened that she forgot it was the day our brother was having open-heart surgery, and if we're unstructured and spontaneous then we may be disheartened by her request to schedule her three weeks out if we want to spend time with her.

Even in our new friendships we disappoint each other since we're co-creating a path that has never been before. We have expectations of how we'd like it to look, what we'd like her to say or do, and what we think we need. We will inevitably be faced with letdowns when she doesn't e-mail us back, dashed hopes when she talks more than she listens, and chagrin when she says something that feels judgmental. We question her motives, judge her actions, and conclude she isn't the kind of friend we'd want.

Forgiveness Leads to Our Peace

In her article "The Myth of Forgiveness," Dr. Tian Dayton, a clinical psychologist and author of over a dozen books, says, "Forgiveness, for starters, is a process not an event. . . . Carl Jung felt that we don't really solve a problem, rather we go to the mountaintop, figuratively speaking, and learn to 'see it differently.'"

Having "Magic Eyes" is what Lewis Smedes called the choice to "see it differently" in the fable that opens his book *Forgive and Forget: Healing the Hurts We Don't Deserve*. Magic because it's the greatest miracle when we forgive—the changing of our thinking from one thing to something entirely different. Our egos like to tell us that we've perceived the situation correctly, that we are right, and that our lack of peace is someone else's fault. But our prayer has to be for those magic eyes. Eyes that give us extended vision beyond our own interpretation.

One of the most popular definitions of forgiveness, made famous by Oprah, who claims it as her favorite, illustrates this required shift of perspective: "Forgiveness is giving up the hope that the past could be any different." Not easy to do. Especially when we believe our present could look different if that past had been different. But accepting the truth that our peace is ultimately in our hands, not theirs, is life-affirming and powerful.

Our freedom comes when we give up wishing the offense were different and choose now to make sure the effects are different. Did I wish my sister weren't moving? Yes. Her choice impacted me and would change my relationship with her. But the outcome wasn't attached to the change as much as it would be based on my response to that change. In these cases I must forgive not because they did anything wrong, but because I crave peace. And if peace is the destination, then forgiveness is my road there.

Even if we convince ourselves that we aren't the one in the prison of our own anger, be reminded that the prison guards also spend most of their time in prison, surrounded by bars. And that's no way to live for the prisoner or the guard, for the slave or the master. It was Gautama Buddha who said, "Holding on to anger is like grasping a hot coal with the intent of throwing it at someone else; you are the one who gets burned."

What I call unconscious resentment, Joyce Meyer, author of the recent book *Do Yourself a Favor . . . Forgive* calls "hidden unforgiveness." Helpfully, she highlights six attitudes or patterns that might reveal unforgiveness if we find ourselves engaging in them: 1) keeping score, 2) boasting of good behavior, 3) constantly complaining, 4) subtly alienating, dividing, or separating someone from someone else, 5) continually bringing up the same offense, or 6) resenting the blessings enjoyed by the person we think is the offender. Many of these attitudes show up in our friendships in a variety of sneaky ways.

In many situations like mine with my sister, we feel guilty or embarrassed even having the feelings surface, let alone admitting them. We wouldn't feel comfortable asking our friends to apologize to us for these things that may not qualify as blatant wrongdoings or sins, but that's not to say we don't feel hurt or disappointed. And that's where it gets super confusing for most of us.

Some psychologists would claim that many of the actions listed above don't require forgiveness since they aren't intentional wrongs done against us personally. In agreement with these trusted sources, we have our own nagging voice in our head saying, "You can't be mad at her for getting married. You should be happy for her!" or, "She shouldn't have to apologize for forgetting your birthday . . . that's just the way she is. Your expectations are too high . . . you just need to accept her and get over it."

Our egos, in their attempt to keep us feeling good about our self-perception, can be both quick to blame the other person for our feelings and deceitful about it since we don't want to see ourselves as judgmental or angry. So our brains get trapped between two conflicting beliefs: that she did something that hurt our relationship *and* that she's not guilty because she didn't do anything blatantly wrong. It may be hard to say, "I need to forgive her," since we wouldn't necessarily claim she owes us an apology.

But what it comes down to most often is that we are frustrated because she is living her life or making a choice in a different way than we would choose or prefer. The frustration often builds up slowly and can seem so insignificant that we try to avoid it or talk ourselves out of it. But everyone annoys someone, everyone disappoints someone, and everyone hurts someone. If forgiveness is the letting go of our resentment or anger, then one can see why the need for forgiveness can become more complicated in female friendships, in which we're often hesitant to even admit we're ever angry in the first place. It's increasingly difficult to let go of what we don't realize we're holding.

Forgiveness Includes Sadness, Fear, and Anger

Unlike IQ, which measures our (largely inborn) intelligence, EQ measures our emotional intelligence, which can be, to a large degree, learned in our lifetime. Dr. Arlene Taylor, a neuro-function specialist who teaches on brain health, defines EQ as the "ability to know what feels good, what feels bad, and how to get from bad to good in a healthy, efficient, and functional manner that results in positive outcomes." This capacity to recognize our feelings and choose healthy ways of acting gives us permission to notice when we've been hurt, disappointed, or scared.

Simply putting on a supportive, happy face for my sister's move wouldn't have been authentic. But the alternative—being mad at her—felt embarrassing and wrong. Many relationships break down at this point for lack of recognizing the inner conflict. We may subconsciously blame her for whatever is hurting us and if, for any reason, we avoid looking at the root of that hurt, we risk not gathering the information our brain is trying to send us. In our haze of denial we might also begin to look for other annoyances to justify our feeling of frustration.

One of the most interesting statements Dr. Taylor makes in her workshops is that, out of the five core emotions—sadness, fear, anger, joy, and euphoria—men have the hardest time identifying sadness, often mislabeling it as anger; and women have the hardest time identifying anger, often mislabeling it as sadness. We have to learn to check in with ourselves and accurately recognize our emotions, be they anger, fear, or sadness. These three emotions are normal and will be a part of every healthy relationship we have.

It's impossible to avoid experiencing these feelings in our relationships—even if they feel awkward—since the one constant in life is change. And with every change or transition there will always be aspects of loss and aspects of gain. Sometimes what we will gain—the husband with the wedding, the backyard with the new house, the extra money with the promotion—will be easier to see initially than the losses of time, identity, options, and ways of being that also come with those gains. But the reverse is just as true: sometimes we see the loss first—less time with her when she has a baby, less in common with her when she retires, fewer options when she lives too far away—before we're able to appreciate the gains in wisdom, new activities we can engage in together, and new roles we can play in each other's lives as a result of the changes.

Accept that every change—every single one in her life and ours—brings some kind of loss.

With any loss comes the need to grieve.

With grief comes anger.

And with anger comes a call to forgiveness.

Anyone who knows the stages of grief will know that within that process of healing from a loss or sadness is included a stage of anger and blame. Therefore not only is it normal to sometimes feel those emotions, but it's also healthy as they contribute to returning us to a state of joy. What isn't healthy is denying them, mislabeling them, or covering them up out of guilt. In these cases our anger doesn't demand fault or apology from our friends as much as it demands us paying attention to our own emotions.

People with high EQ's aren't those who never feel mad or scared or hurt or depressed, rather they are those who are skilled at going through the process—articulating their feelings, gathering the information that the emotion gives them, and acting in a way that will propel them forward. In other words, not only can we not create friendships devoid of fear, sadness, or anger, but neither should we want to. These normal emotions provide invaluable information about where we need to keep growing and practicing love.

So taking my sister's move as an example, I accurately identified sadness as my first emotion. I could list pages of losses that I anticipated—losses that ranged from not having someone from whom I felt comfortable asking for rides to the airport to things like not getting to watch my five-year-old niece and two-year-old nephew grow up. Naming those losses helped me gather information about whether, and how, I wanted to re-spond to any of the things on the list. The honesty moved my brain into thinking who else might be willing to drive me to the airport in the future and started me thinking about creative ways I might stay in touch with my niece and nephew. Feeling the sadness served me as I learned what was important to me, gave myself permission to grieve, and entertained ideas for minimizing the losses in some cases.

It wasn't as easy for me to identify the sadness when my friend Daneen announced she was pregnant. I was *supposed* to be excited for her so it took me longer to be honest with myself that I actually did feel sad. My perceived losses included things like grieving that we'd no longer be at the same stage of life and that I'd have to give up time with her as her list of responsibilities grew. I also felt fear—fear that maybe she'd want to move out of the city now, fear that I'd feel left out since I wasn't a mom, fear that I'd lose value or interest to her, fear that she'd change. And since anger is a part of grieving, I also felt anger. (Wow, that's so hard to admit, huh? No one wants to be that friend! No wonder we avoid admitting it!) But in honesty, I felt anger that she was risking our friendship, that she just expected me to be excited, that she needed new things from me, and that I never felt like I was doing enough to support her.

Forgiveness Gives Us Valuable Information

When my husband went through his divorce from his previous mar-riage, his counselor wisely said to him: "How others treat you will say more about their story than it will about yours." And how true that proves to be for everyone. When two people can show up in one setting with opposite emotional reactions, it reveals that the situation doesn't determine the feelings as much as the meaning that each person places on the situation does. We come to every moment with our own lens trained to see whatever will validate our judgments, justify our insecuri-ties, and affirm what we hold valuable.

Listing those things—losses, fears, and frustrations—moves the spot-light in my brain off of *her* and shines it squarely on the *information* that I need to process in order to serve my life and empower me to be able to serve her in the new ways she will now need. When the attention is exclusively on her, my brain looks for more ways to keep validating my frustration. We've all been there . . . getting to the place with someone where everything they do annoys us. We're just stewing over the person, continuing to heap blame on them for the dissonance we feel. But when the attention is placed on the actual issues, then we actually have information about us, for us.

In our friendships we are too quick to attach meaning to *her* when really how we feel reveals more about *us*. Subconsciously, every time our friends speak or act, we're running their story through our filter and asking, "What do I think about that? How am I impacted? What am I feeling? What does this say about my choices and my life?" So when I react to my sister's move—rather than being able to stay in her story and ask questions about how she's feeling and what she's thinking—I'm now more concerned about *my* life and how her move will affect *me*. Likewise when Daneen announces she's pregnant, I'm not just reacting to her, I'm also subconsciously reacting to how *my* life might be impacted.

When we're reacting to how silly it is for our friend to spend that much money on a pair of shoes, we're doing that to justify our own choice about why we wouldn't or couldn't choose the same. When we're reacting to a friend's divorce, it's coming from a place of how we feel about our own marriage, the choices we've made, how this will change our friendship with her, or how we felt as a kid when our parents went through their divorce.

When I see my losses clearly, then I can make decisions about whether there is anything I can do, or want to do about them. I can give myself the space to grieve some of them and perhaps even come up with solutions that will prevent others from happening. When I can see all my fears I can then begin to assess which of them might be real fears that I can react to, and which ones might just be my imagination pushing me into worrying about things I cannot control. I can choose to take steps to protect myself if needed. When I see all the things I feel angry about, I can begin to evaluate whether I need to put any boundaries in place to prevent being violated next time, or maybe I'll start to see that I'm not really mad at her for having something as much as I'm mad at myself for not having that thing. With that valuable information I can begin to take the steps of seeing what's important to me and what I might choose to do or see differently going forward.

The same process can be used in every place we feel angst, frustration, or annoyance: What am I feeling? What information can I glean from this feeling? Is there anything I am being invited to do in response?

Even when we're provoked by things like her spending money she claims to lack on a designer purse or a family trip, her putting more energy and time into her kid's birthday party than we think is worthwhile, or her forgetting to call us on the day that our brother was having open-heart surgery, we can begin to see them as opportunities for us to pause and own our own feelings, asking ourselves where the dissonance is for us in these perceived grievances. These moments where we don't think she's doing it "right" can be trickier situations to process than the obvious ones like moves, weddings, achievements, births, and retirement. But in all cases we're tempted to make the same mistake of keeping the attention on her and whether she's living her life the way we want her to, rather than shining the light back on us to see if we're living the life we want to.

So forgiveness—our willingness to take a step back and see the situation from a bigger vantage point—provides the opportunity to reflect on why we're feeling what we feel, acknowledge the losses and gains in this new situation, and then consciously choose willingness to let her off the hook from being responsible for our feelings and responses.

If we don't identify that this is about *us* then we end up doing a double-whammy against our friend. She not only ends up getting blamed for our feelings, but she is also at risk of not getting our full support. When we're more worried about how we feel about her life change, it's harder to validate her feelings, affirm her process, express genuine love, and give to her with acts of service.

Forgiveness allows us to reverse the default process: owning our feelings instead of blaming, and supporting her life instead of getting distracted by our own.

CHOOSING TO SEE IT DIFFERENTLY

- *When She's Late:* Instead of being mad at her for being chronically late, decide ahead of time how you will spend the extra time waiting for her (playing Words with Friends on your phone, reading another chapter of the novel you're enjoying, or thinking through tomorrow's to-do list).

- *When She's Inconsistent:* Instead of harboring resentment that she claims to have no money and yet keeps spending on things you don't think she needs, affirm her when you do see an area she's sacrificing in or being thrifty, and take the time to see an area in your own life where you complain but don't always act immediately and fully to resolve.

- *When She Always Forgets:* Instead of being constantly dismayed at how she keeps forgetting your birthday, or other big dates, choose to send her an e-mail or a text ahead of time saying, "Just a reminder that my dad's surgery is next Tuesday—it would mean so much to have you call." Or, "I'm feeling sad as I approach the one-year anniversary of my divorce, any chance you have time for drinks?" Or, "I can't believe I'm turning 48 next week! Hard to believe. Just wanted to say thanks for your friendship."

- *When She Gets Too Busy:* Instead of taking it personally, choose to see her exhaustion as a place to show up and help. Send her a card in the mail cheering her on with her taxing job, call and ask if there is an errand you can run for her, point out all the things you see her doing since few others will validate all that she's giving, and invite her to commit to a celebratory dinner "when one of her massive projects is over" or to spend an afternoon at a spa with you "to make sure we rejuvenate you in the midst of all that you're doing."

- *When She Makes the "Wrong" Decision:* Instead of judging her, try to give her an even bigger circle of acceptance and grace. Most of us want to be understood, so it's always better to ask questions to *hear* her process: ask her to share the positive things she's choosing or to explain what she hopes will happen (i.e., why she likes him or what she thinks is the gain in loaning her sister money). There are few times we need to weigh in someone else's life—even if she's marrying the wrong guy, we cannot rob her of her own life lessons. Yes, she may end up hurt. No, we cannot prevent that. We're called to be present along the way for both good choices and bad choices.

A FRAMEWORK FOR FORGIVENESS:
GUIDELINES TO CONSIDER

But what about in situations where we can clearly see them doing something we'd label as wrong, annoying, or unhealthy? Perhaps they said something hurtful, have a repetitive pattern of competing with us that we find exhausting, or seem completely self-absorbed in their own life? I wish there were a one-size-fits-all answer, but there simply isn't. We all have a varying range of what we'll tolerate and we possess different communication skills and experiences in being able to handle tough conversations. Unfortunately, too few of us have seen conflict modeled well.

With that said, there are five principles I'll put out there for our consideration in knowing how and when to let her know that there are issues in the friendship that we're feeling.

1. Choose the awkwardness of a conversation over the risk of losing each other. We too often choose to avoid the pain and discomfort of a conversation, and unwillingly end up choosing the pain of a strained relationship or the loss of a friend. Will it be awkward? Yes, possibly. Is there risk? Yes, indeed. But do we love her enough or value the potential of what we could have as greater than that risk? Hopefully.

In romance, we'd never walk away without giving each other a chance to hear what is bothering us—there's no such thing as a "drift apart break-up." We women will always tell them what we wish were different and what we think will fix this tension. We have to love our girlfriends enough to give them that same gift of trying to make this work.

2. Never wait until the "last straw." It can often be too late to salvage a friendship if we wait until we can't handle it anymore. If we look down the road and can see this habit or interaction getting more frustrating, then we should choose to bring it up now. Or, if we can see something she could do if she knew how we felt, then we must bring it up sooner, rather than later. Few annoyances get better with time.

3. Pause for wisdom. I always sit with my angst for a short time, not to avoid it, but to get clear about it. I pray for wisdom, that I will be clear what part of this issue is my work, and what part I think would be helpful to share. I pray for clarity that I'll be able to see the outcome I'm hoping for—if only that we'll feel closer to each other when we talk. I pray for love that I'll be able to show up in conversation from a place of acceptance, not fear or blame. I pray for courage that I'll be willing to start a conversation that most of us would rather avoid.

4. Ask questions to brainstorm the best approach. Do I think she's already feeling the strain, too, or will this be a surprise to her? What is it I think I need—am I hoping she can change, or am I asking her to do something differently, or do I just need my feelings to be heard? What can I own in this situation—where do I owe her an apology or need to take responsibility for my feelings? Do we have a comfortable history of honest conversations or will this be our first one? How do I anticipate her reacting—will she fly off the handle, feel horrible and apologize profusely, or deny it and change the subject? Is this a habit of hers that she's already aware of and working on? Am I bringing this up because I think it will help me or because I think I need to help her? Have I seen her work on this issue—if so, can I point out some growth I've seen and affirm her for her attempts? Am I prepared to receive the frustrations she might be holding about me, too? How can I be ready to model the hearing of her complaints in the healthiest way possible? Does this subject demand a big conversation with lots of time or can I just casually bring it up the next time it comes up?

5. Come from a place of gentle strength. To bring something up means we care about the relationship and the person. We want to be conscious during the entire conversation that our goal is forward progress, increased commitment, and more mutuality, rather than getting sidetracked by wanting to be right, defending our ego, going overboard, or shaming her. If appropriate, it's always good to point out our commitment to her and the relationship lest she start pulling away from fear of rejection. The more we can communicate how much we value her and want a continued relationship, the more she'll be able to hear our needs.

THREE DIFFERENT WAYS TO SHARE OUR FEELINGS AND NEEDS

1. The Gush: This is a good approach if we don't feel too much anger and can easily take responsibility for the processing we're doing, but still want to open up communication in an area that could be divisive or difficult for the friendship. Sharing our feelings and needs with context builds connection and intimacy.

Examples:
Regarding a Life Change: "Just in case you've noticed that I've been acting a little distant lately, I just wanted to tell you some of what I've been feeling so you wouldn't be left guessing. I value our friendship too much to risk that, so wanted to take a moment to honestly share. I've had conflicting feelings—being so excited for you dating this new guy and then also struggling with my own insecurities and fears that it brings up. Please know I only want to cheer for you and will do everything I can to support your relationship. I just start getting nervous that maybe I'll never find the right guy, or maybe you won't have time for me anymore, so I think I started to withdraw. But that's the opposite of what I want! It would mean so much to me if we could be more intentional

in scheduling consistent time with each other. How can we best do that and not take away time you need with him?"

Regarding a Habit of Criticizing: "Can I talk to you about something I'm feeling because I value our friendship so much and want to make sure we're giving to each other in the best ways possible? I realized last time after we had dinner that I felt kinda bad about myself when I got home. Thinking back on our conversation I think I took some of the things you said personally, which left me feeling criticized. I know you like me and aren't trying to hurt me in any way so I just wanted to let you know that when you point out my faults I end up feeling super insecure. I'm appreciative that you know my faults and love me anyway, but I was wondering if you'd be willing to make a more concerted effort to join me in recognizing more of the things that I can like about myself?"

2. The Question. This approach is good if there's a repeated experience happening and we don't feel like it requires a big conversation in order for us to stand up for and point out our needs.

Examples:
- If she's always late, then when we schedule the next date, ask, *"What time can I honestly count on you to be there this time?"*
- If she talks more than she listens, then ask, *"Hey, before we go, can I give you a bit of an update about my life?"*
- If she withdraws in a conversation, then ask, *"Did I say something that bothered you? What are you feeling?"*
- If she flakes out on a commitment again, then ask, *"Do you realize you've canceled on me before?"* and let her respond. Maybe follow up with, *"I want to trust you when you commit, what can we do to avoid being in this place again?"*

3. The Non-Violent Communication Approach. What I love about this approach is that it invites us to state our needs without judging her. By not judging, we are also reminded that our girlfriend has needs, too. And no matter what she's "doing to us" that has upset us, she's also attempting to meet some very understandable human need. Unfortunately, it happens to be in a way that isn't meeting one of our needs, so this approach allows us to sidestep a conversation of blame and engage in a deeper conversation about each of our needs.

In real life we may only include one or two of the first three steps to help our friend really understand what's behind our request in the fourth step.

We can: 1) clarify what we are *observing* with no evaluation, 2) share what emotions we are *feeling*, 3) express the *need* that is connected to those feelings, and 4) make a *request* of the other person to help meet that need, understanding that they can say yes or no or help come up with an alternative. (For more information, see www.cnvc.org, where much of this information, including lists of possible feelings and needs, can be found.)

As with any tool, starting with a sincere heart that's willing to be vulnerable and compassionate is more important than trying to state everything perfectly!

Examples:
Instead of: "I hate it that you're always one-upping me."
Replace with: "When I hear you tell a story directly after I finish telling a story, I feel sad. I want to trust that I matter to you, and knowing you heard me would help with that. Would you comment on some part of my story before telling me yours?"

Instead of: "You're never there for me when I need you."

Replace with: "When I moved last month and you didn't offer to help pack boxes, I felt disappointed. I really needed support. If I'm willing to tell you in advance when I could especially use your support, would you try to arrange your schedule to be there?"

Instead of: "*Your kids are too demanding, you don't have time for me.*"
Replace with: "I see you've become very busy, and I'm starting to feel scared that I'm losing you. I need to know we're still friends and can be there for each other. Would you be open to coming up with some creative ways to stay connected?"

FORGIVENESS LEADS TO PEACE

Everything we do is a search for peace.

We save for the bigger house, leave the corporate job, lose weight, raise well-behaved kids, and search for love—all in the hope that in our achievements and destination we will feel like enough, feel worthy, feel successful. And, we presume when we feel we've got it made that we will then feel peaceful. Settled. Content. Happy.

In our chase, it's not just peace we're running toward, but also fear we're running from. We're not just running toward our castles of perceived peace, we're also slaying dragons in our dust, trying to fight the threats nipping at our heels. Whether it's an annoying ingrown toenail, an overwhelming bill, a computer that doesn't work, a phone call we don't want to make, an appointment to be scheduled, discipline to dole out, wrinkles to eliminate, or gray hairs to cover—these stressors are things we keep trying to eliminate so that we can feel peace.

If we could just defeat that dragon, swim this moat, and rule that kingdom, then we believe we'd reach that elusive state of Zen. In our balance-obsessed culture we are constantly striving to add enough good things and decrease the bad things, all in an effort to achieve peace.

At first glance, the lists of things to eradicate or acquire don't seem directly related to our relationships—but that doesn't mean they aren't.

For the temptation we live with is one of always trying to impress others and impress ourselves. We walk this tightrope because our egos would have it no other way. We want to believe we're enough, and we're willing to try to prove it. Therefore, until we can forgive ourselves for not living up to whatever our expectations are, and forgive others for the same, we live with angst and fear, stress and uncertainty.

The world's leading theologians, philosophers, spiritual teachers, psychologists, sociologists, wisdom thinkers, healers, and enlightenment seekers all speak to the connection between our peace and happiness and our ability to forgive. Beyond lowering our blood pressure, helping us sleep better, adding joy to our life, and improving our relationships—forgiveness is the key to the peace we crave.

We are responsible for how we experience our reality, says *The Course in Miracles* teacher Marianne Williamson. She defines forgiveness as the correction of our perception. In her bestselling book *A Return to Love,* she writes, "Forgiveness is the key to inner peace because it is the mental technique by which our thoughts are transformed from fear to love." We are not meant to hold both fear and love, both peace and panic. Having heard her speak on the miracles we all seek in our lives, I can attest to the fact that she is adamant that miracles occur naturally when there is love flowing, not fear or judgment blocking. Therefore, in order to receive the gifts we have waiting for us, we must offer forgiveness, the humility to admit we don't see things clearly, but that we'd like to "see as God sees, think as God thinks, love as God loves." A belief in God isn't even necessary for having the humility to acknowledge that we are limited when we are assigning meaning based on our own experiences. There is a wisdom and love that we can choose as our lens. It's hard to see someone else's motivations, wounds, and insecurities, unless we simply remind ourselves: "If it's not love coming *at* me, it's a call *to* love."

I am reminded of a Biblical scripture in which the author, the apostle Paul, tells his followers that their purpose in this world is to be ambassadors of reconciliation—people who receive and give grace, messengers of the truth that, since God does not hold anything against anyone, neither does anyone else need to (2 Corinthians 5:19–21 NLT). Paul illustrates how the majority of people during Jesus's life trusted their judgments and ability to evaluate Jesus based on his unimpressive looks and unconventional actions, and they got it wrong. He didn't live up to their expectations, or make them feel the way they wanted to, so they blamed him and crucified him. His death is a symbol for a billion Christians around the world to remember how justified they can feel in their judgment yet perhaps still be mistaken. Crosses are a sacred symbol for many people to invoke our own need for forgiveness and to more easily extend it to others.

But, reconciliation, or forgiveness, is not just a Christian value—in fact, Christians often seem to struggle with it the most. My experience, and perhaps yours, is that even in a tradition steeped in the value of peace and forgiveness, frequently the need to feel right wins out over the theology. It proves that we all face the limitations of our ability to forgive. Beyond any one tradition, I genuinely think it's the hunger of humanity: we all want to be loved, accepted, and chosen—gifts we cannot come to without forgiveness.

Therefore, it's not merely a skill we must practice, as much as it is to be our role, our calling in life, the way we commit to showing up as often as we can. For no matter our shortcomings, the invitation remains to use this present moment to push the boundaries of our love out a bit further. We all have a boundary somewhere: there will always be some people and some actions that we will find easier to forgive than others, and there will always be a line that feels "too far" for us to extend forgiveness. With every situation comes another opportunity to increase our capacity for forgiveness.

And sometimes the hardest part of forgiveness is in offering it to ourselves. We, too, will stand next to the people we love and bump into them, hurt them, disappoint them, and fail them—not to mention hurting, disappointing, and failing ourselves from time to time. And we're called to keep going, continue growing, and maintain our self-love.

That's why I title this chapter with the word *practice*. Because it's not something we'll perfect, but something we must keep practicing, continually making our circle around what and who we will forgive a little bit bigger.

HOW TO APOLOGIZE

Ground yourself in humility. Humility means knowing your

inherent worth so that you can see yourself clearly, without the need to impress or overexert. Apologizing doesn't mean beating yourself up and thinking less of yourself; it means that coming from a place of worth you can better admit your imperfections. Show up as genuine, gentle, loving, and peace-filled as possible. Be willing to admit that you could have done it better.

Fully acknowledge the offense. Describe what you did wrong, taking full ownership. Once the facts are out, admit that your behavior doesn't live up to your standards or that it violated some expectations or commitment. This is not the place to say, "I'm sorry you feel that way." This is the place where you say what you could have done that would have been more meaningful, healing, or loving.

Express awareness for the why. We don't want to make excuses, as though we're trying to avoid taking responsibility, but our ability to articulate *why* we did what we did does help show that we understand our mistake, which is key to being able to make the changes necessary in the future to prevent a repeat. For example, "I know when I get scared, I tend to do x. I want to learn to catch myself in those moments better." Understanding the real reasons we act out can help rebuild the trust in a relationship.

Come prepared to act. Our words need to be backed up with our actions. Sometimes there is a clear way we can make it right—stop being late and show up on time. Sometimes we know we've hurt their feelings and we need to do our best to restore their dignity or remind them how much we adore and respect them. Sometimes the best way to end an apology is with the question "Is there anything I can do to make it up to you?" Sometimes the most important thing we can do is to be willing to talk about what we hope for our future.

Sometimes forgiveness will only recover us, not the friendship. Forgiveness doesn't mean we stay friends, continue to reveal our secrets, or refuse to put better boundaries in place. There are times for those actions and decisions, and they can be a response given for love and in forgiveness.

But most of the time forgiveness not only salvages friendships, but also maximizes them, taking them to places of trust and Frientimacy that can be reached no other way. Remember, every relationship model includes a stage of conflict and tension that is expected, anticipated, and normal. On the other side of that stage is where we experience the intimacy and true belonging we crave. Should we turn back every time we get to this point in the road, we will never get to where we're going. Should we walk away from every person who hurts us, we'll never know real love. Should we end every friendship when someone disappoints us or we disappoint them, we'll never have that friend who is there "no matter what."

Relationships exist because of, and for the purpose of, our practicing forgiveness. The same is true of religion, no matter what spiritual path is chosen. Our goal is peace and happiness and our only way there is through forgiveness. There is no greater skill to possess, no more meaningful choice to be made, no further place to grow our maturity than in the moment where we are provoked to forgive.

And in that moment of forgiveness will be the seeds that will produce the fruits of peace that we chase.

IDEAS FOR PRACTICING FORGIVENESS

There are no magic words that will change our hearts overnight, no pills we can swallow that will lessen our grudges, no easy three-step plan to forgiveness that works for everyone, no effortless and uninvolved way to admit our wrongs, and no formula that can guarantee a specified outcome on our timetable. All we can do is keep choosing to practice increasing our capacity to return to love.

1. Forgive yourself. We give what we know—forgetting some-times that what we give and receive is the same thing.

2. Ask for wisdom. Whatever name you give your trusted source—God, Universe, Higher Self, Love—invite that wis-dom to journey with you, helping you make decisions and leading you to peace.

3. Whisper a mantra. My favorite is: "I'm willing to see this differently." Others might be: "I offer grace," "I am here to learn to love and be loved," "Let me see her as God sees her," or "I choose peace."

4. Pray for her. Pray for her healing, her joy, her personal growth. When we pray for others, we are aligning our inten-tions with that of the Divine, not only giving healing energy to her, but also to us.

5. Choose perspective. There are definitely some wounds that are unspeakable, life-altering, and fatal. Is this one of them with your friend? If not, step back and see if there is a way to diffuse some of the anger or frustration. How con-suming do you want this to really be? If she's always late, rather than end the friendship or insult her again, maybe just bring a book along with you and know that once she arrives you'll enjoy your time with her, but until then you'll be happy, too.

6. Make your peace with imperfection. Every single person is imperfect. To expect otherwise is unrealistic. Is this an issue where you're reminded she's not perfect or did she really harm you? Was she morally wrong or just didn't do it the same way you would? The more you accept your own unique wiring, the more you can accept it in others. Say, "She's doing it differently than I would, and that's okay."

7. Embrace her shadow side: We all have a soft underbelly, with wounds that can manifest themselves in unhealthy ways. Even our every strength is a double-edged sword that can also be a weakness. The goal is to accept each other "for better or worse." Books like *Please Understand Me II*, which reveals the 16 Myers-Briggs Temperaments, or *The Wisdom of the Enneagram,* which highlights the growth opportunities for each of the 9 Enneagram types, can teach us more about ourselves and how different we may be from others.

8. Favor gratitude. If it's too easy to dwell on what she's doing that annoys you, then commit to writing down at least 30 things you like about her. The list can include things she's done for you, qualities you admire, and good memories you have. Be as specific as possible. Read the list frequently and continue to add as needed.

9. Live in the present. Let go of the temptation to keep retelling yourself the story of what happened that's bothering you, further pushing your stake of anger into the ground. The painful act was done in the past; all we have in the present is how we want to respond and who we want to be.

10. Gather knowledge. Buy a book and commit to studying the subject of forgiveness. Also, *The Power of Forgiveness* movie page (http://www.thepowerofforgiveness.com) has a fabulous list of resources from which to choose. Sometimes as our heads better understand what forgiveness is and isn't, how it impacts our health, and what damage it can have on our thinking process, our heart may become more receptive to practicing.

11. *Try the triad.* Stand in one spot and speak to an empty chair/spot that represents the person you're mad at. Tell them how you're feeling. Next sit/stand in that empty spot to embody that person as best as you can. Look back at where you were—speaking to yourself in the voice of the person you were addressing. Make sure they tell you how they feel. Then, stand in the third point of the triangle and become Wisdom—speaking to the relationship—telling both people what you saw, witnessed, heard. Finally, return to your first position that represents you and answer, "Is there anything else I'd like to say or do now?" While this method feels awkward, its effectiveness is time-tested. It may be best practiced with a life coach or other trusted friend who can bear witness.

12. *Give a blessing.* We know when forgiveness is underway, when we don't want the other person to suffer anymore, when we can wish them well. Practice it now even if it feels contrived. Say their name and wish them love, peace, healing, and joy.

13. *Hire a guide.* If you are carrying a wound that just feels too big and too painful to release, I encourage you to hire a professional to walk the process with you. It's that important.

14. *Honor grief.* Sometimes it's just too soon to forgive—you still need to go through the grieving process. Give yourself that significant healing step.

15. *Clarify boundaries.* What feels violated that we want to protect in the future? Does it need to be all-or-nothing with this person to best protect ourselves or do we just need to only trust in smaller ways for now? What do we know we need? What will we not put up with? Which boundaries need to be communicated with others and which ones do we just quietly implement? Reading the book *Boundaries* by Dr. Henry Cloud and Dr. John Townsend might help.

part three

FRIENDSHIPS DON'T JUST KEEP HAPPENING: BE INTENTIONAL

FOLLOW GRACE:
Responding to the
Five Friendship
Threats

JULIANA   AIIN   LYNNE

ROBIN   JACQUELYN

NANCY

CHRISTINA

KYM   ANGIE

ne of the ironies about Frientimacy is that while most of us crave it,
it is a stage filled with things we often want to avoid.

While having a BFF sounds so good, even with people we love and
respect, there is no way to be friends without bringing our personal insecurities, fears, and baggage to the relationship. It's hard to celebrate
each other's joys when we're jealous. It sometimes seems impossible to
hold others' pain without projecting our own story into it. There are
awkward moments.

We often step on each other's toes—and hearts.

Once when one of my friends was sharing her frustration with us
about her medical team during a painful hospital visit, a physician among
us started trying to explain why those doctors had to react the way they
did. Our friend simply wanted her feelings understood; the physician
friend wanted to defend her profession. Both needs were valid. But it's
hard to fulfill both at the same time perfectly.

Another time, one of us was trying to explain her reasons for deciding to not have children. That's a hard conversation to have at any time,
but doubly so with mothers in the room who can't imagine life without
their kids. To be able to support the decision of one without anyone feeling as though her life choice is any less valid or significant can be com-

plicated, to say the least. And the reality that everyone comes into the conversation with insecurities heightens the risk that someone might not feel understood.

Once one of us confessed to the group that she was engaging in a romantic relationship outside her marriage. How does a group of women give her a safe place to share that reality of her life (knowing the courage it took her to confess it to us) while also dealing with our own feelings about her choices? For those who have been cheated on, it can be hard to not project that pain onto the friend. For those who have found themselves in similar shoes, it can be hard to not give advice. For those who think her behavior is unforgivable, it can be hard to figure out what a friend is supposed to do or say in such a situation.

Sometimes it's not as much about agreement as it is about finding ways to stand in front of each other with humility, vulnerability, and hope. But that doesn't always happen without someone saying words that hurt or damage.

And this is where many of us walk away. We chalk it up to one more person who wasn't good enough to be our best friend, convinced that now we've seen her real side. Too often we label people at such moments with judgments like "selfish" and "toxic." We tell ourselves that we don't need to put up with this kind of behavior, that we deserve a *real* friend, and that we're too healthy to be in this kind of drama. Or even more commonly, we drift apart because "we're just too different."

It is normal for friendships to shift and change. I'm not against drifting apart, breaking up, or setting clear boundaries. But if we find ourselves without close friends, it might be worth examining our expectations of a "real" friendship. Is someone a bad person if she disappoints us? Is the fact that our lives have changed an automatic reason to assume we can't understand or support each other anymore? Do I have to agree with all her decisions in order to love her and support her? Can she have an annoying trait (always talking about herself, showing up late repeatedly) and still be part of a healthy relationship?

We have to remember that *every* healthy relationship model put forward by psychologists and sociologists has within it a stage that is described with labels like disillusionment, conflict, questioning, tension, storming, chaos, and struggle. With words like that, it's obvious why we'd be inclined to stay in the earlier phases of friendship where it's described as pseudo-community, the honeymoon stage, or forming. Those early stages often feel fun, good, and energizing. When we're both on our best behavior, still trying to impress each other, the relationship doesn't yet feel fraught with emotions or apparent flaws.

In the friendship process, though, I have found that too many of us end things before we ever get the chance to experience the ultimate rewards. For it's in the phases that follow both the honeymoon and the disillusionment that we step into intimacy, commitment, and true belonging. Had we given up when we were disappointed, exhausted, and drained then we may not have ever experienced the fulfillment that comes from the real closeness on the other side.

Cutting people out of our lives or "kicking them to the curb," as many self-help voices are urging us to do, may make us feel momentarily strong, but it could also mean we rarely reach real intimacy, an experience that appears to be in short supply these days.

If we don't brush our hands off and walk away, our other temptation is to merely stay and put up with behaviors or qualities in others that we aren't comfortable with: narcissism, neediness, or pessimism. But then we're forced to hide our true feelings, walk on eggshells, pretend it's okay, and just silently fume. These avoidance behaviors keep us in the early stages of a relationship, in the pseudo-community phase where we may look like friends, but the friendship is not safe or meaningful.

Rather than walk away or just put up with it, there is a third option. The healthiest (and often most difficult) option is to "grow through it"— seeking to repair the relationship. This will definitely feel awkward at times, and it takes energy. We'll risk disappointment and possibly reveal our own shortcomings. It requires being forgiving. It's clear why so few of us step into it. It means we have to step forward together. Repeatedly.

It might mean we'll sit in a circle with the one who is having an affair, perhaps next to the one whose husband cheated on her. It might mean we'll cheer for the one who just hit her biggest career goal, and cry with the one who was just fired. It might mean we'll commit to seeing that the one who we think talks too much also makes us laugh the most. It means we'll see her imperfections, and she'll see ours too.

It means we know that none of us is perfect. And none of us is without goodness. We forge on. There will be lots of awkward moments we will witness and hold.

Frientimacy takes practice. We have to make commitments to be generous and honest with each other. We trust that the benefit from the commitment is bigger than the pain of the process, and that the history we eventually forge will be deeper than the present moment feels.

That we have this privilege to grow is nothing short of grace. That we can show up differently and influence different results is nothing short of grace. That we can offer love instead of fear is nothing short of grace. That we have this moment to choose extended vision, greater compassion, and deeper insight is nothing short of grace. That we can participate in the miracle of seeing our perspective shift is nothing short of grace. That we can choose to do differently today than we did yesterday is nothing short of grace.

THE FIVE FRIENDSHIP THREATS

In the last chapter I talked about the overall importance of having a heart determined to forgive others in order for us to experience the peace we crave. In this chapter I want to be a little more practical about how we can shift our perspective and do the work of protecting and repairing our friendships in some of the areas we find most threatening. Most of our friendship frustrations seem to fall under five main categories—blame, jealousy, judgment, non-reciprocation, and neglect—so that's where I want to focus our attention now.

Parenthetically, let me just say (since you're the one reading the book and not your friend—though I do think this book makes a fabulous gift!), I'm going to be focusing on how we can change and show up differently. That's not the same as saying that everything, or even anything, is our fault, only that there is always capacity for our growth. Because while we call it "personal growth," it's not when we're alone that we most see the results—but rather it's when we're facing another human being. How I treat others is the litmus test for whether my counseling-meditation-church-attendance-book-reading-workshop-going-yoga-stretching-journaling-reflecting efforts are doing the necessary work.

How I keep my own light in their presence. How I practice compassion in situations I don't understand. How I learn to let myself grow in both chaos and peace. How I allow my rough edges to be polished. How I learn to see people in their innocence and purity. This is our life work.

1ST THREAT: BLAME. OR, "I FEEL BAD WHEN I'M AROUND HER— SHE MUST BE BAD."

Names like *frenemy* and *toxic friend* are becoming part of our vernacular. Books and articles continue to warn us about unhealthy women with cute names like Negative Nellie, Sabotage Suzie, and Fault Finding Fran. Do a Google search with two words that by definition shouldn't be in the same sentence, "avoid" and "friend," and we'll get a list of 409,000,000 articles helping us figure out which friends to drop. I'm a bit dismayed at how popular it is right now to label people with their weakness and act like we are somehow too good, too self-righteous, too enlightened, and too healthy to hang out with anyone who isn't perfect yet.

It's certainly true that there are extremely unhealthy people who can hurt us and drain us, with whom we need to set very firm boundaries. But before we too quickly label someone as "toxic," I'd like to suggest that we consider four potential personal and relational consequences that happen when we get label-happy.

When we label a person, we are buying in to a fear-based belief system that people are inherently one thing: unhealthy or healthy, bad or good, toxic or non-toxic. If people are only one way or the other, our highest priority, then, is to vet them, judge them, and weed them out of our life. If we don't, they will bring us down (assuming, of course, that we're not one of them).

Labeling Distracts Us from Our Growth

Recent research suggests that eighty-four percent of women admit to having had a toxic friend. That means we either all know the same remaining sixteen percent of women who are the poisonous ones, or that some of us putting the labels on others are also the ones wearing them.

I'm repeatedly reminded that we all have a shadow side, a place where our tireless egos try to hide our wounds from others or seemingly protect us so we don't keep getting hurt. Don Riso and Russ Hudson, in their book *The Wisdom of the Enneagram,* point out that "we tend to see *our* motivations as coming from the healthy range. The defenses of our ego are such that we always see ourselves as our idealized self-image, *even when we are only average or even pathological.*" That's humbling enough to remind me that I have a good chance of exhibiting the faults I see in others, even if I do it in different ways.

Look at the list of what we think makes someone toxic (according to the recent survey conducted by TODAY.com and SELF.com) and tell me if you haven't exhibited one of these at some point. The number one source of toxicity, say experts, is narcissism (sixty-five percent). The list continues with being too needy (fifty-nine percent), too critical (fifty-five percent), giving backhanded compliments that undermine (forty-five percent), and proving to be flakey or unreliable (thirty-seven percent). I'd say, to some extent, that's a list that we all struggle with, not because we're all poisonous, but simply because we're human.

I don't condone these behaviors, but I can acknowledge that they're normal, albeit unhealthy, habits that develop out of our own insecurities. None of us started our adult journeys from a place of enlightenment. We are all still on our own paths toward becoming centered, present, and awake.

But pointing to someone else in a devaluing way, while it may make us feel healthier/more righteous, could distract us from the growth we need to be stepping into ourselves.

Labeling Risks Victim Mentality

Believing someone is toxic undermines our own power. The obvious loss of strength comes just in merely believing that someone is inherently poisonous.

First, this is a value judgment that weakens how we feel about ourselves since it's impossible to put out judgment on others without also putting it on ourselves.

And second, we destabilize our peace when we dare to believe that someone else can affect us the way that drinking poison would, as though we're victim to them once we've allowed them into our lives, unable to withstand their toxic fumes. It gives them the power that we should hold for ourselves: the power that says my peace is mine—no one gets to vote whether I have it or not.

We give too much power away when we use the word "toxic," subtly telling ourselves there is nothing we can do about it. Believing that anyone has that kind of influence on us doesn't remind us that we choose our own feelings and responses.

Labeling Is Harmful to Others

Labeling people as toxic doesn't inspire loving transformation. It is not only ineffective, but also damaging.

It's ineffective, in part, because blame and shame only invite egos to yell louder in an effort to defend themselves. People often cannot see their own flaws or the impact they are having on others. So to have it pointed out in a way that stems from judgment almost guarantees that the words will not land on fertile or transformative soil.

Labeling is damaging because we're risking someone believing the label as an indictment of her personhood, her being, rather than her behavior. That's a crucial difference. It's the equivalent of a parent disciplining a child by saying "You're a bad boy" versus "What you did was a bad thing." For anyone to believe that they are inherently bad, toxic, or irreparable prevents them from ever trying to change. (The term "unhealthy" at least suggests there is the expected state of health.) What we want is to put the focus on the behaviors that are impacting us and therefore on the possibility of transformation for both of us.

We each, even the most damaged among us, have a blessing to offer the world. A label doesn't remind us, or them, of their essence, their spirit, their being, their potential gift.

Labeling Minimizes the Role of Relationships

And here's the ultimate irony. The truth is we cannot all wait to be in relationship *until* we are healthy, for it is in our relationships that we can *become* healthy. We don't grow more loving in a loveless vacuum.

We are relational beings. Which means that relationships are the curriculum and context for our opportunities to grow, mature, and become more whole. If we jump out of them when they get difficult and tense, for whatever reason, we can short-circuit our growth and the growth of this separate organism of life called the relationship.

Before I go on, let me give a caveat: I am not encouraging anyone to stay in abusive situations or to put up with unhealthy behaviors that are damaging. Sometimes we have to be willing to establish very firm boundaries with people who continually hurt us, and that might mean separating ourselves at some point.

That said, what often gets labeled as toxic (as we see from the list on page 200) are actually quite subjective designations often given too quickly.

For example, few of us are qualified to diagnose someone with the emotional disorder known as narcissism. And yet what happens is if someone doesn't live up to our expectations, most of them unstated, it is far too easy to feel like we've given more than we've received. We then conclude that the other person is inherently selfish—that he or she is incapable of understanding us and giving to us. They think only of themselves, period. We are using our feelings of lack and our own unmet desires to then label them toxic. There may be a different way of seeing the situation.

Imagine entering into our relationships with the purpose to learn our personal and relational lessons in our journey toward becoming more mature and whole. That could mean choosing to withhold slapping the label of toxic onto her for a while as we together work in our laboratory of love to grow this relationship as far as it can possibly go.

In the end, if we both need to separate from each other, we do so having learned our important lessons and grown in our ability to love more effectively.

The good news in focusing on the *interaction between us* that *can* change, versus only focusing on the *label we've judged her with being* that implies it *cannot* change, is that now there is space for both of us to grow together.

A Better Way to Respond

Now, if there were half a billion Google search results on how to avoid irritating people, that I could comprehend. I understand that there are people out there who drain us, annoy us, and repeatedly exhaust us, and we may often make the choice to avoid people that make us feel that way if we can. What I have a harder time understanding is how those people ended up getting labeled as our friends to begin with, when the very definition of "friend" implies affection and positive feelings! The fact that we have called these people our friends leaves me thinking that there might be something worth restoring.

The irony is that much of what we experience in Frientimacy could look like toxic behavior! What I mean by this is that we will invariably know more negative things about the people that we are closest to. As we foster a friendship we are inviting her to let her guard down, which presupposes us seeing her flaws. The more intimate we become—the closer we get to someone—the higher the chance becomes that we will metaphorically bump into each other more often.

So if we can resist the temptation of believing someone is toxic (which is far different from acknowledging that we can be hurt by their behavior), then we can acknowledge that all of us have the capacity at times to express unhealthy behaviors, just as we can also all show compassion and thoughtfulness.

In real-life applications, just because a new mom is needy and insatiable (a characteristic that fifty-nine percent of us would say makes her toxic) doesn't mean she'll be that way forever, or that she can't also be filled with love and joy at the same time. Just because a friend is starting to sound too critical, a reaction from her own insecurities (a characteristic that fifty-five percent of us would say makes her toxic), doesn't mean she won't grow into her self-worth, and that in the meantime she can't also be someone who would drop everything in her life to support us.

We are all meant to be a blessing on this planet, even if we do adopt behaviors that can damage one another. This worldview invites us to see our relationships as our self-growth laboratory, a context in which we learn the genuine dynamics of who we are and who our friends are.

When we show up, really show up with someone, seeing them past the healthy, non-toxic facade we saw initially, it allows us to ask: "What does this relationship tell me about myself, about what I value, about what edges I need to smooth? Have I clearly communicated to her what I want and need from her and how her behavior impacts me? Have I sought to understand why she's acting out her insecurities with me in this way? And what does this relationship tell me about her and how I can give to her in ways that will be meaningful to her?"

I'm not saying we need to get closer to everyone whom we consider toxic. But I am saying we'll have to do it with a few of them if we want Frientimacy—friends with whom we experience familiarity, safety, comfort, and acceptance of both our good and bad sides.

2ND THREAT: JEALOUSY. OR, "SHE THINKS SHE'S SO COOL."

When we're not grateful, we tend to be much more susceptible to jealousy, envy, and competition. It doesn't take an expert to see how these characteristics might not contribute to healthy friendships!

I notice that when I'm grateful and have a sense of my own well-being, I show up in relationships with more light. It has something to do with self-esteem, but also with simply holding a peace about my own life, that invites me to not feel threatened by theirs. I repeatedly watch in others, and in myself, how easy it is to project personal insecurities onto other people.

If we're not happy with being single then it's harder to want to be at parties with couples. If we struggle with our weight then it will annoy us to have our skinny friends complain about not fitting into their little black dress this weekend. If we're exhausted by being up every night with a teething toddler then it's easier for us to judge others who seemingly have an easier life. If our marriage is going through a rough patch then we tend to feel more frustrated with other couples expressing public displays of affection. If we don't have kids, we become more annoyed by those who aren't willing to get a babysitter in order to come to a party we're throwing. If we are working overtime this month, we'll feel frustration at the woman who seems to have all the time in the world to be baking and crafting for her kid's birthday party. You get the idea.

Jealousy. It's one of those tricky and counterintuitive feelings. For it's easy to misinterpret the feeling as being about something that someone else is doing wrong and be frustrated with them. But really, it's reminding us that we have an issue that matters to us. It's not about them. It's our own stuff. How we react says more about our story than it does about theirs.

We push down on others, hoping it will raise us up. It's almost as though we think life is a seesaw where only one of us can win.

I see it in breakups frequently: the person that was most cherished only weeks ago is now criticized in an attempt to comfort us that we are better off without that person. As though we can't admit their worth and hold ours at the same time?

I see it in friendships where two women make different choices: the one who had the baby, took the job for money, decided to move away, chose a private school for their child—both women, to hold the belief that they made the right choice, are tempted to devalue those who make an alternative decision. As though we can't hold the belief that we could both be making the right choice for our lives, even if the choices look different?

I see it where there appears to be an inequality that provokes our jealousy: the person who seemingly has the fame, the power, the money, the happy family, or the good looks receives the most criticism. Ironically we secretly want something they have, but instead of using their success as our inspiration, we attack them with our insecurities disguised as complaints. As though it's their problem for having what we want.

Certainly their actions or choices might trigger our feelings. But we'd be wrong to assume that they did something wrong, when in fact, the moment serves as an opportunity for us to look at our own life and ask, "What is it that I want?" And just as important, "Can I be around people who have that without holding it against them?"

Three Responses to Jealousy

The real question comes down to whether someone else's happiness threatens my own. In other words, can I figure out a way to not only show up with gratitude for what I have and hope to have, but also show up with gratitude for what they have?

Here are three ways to respond to jealousy.

First, increase your gratitude. Keep a daily journal if you can, where you write five things down every day. Or, make one long list today where you force yourself to list up to fifty things. Or, attach the practice of gratitude to something else you already do regularly like brushing your teeth or waiting for yoga to begin. Or, spend an afternoon looking back over the year to identify milestones you're glad you reached, moments that mattered, growth in your life that you witnessed.

You may not have what you want yet, but what little glimpses gave you hope that you might reach your goal? For example, with friends, you may not yet have that circle of local friends that nurture your life, but maybe you can celebrate that you joined GirlFriendCircles.com to do something about it.

Second, increase your awareness of your jealousy. When you feel jealous, use the moment to ask yourself why you feel this way. What do you feel is missing in your life? As you take more responsibility for your feelings, you'll gain awareness about who you are and have more opportunity to respond to that desire in positive ways. Don't beat yourself up! Just gently hold those moments as touchstones that remind you of who you want to become and what you want to invite into your life. And own it for yourself. No need to punish others. Their joy will not diminish or steal from yours. There is enough joy in this world for all of us.

Third, increase your trust in an abundant world. Above all, trust that the world functions from a place of abundance. There is enough. Enough joy for all of us. Enough peace for every single one of us to experience, no matter our circumstances. Enough love so that we can all choose to give and receive this fruit. Albert Einstein wrote, "The most important question you'll ever ask is, 'Is the universe friendly?'" How we perceive this world will determine whether we show up with fear or love. That choice leads to everything else.

My favorite mantra to whisper whenever I find myself focused on lack or worry is, "In this moment, I have everything I need." And, while it may be more tempting to focus on what I think I'm missing, that truth about the present moment remains.

3RD THREAT: JUDGMENT. OR, "I WISH SHE WOULD DO IT THE WAY I DO IT."

While there may have been a time in history where we all married by a young age, started having kids around the same time, and presumably all gave up careers to raise our families—we definitely now live in a culture where very few of us are on the same schedule. It is not to be assumed that someone our same age will be in the same life stage. We can be new moms at seventeen or forty-five.

Most articles and books focus on the logistics and the "how-to's" (i.e., what do we do when we used to plan trips together but now she doesn't want to get away due to the baby?) But while the *how* is important, even deeper is the *why* is it so hard? I think it's because we judge each other.

With all the choices women have before us now, our life paths can seem increasingly disparate. We're no longer just talking about someone getting married a year ahead of someone else (or any other major life change—empty nest, retirement, divorce, kids) as much we might be

talking about a woman deciding to never marry and a woman who decides to marry someone different every decade. The freedom we have to
choose from a myriad of options heightens the reality that few of us will
travel it in sync.

In our effort to come to peace with our own choices, we risk making
judgments about someone else's. It happens with stay-at-home moms versus work-outside-the-home moms. It happens between single women and
married women. It happens between those who make amazing money at
their jobs and those who don't. It happens between those who live in the
city and those who don't. It happens between those parents who let their
kids come back home to live late in life and those who don't. It happens
when she goes back to him, or when she gives up on a marriage we think
she should fight for. It happens when she's too lenient with her kids or
too strict with them. It happens when we roll our eyes that she's taking
this religious thing too far and it happens when we question whether she's
devout enough.

Naturally, we judge because we assume that we're in the "middle" and
everyone else is going too far one direction or another.

The subconscious temptation is to devalue the other person's choices
and gains in order to make ours feel better. We sometimes do it blatantly
because "we would never choose that," but sometimes it's subtle where, in
our effort to convince ourselves that we made the right choice, or that we
had no control in our choice, we can often pull away from those we think
cause us to feel ambivalent. But is it them "making" us feel that way or is
it our own stuff?

Judgment springs from fear. If we don't understand something, don't
know how to change it, or are somehow concerned that it can threaten us
in some way, then we will judge it as something "out there," apart from us.
When we see a choice or decision as separate from something we would
do, it's only one step further to see the person as separate from us, too.
And when we feel any fear, our most basic reactions are fight or flight.
Fighting is when we attack the other person or situation, directly or indi-
rectly, to feel safer—or more superior. Flight is when we use our judgment
to give ourselves permission to dismiss the person or situation as hopeless
and walk away. In either reaction, we have forfeited the opportunity to
connect and create peace in the relationship.

Our friendships don't end because we don't know how to call the other person and schedule time together. No. They end too often because we don't know how to feel excitement and joy for someone else's choices and stages while also staying in a place of contentment and joy for our own.

Two Prayers that Decrease Our Judgment

"Help Me Trust Her."

In general, everyone's worldview makes sense to them. We aren't always privy to their process the way we are to our own, but we can assume she's not waking up with the intention of ruining her life. She's doing the best she can with what she knows right now. We can choose to increase our trust in her, believing that she is moving toward what she thinks she needs. And if, in the off chance her choice leads to pain or disappointment, then we can trust that she will grow through that, too. We can trust that she will learn the life lessons she needs to learn without our lectures or judgment. We can let go of the need to be her compass, and instead choose to be her friend no matter what her choices are.

"Help Me Trust Me."

Perhaps most important of all is our ability to give the same gift of inherent trust to ourselves. I once heard Tim Kelley, a life purpose expert, say, "Your ego cares how you get there, your soul only cares that you do." Our soul, the part of us that cares deeply about our growth and development, cares less about our image, what the world values, and whether something hurts or not; rather, it cares far more that we are becoming the people we are meant to be. In his book *True Purpose*, Kelley says, "Your soul isn't that concerned about how much money you are making at work. . . . It cares whether you are learning, growing, and transforming from the experience."

On the one hand, this awareness can make it much harder to always know what is the right choice since we don't always know what the highest priority is or what value we should let guide us in making our decisions. But on the other hand, knowing this truth makes it much easier to trust ourselves as we can simply commit to learn from anything we experience. We don't need to ever beat ourselves up over any choice if we can rest in the reality that every experience, even the ones that brought pain, can be used to produce maturity, provoke compassion, and practice forgiveness.

David Whyte, in his classic book *The Heart Aroused,* says it this way: "For the personality, bankruptcy or failure may be a disaster; for the soul, it may be grist for its strangely joyful mill and a condition it has been secretly engineering for years."

Indeed, we can trust ourselves to grow and become better. Which really is a far more worthwhile goal than to simply try to get through life with as little pain as possible.

4TH THREAT: NON-RECIPROCATION. OR, "I'M ALWAYS THE ONE GIVING."

If there is one thing I hear all the time from women, it is some variation on the theme: "I'm tired of being the one who gives more than I receive."

The details change depending upon the stage of the friendship, but the implication is always that we are tired of being the initiators, the givers, the schedulers, the inviters, and the ones who do the most for the other. We apparently listen the longest, serve the most thoughtfully, and show up the most consistently. In short, it's easy for us to often think of ourselves as the "better friend."

From all my interactions with women, you'd think the odds are probable that I'd eventually connect with these blessed beneficiaries, these friendship winners in the life lottery of our giving. One might think that for every woman who gives too much that there would be at least one woman out there who admits getting everything without giving anything.

Ironically, I haven't yet met her.

I am curious about this apparent vast imbalance, and I'm not talking about a healthy friendship where life circumstances mean that one of us needs to receive more than we can offer, for a time.

My inquisitiveness leads me to ponder possible theories about why women seem to often be giving to each other without ever feeling full in return. Could any of them be true?

Seven Possible Explanations for the Giving Disparity

1. *Maybe everyone, except me, is selfish.* This is possible, I suppose. Likely? I think not.

2. *Maybe we're all paying it forward.* Maybe it's like a big love triangle—where he likes her, but she likes the other guy. Maybe we all are over-giving to someone, and that person is over-giving to someone else, who is over-giving to someone else, which means we're all giving, but it never feels reciprocated by the right people.

3. *Maybe it's easier to see what we give than what she gives.* In one case, I knew both of the women in a friendship, each of them thinking they gave more than the other. One said, "I'm always the one initiating our time together," while the other said, "She does all the talking—I am always the one listening to her life." They were both accurate, but it didn't mean that the other wasn't contributing; it was just in a different way. Some of us are better at scheduling, others at remembering birthdays, and others at asking meaningful questions. Maybe we tend to only have eyes for how we give.

4. *Maybe we're scared.* Maybe we don't over-give at all, but our insecurity heightens our fear of it. Perhaps we hold that memory of one person who walked all over our boundaries long ago; and now, to prevent getting hurt again, we are super-sensitive to anyone who doesn't reciprocate immediately in big ways. Maybe we don't remember that we've become better at setting boundaries since then and can trust more people than we do.

5. *Maybe we give more than anyone needs or asks.* I once had a friend who kept buying me trinkets from different shopping expeditions. It was so thoughtful of her even though I didn't need those little things. She was giving to me in a way that I wasn't asking her to give, didn't need her to give, and certainly wasn't reciprocating back to her. I probably didn't value receiving the small gifts as much as she valued buying them for me. If she ever felt it was disproportionate, I'd rather her have cut back on what she bought me than to resent me for not matching her style. Maybe we need to look at where we give and see if we think it's really meaningful to the receiver.

6. *Maybe we are leaking what we are given.* Maybe other areas of our lives drain us so much that even if our friends are giving to us, we can't hold it. Maybe she affirms all the time, but it just bounces off you. Maybe she initiates get-togethers frequently, but you're too stressed to hear them. Maybe there is no one else who can fill the emptiness you feel except you, doing the work of self-care and personal growth.

7. *Maybe we're not over-generous at all.* Perhaps to prevent feeling rejected we only give an inch and retreat, calling it imbalanced when really it was just one e-mail that went unreturned. Maybe the one clue you dropped—that you'd be open to getting together again—wasn't really disproportionate. Maybe we're only putting our toe in the water and calling it over-giving when it's not. Maybe we can e-mail her a second time, or follow up again, without it falling in the category of too much.

Though I won't go so far as to say I don't think there are needy, insatiable, and self-centered people out there, I will say that I don't think everyone but us is one of them. From my experience, almost every woman I interact with truly wants to be in a mutual friendship.

In fact, in his book *The Happiness Hypothesis,* Jonathan Haidt devotes an entire chapter to the law of reciprocity, saying, "Reciprocity is a deep instinct; it is the basic currency of life." He highlights the research that suggests we actually might have an "exchange organ" in our brain that keeps track of give-and-take—as though it's hardwired into our very DNA. Everyone seems to feel best when we feel like the gifts are going both ways, no one wants to be the leech.

It's just sometimes harder to see reciprocity when two people are keeping track on different scorecards with incomparable game rules. With the exchange of money, we know how much is spent and received. In relationships, few things have such tangible and agreed-upon value. When one woman continuously initiates keeping in touch with her friend and the other tends to be the one who does most of the listening during the call, who is to say which one gave more?

Five Principles to Help Increase Our Relationship Balance:

1. *Never give more than we can afford.* Let's state the obvious up front: it's our responsibility to give in ways that don't drain us. Financial advisors caution us to never give a loan that we can't afford to lose. I'd gladly cover a new friend's coffee if she didn't have cash with her, but I wouldn't agree to give her a business loan. With a friend with whom trust had already been built, I'd gladly risk more if both people agreed upon clear parameters. Whether it's with acts of service or emotional availability, we don't give any gift that will leave us feeling resentful if it's not reciprocated in a specific way. We want to ask ourselves whether this is a gift we're giving (no strings attached, no expectations), or whether it's a loan (hoping for a payback). Being judicious with whom we give to, how much we give, and why we give is our responsibility. If we repeatedly give more than we receive and feel bitter about it, we may want to explore why we go beyond our limits.

2. *Expand our circle of friends.* We all give in different ways— it's why I'm a big proponent of having several close friends. We get different needs met and can appreciate how different people give to us better when we can see the differences. We'll need less from any one friend when we feel supported

by several. When we have a friend whose shoulder we can cry on, we can better appreciate the other friend who simply makes us laugh. The best way to feel more full? Receive from more women! This is especially true if we feel that one friend keeps disappointing us. It's our responsibility to build a circle of friends around us, not any one friend's obligation to be everything we need.

3. *Acknowledge that balance doesn't mean identical.* It's important to note that we not only give in different ways, but we also give at different times. Going through my divorce, I monopolized more than fifty percent of many conversations with friends. And the roles have been reversed at various times. When my friends start new relationships, launch new businesses, have babies, or go into long months of depression or low energy, I notice them pulling back a bit. Life can get all-consuming in ways where scheduling a pedicure with a friend simply doesn't make the list of things we have time and energy to do. We don't all give fifty/fifty in every area, all the time.

In his bestseller *The Five Love Languages,* Gary Chapman says we all have a love tank that must be constantly replenished. The gas for those tanks comes in five different communication styles, each of us preferring one or two of them more than the others. To recap, the five love languages are: quality time, words of affirmation, gifts, acts of service, and physical touch. We tend to speak a primary love language, invariably also looking to receive in that same one.

While most of the research pertains to romantic love, parenting, or workplace interaction—I think the five love languages can be helpful in friendships, too. It makes sense if my love language is gifts that I would find it enjoyable and meaningful to pick out that perfect birthday card for a friend, knit that homemade scarf, or even buy those exquisite earrings for her while traveling far away. Conversely, if gift giving isn't our language then the need to buy a gift can feel more like a task to do on our never-ending list. Which doesn't mean that, for our friends, we wouldn't want to make the time to do it, but this example does show that we all give and receive differently.

If we're looking to get a gift for every time we give one—we may only be keeping track in the language of our choice, not in hers. She could very well be counting all the times she's offered to help take pictures at our son's birthday party for us so we have one less thing to worry about, baked extra cookies on our behalf for the bake sale, and dropped off soup when we were sick—and we might be found lacking if our love language isn't acts of service like hers is.

I have one friend with the love language of quality time who impressively always invites and schedules time with my husband and me. I don't reciprocate evenly in that area as I tend to guard my free evenings a bit more, but I've provided her coaching, have held her heart through pain, and have been a safe place for her to process life out loud as someone who cares. The point is that mutuality doesn't mean we both give in the same ways.

Marcus Buckingham, in his book *Find Your Strongest Life*, suggests that we each have a lead role to play in life that makes us happiest and strongest. You can find out for free online which of the nine roles is your primary: Advisor, Caretaker, Creator, Equalizer, Influencer, Motivator, Pioneer, Teacher, or Weaver. An Advisor may feel as though everyone always calls for her opinion, while a Caretaker may be able to best see what needs to be done to relieve someone's stress. An Equalizer will be the one who tells us the truth, while the Motivator will be the one who cheers us on.

There are some actions that we will do naturally, easily, repeatedly. The same is true for our friends.

4. *Bask in the ways we receive.* So you give a lot. Congratulations. We must also make sure, however, we notice what we're receiving, too! She may not be great at remembering our birthday, but does she love us in other ways? Why were we

drawn to her initially? We want to take time to look for all the ways she might be giving that we don't initially see. Pulling out a pad of paper and listing everything we can think of that she does for us helps us see her contributions. This includes things like easily forgiving us, brainstorming our business with us, encouraging us to be an individual, standing up for us, making us laugh, remembering to ask about our mom, and so on. We definitely want to receive what's being given!

5. *Continue to give our best.* If we're the friend who's good at scheduling time together, then we should do it! If we're good at listening longer, asking better questions, and validating feelings, then let's do it freely. If we're the one who remembers birthdays and buys presents for her kids, then let's do it with joy, harboring no resentment. If we're able to pay for meals, we can tell her that it's our privilege to give to our friendship in this way. We will love on her in the ways that are easy and natural for us, knowing that is our contribution to the friendship we share.

The truth is that we're all trying to give what we can, when we can. Withholding the love we can offer will only starve a relationship to death. If we're going to show up, then let's do so with as much generosity as we can give, trusting that as we help fill the love tanks around us that what we give will come back to us.

5TH THREAT: NEGLECT. OR, "SHE'S NOT HERE FOR ME."

I find it interesting that most of our disappointments with friends come from having a different definition of what "being here for me" means.

Most of us have this sense that our good friends would be here for us in some major life crisis: our child goes missing, a breast cancer diagnosis, the decision to take mom off life support. But usually those are once-in-a-lifetime calls and it's the other thousands of life moments where we can start feeling forgotten. Sometimes we just need to talk to her about our fears of just how fast our little girl is growing up, our angst at how our body doesn't perform the way it once did, or the annoying statement our mom made last week. When we start feeling unknown, that sense of detachment can quickly translate to feeling uncared for, which then leaves us feeling forgotten and alone.

We digress to either taking it personally, where we assume we're not worth their precious time or that maybe they don't really like us as much as we thought they did; or we blame them for being an awful friend. We find ourselves saying things like, "What's the point of having friends if she can't even be here for me?" and, "Well, if her life is too busy for me then I guess I know where I stand on her priority scale. I shouldn't have cared so much!"

For me, when I start getting whiny about my friends not being ever-present, there are three responses I try to practice:

1. Ask for what I need.

This one point could save many a friendship from ruin.

In the 2010 movie *How Do You Know,* Reese Witherspoon plays a character whose entire life is turned upside down when she is cut from the professional softball team that has been her entire career. She obligingly goes to see a therapist but before the session starts she talks herself out of it, willing herself to believe she doesn't need it. The psychiatrist, who knows nothing about the situation that his new client is struggling with, watches her walk out the door before any conversation occurs. And in what I think is the best scene of the movie, Reese sticks her head back in the doorway and basically challenges him to sum up his best therapeutic advice for life before she leaves. Without batting an eye he responds, "Figure out what you want and learn to ask for it."

I've come back to that mantra repeatedly in my life. It's two-fold, neither side being easier than the other: figure out what I want and learn to ask for it. Neither action comes naturally.

My mother, who birthed me, still can't always figure me out and my own spouse, who lives with me, can't always read my mind—it's asking a bit much of my friends to do more than that! We don't need to leave our friends guessing—they have enough on their own plates. We can give them the gift of telling them:

- "I need help in crafting a birthday experience that will be meaningful to me. I am hoping that for my birthday this year I could do . . . Will you help me plan it?"

- "I need someone I can be honest with. Everyone just keeps talking about my baby, as though I no longer exist . . . Do you mind if for this afternoon we just focus on me, not as his mother, but just me?"

- "I need support. I think I'm struggling with depression after losing my job. Would you be willing to call me at least once a week and just stay in touch a bit more during this time?"

- "I need to feel like I have your undivided attention when we talk about this subject. Would you be willing to turn your phone off for an hour?"

In romantic relationships we seem to be much more practiced at these conversations. Every day we can easily come up with a list of things we need from the other person—changes we want them to make, chores we expect them to do, attitudes we hope they'll adopt. It's a sign of intimacy, commitment, and safety when we begin to express our needs with the trust that the other person would be honored to help.

I don't know anyone who wants to feel like they are disappointing even one more person in life. Most of us live with the awareness that there is always more we could be doing. So we give others the gift of telling them what they can do that will make the biggest difference to us.

We can let go of the fear that asking for help means we're selfish. News flash: we have needs. That shouldn't come as a shocker. And it certainly doesn't make their gift any less genuine or sincere just because they didn't come up with it themselves! All we're doing is helping them help us in the most effective way possible. When they know what they can do to support us, it saves them time and energy that could otherwise get wasted in them trying to guess.

Recently, one of my girlfriends was telling me about a fight she had with her closest friend two weeks before. As the outside observer who had no emotion tied up in it, it was easier for me to see past all the hurt feelings to what was never said that day; it sounded like good intentions gone horribly awry, as well as miscommunication—one little comment here, one little judgment there, one unfortunate joke here, and an overreaction there. My friend had shown up at her girlfriend's house because she was hurting from a recent engagement breakup and needed attention. Her friend had just told family the night before that she was foreclosing on a house. She probably needed validation and love to fight against her own sense of failure and the fear she was inevitably feeling. Neither of them showed up wanting to hurt the other, in fact they showed up wanting to love each other. But neither of them told the other what they needed which resulted in the opposite outcome as they pushed each other away. There is something hugely vulnerable and beautiful when we can look at each other and say, "I need you, and here's how."

It's all a dance of stating our needs, hearing what the other person needs and wants to give, and then both people having to make a decision about how to move forward. Sometimes the answer is no to a request we've made and we have to try to renegotiate for something different, or tell her thank you and go find it from another friend. In our friendships the good news is that we rarely should need to walk away from someone just because they aren't giving us one hundred percent. We have room in our lives for many friends, even if they can only give sixty percent right now. Or forty percent. It's not all-or-nothing, all the time.

Sometimes it's less about making a big ask for a favor and more about just making sure we help our friends respond in meaningful ways to our sharing. My Tuesday night girls group is in the habit of asking each other every week, "How can we best support you? What do you need from us?" Simply asking that question puts it on the person giving their update to check in with themselves and clarify: "Actually, I don't need you to try to solve this, I just want you to groan with me as I tell you what I'm struggling with this week," or, "Honestly, I know it sounds crazy but I just need you to tell me I didn't ruin this situation. Tell me it's going to be okay," or, "I'm really open to your advice—you know me—what choice do you think is best for me?" This prevents us from walking away from each other feeling judged, misunderstood, or frustrated that they didn't say what we wanted to hear. The truth is, we want to help each other—sometimes we just don't know the best way to do it.

Taking the time to see what we need, what we want, and what we hope for is our work. We can't expect them to do for us what we aren't even doing for ourselves.

BE CLEAR WHAT WE'RE ASKING FOR

There's nothing worse than sharing a feeling and having the other person start problem-solving when all we wanted was validation, or to have them start telling us about a time when they felt that way when all we wanted was some attention. It's our responsibility to tell our friends what we need.

Specific Action Needed

We have to ask for what we need. Depending on our relationship commitment and history, it's good to err on the side of offering something when we're asking for something we need.

- Is there any chance you can drive the carpool tomorrow for me? I have a dentist appointment. But I'd be happy to drive one of your shifts next week or pick up some of your groceries and drop them off while I'm running around today.
- It would mean so much to me if you were able to attend my son's wedding—tell me what you need to help make that happen.
- I need a girls night out, can I take you to drinks next week?
- You're such a great interior designer, would you be up for helping me think through a living room redecoration sometime over a glass of wine?

Listen/Validate/Affirm

Sometimes we just need a witness to the craziness of life,

someone to hear the ups and downs of the last week. We might just need to talk out loud as we vent, share hard things, and process our feelings. But it's best to tell our friends what response we're hoping for so we don't get advice if we don't want it.

- I have to tell you how crazy my mom/boss/hubby is being, but I have to beg you to not defend them or put me in a place where I need to defend them. I just want to vent.
- My business is stressing me out . . . I don't expect or need you to fix it, I just want to complain a bit and be told that I'm amazing even if I don't feel like it! Help me remember why I started this thing!
- I'm embarrassed to tell you about what my daughter did yesterday. . . . Please don't think less of her or me . . . I just need someone who can empathize with not having perfect kids.

Provide Advice or Knowledge

We need to give our friends enough information to see clearly our problem or our intended solution to which we want feedback. Sometimes hearing their stories is helpful when we know our options but just want to hear others share their regrets, lessons learned, and perceived gifts from similar experiences.

- How did you and your ex tell the kids you were getting divorced?
- Did your mom have a hard time giving up driving? I think I need to approach my mom about possibly not getting behind the wheel anymore.
- I can't get my daughter to eat any vegetables, any ideas?

Vote or Not?

As friends we often weigh in with our opinion, trying to

help, but sometimes it's overstepping. We can tell our friends when we are open to their vote and when we're not so we avoid disappointment if they don't guess correctly.

- I know that no one can make the choice for me whether to have another baby or not, so I was just hoping I could talk out loud and that you'd help me figure out what I'm really thinking and feeling OR I was just wondering what you think since you know me.
- I'm guessing you won't be thrilled to hear I'm getting back together with him, but I just need your support right now as I figure out for myself whether we can make it work OR I'd love to hear what you've observed about us and why you don't think we're good together.
- I can't decide if I should retire this year or if I need to wait, can I tell you all the reasons I think I should wait, OR what do you think I should do?

Ask Questions Back

In this option, we invite our friends to ask us clarifying questions that can help us process a decision we are making. We give them our permission to ask us questions that might help us see our own motives, intentions, hoped-for outcomes, expectations, and best methods. Remind them that the focus is on helping us come to our own wisdom by only asking questions, not for them to give advice or opinions.

- Would you do me a huge favor and just help me sort through whether I want this job by asking me every question you can think of that might help me figure it out?
- I feel conflicted about whether or not to have my dad move in with us, would you just ask me questions about it that might help me see my own answer?

The Quakers have a tradition called "Clearness Committees," where they bring trusted friends around them for the sole purpose of asking questions of the person who has a decision to make or feels blocked on something. It's a beautiful practice that I think friends could adopt as a way of showing trust that most of us have our own wisdom, we simply need others to give us the space to think it through. The purpose isn't to give advice or counsel, but to open space for light.

Sample Questions could be: What would energize you the most if you did x? What scares you about it? Where do you feel guilt come up when you think about it? What parts of your skill set would be maximized? How do you see this decision affecting your health? Where do you see joy in this choice? What does the critic voice in your head say? What does the confident, strong part of you say? How would you guess this option could change you?

2. Engage in Self-Care

We are most aware of what we lack when our own tanks are perilously low. Like kids who throw their temper tantrums, it's often less about what the parents are actually denying them, and more about whether they've gotten enough sleep, have full tummies, and feel as though they are getting enough attention. It's easier to cry over the toy we didn't get if we're feeling drained, tired, and filled with self-pity.

We are susceptible to blaming our friends for not giving us what we need when it may be that we haven't yet given ourselves what we need. Why should we expect her to give up an hour of her life for us if we're unwilling to give up an hour of our own time to get extra sleep tonight? It's insane to expect her to do for us what we're not even doing for ourselves.

What does our body need right now to feel more grounded and strong? Is it extra sleep? Yoga? Consistent exercise? Healthier eating? A massage? Meditation? A long walk? A concert? An afternoon of crafting?

Sure, it would feel good to vent to her, and it hurts that she's not easily accessible. But what other ways can we reduce our stress? Listen to music? Hire a counselor? Go for a run?

Yes, we want her to tell us how amazing we are, but how can we give that gift to ourselves? Can we journal? Read an inspirational book? Make a list of what we like about ourselves? Schedule an afternoon away to let our hearts catch up with our bodies?

Self-care doesn't mean that we become independent, never needing anyone. On the contrary, it means we can show up with more peace, knowing we can do for ourselves so much of what we demand of others.

3. Say a Prayer for Them

It was Plato who purportedly said, "Be kind, for everyone you meet is fighting a great battle." Indeed.

Praying for the other person reminds me that most people in our culture are running on fumes. Especially women. We are sleep-deprived, worried, stressed, and scared. It's really never her intention to neglect me; rather, her life is just pretty consuming, too.

One of my friends looks vibrant and energetic on the outside—having aged into her sixties in a way that thirty-somethings would envy. From all outward appearances she looks as ready for life as they come. Pull back the curtain, though, and you'd see that she takes pills to fall asleep every night and pills to give her energy in the morning. Her finances have been maxed out. Her health yo-yo's as she simultaneously gives herself life by running every day and takes away her life as she holds massive stress and resentment inside her body. The health of her marriage fluctuates, often to a precipice where I doubt they will survive. But then they do. Her youngest daughter still lives with them and contributes to the stress even though she's in her thirties.

Change the details and I could be talking about any number of us.

The point is that while we look happy, clean, and successful on the outside—our lives are exhausting us. Most of us aren't ending our every day with tons of extra energy just looking for demanding ways to give it away.

No, the truth is that we aren't sure we are going to get the things done on our own to-do lists, come through for the people who rely on us, or pay the bills we know are looming. There's a popular cartoon with a woman holding her head moaning "Why, oh why, do they want dinner every single night?"

Life is tiring—it's harder than it sounds to get a birthday card off in the mail.

Sometimes rather than take it personally, I choose to bow my head slightly and pray for her courage, peace, energy, and joy. I pray to see ways I can give to her. I pray that we could both be used to support each other in ways that enrich our lives. I pray that as I want to be given to, help me to see how I can give.

Praying for her reminds me that it's not just my life that feels overwhelming and big. She has her stuff, too. And I want to stay compassionate towards her, loving her well through her daily battles.

W e live in a world where relationships shift. Sometimes, through no fault of our own, we will have to rebuild community around us. And it's hard to start over. But there's no way to Frientimacy without a beginning. So we put in the time. We risk our hearts a bit. We face the fact that not everyone will make the same time for us. We recognize that sometimes—frequently—we need to have some conflict with each other before we'll trust each other.

We know that what happens on the other side is worth this side. So we don't give up. We go on another friend-date. We follow up one more time. We ask her a real question about her life and listen carefully. We initiate a thoughtful act. We schedule our next get-together. Frientimacy takes time to develop.

We will begin to know the value of having people who know us. We will feel the difference it makes to have close friends. Not the kind we have to impress, but the kind we get to be real with.

There will be awkward moments, frustrating behaviors, and uncertain steps. But it will also be so worth it.

You see, it's in these relationships that we learn the real work of this world—how to show up with increased love for others and ourselves.

One spiritual path calls our relationships "our life curriculum, the assignments to realize our maximum growth possible." Other traditions call us to learn how to face each other that we might forgive, bless, feel compassion, and see ourselves most clearly. We cannot stop judging ourselves and grant ourselves the forgiveness we crave without also extending it to others.

Journeying beside people is the honor of a lifetime. These relationships are like emotional gyms where we go to get stronger, lose excess weight, and see what we're capable of becoming. Is it always fun to run on a treadmill feeling like we're literally not moving forward? No. But when you know the goal that you're training toward, it makes the time feel valuable, doesn't it?

Frientimacy is a race worthy of our training. And remember that we don't cross finish lines in victory despite the sweat and hard work but because of it.

In this last chapter I want to take you from reading a book to actually establishing your plan for training—for inviting in the change you feel would be meaningful.

READY FOR CHANGE

Change is not easy. We resist it—sometimes consciously, sometimes unconsciously. Like a sled that has repeatedly established tracks down a hill, it becomes nearly impossible for us to change course midway and decide to veer off into fresh snow. Among other things, that choice requires us to deliberately put our feet down, slow our momentum, risk imbalance, lean far into a new direction, turn our sled where it doesn't go naturally, and then make a new path that will initially feel sluggish and reluctant.

Similarly, our brain has well-worn tracks. We all have routines, habits that lead us to the same place over and over again. It's one thing to come to the place where we decide that those habits are no longer serving our goals or getting us where we say we want to be, but quite another to actually know how to do it differently.

For example, admitting we need friends is one thing, but deciding what we'll actually do differently to make that happen is quite another. Even when we *know* that friendships don't just happen automatically, that doesn't stop us from *wishing* that they would. We can still fall victim to simply hoping that different results emerge just because we now have more information. But information and hope aren't enough.

THE PROCESS OF CHANGE

Let's start by understanding what change looks like when it is broken down into steps. In the process of moving from where we are to where we want to be, there are many steps. In coaching we view those steps as a pipeline, constantly trying to evaluate what step is clogging the way toward the goal. It's crucial for us to be able to articulate where we are in that movement in order to be clear what our next step needs to be.

Here is the pipeline of five steps that produce change:

1. *Insight:* Understanding what need we have
2. *Motivation:* Willingness to give the time, energy, and necessary resources to do what it takes to meet the need
3. *Capabilities:* Learning the skills and knowledge required
4. *Behavior:* Having and taking the opportunities to practice our new skills, behaviors; putting into practice what we said mattered
5. *Accountability:* Internal and external systems that provide feedback, reminding us to change, providing meaningful consequences

So if we set "fostering a healthy circle of friends" as our goal, then we'd start at the first step and ask if we understand what it is we need, what it looks like, what it feels like. The fact that you read through this book suggests you could sense the need you had, and hopefully using the Five Circles of Connectedness helped provide a more clear sense of what types of friends you needed.

The next step, motivation, is one that only you can determine. There is a price tag on creating new friendships—be it time, awkwardness, or energy. Which leads to the question: are you willing to pay that price?

Are you willing to call someone and invite them out when that isn't a habit you've ever cultivated before? Are you willing to give up a night at home where it feels known and safe to go out with strangers where it feels scary and uncomfortable? Are you willing to give her another chance even when she didn't respond the way you wished she would have? Are you willing to expend energy making small talk for a while, uncertain how long it will take before the conversations become meaningful and consequential?

Reading how much our friendships impact our happiness, health, and life success helps motivate us, but ultimately we have to accept that there will be a cost to this choice—something will be spent with the anticipation of it ultimately being worth that price.

The bulk of this book is about the third step in the process: tips, expectations, ideas, steps, stages, and how-to. So now you have a stronger grasp on how to meet friendly people and turn those connections into friendships that matter.

From here, you will have to go do something about it. You need real-world practice now. You have to choose to try new things. You'll have to consciously make different decisions that may not feel natural. You'll have to look for opportunities to apply what you've learned and predetermine that you'll take advantage of those moments to do it differently than you have in the past.

And doing it once won't help. . . . you'll have to do it this new way repeatedly. That's where the need for accountability comes in.

We have to metaphorically drag our shoes in the snow and slow down the sled. We have new tracks to make.

USING OUR BRAINS TO TAKE ACTION

We often think that looking for friends is just a matter of the heart. Our brains beg to differ.

My husband and I taught a series together for our local spiritual community called "Revolutionary Lessons to Overcome Fear," based on Dr. Srinivasan S. Pillay's book *Life Unlocked*. Dr. Pillay is a Harvard-trained psychiatrist who uses neuroscience research to show not only the massive impact of fear on our lives but also some strategies for overcoming paralyzing fear. It struck me as I was pulling my notes together for a recent presentation how much this brain imaging research might inform our process for taking action to make new friends.

First, Stand in Anticipation.

Dissonance occurs when we are in a familiar place and yet choose to anticipate a preferred future. To bring about any change in our lives, we actually have to develop that dissonance—that space between two disparate places that isn't yet aligned. We have to recognize that we need to move from one way of being into a new way. Holding that desire for a different way is crucial to helping our brain look for solutions that will help get us there.

Unfortunately, for many of us, we simply stop dreaming or hoping because it hurts to want something if we're not sure we'll get it. So we've spent more energy trying to convince ourselves we don't really want that different job, don't really need to lose that weight, or don't really need more friends. We end up looking for evidence to justify where we currently are, as opposed to holding the hope out in front of us and looking for evidence to fuel us toward a new normal. It's tempting to spend energy trying to lower the dream rather than standing in the gap. But stand we must.

The old adage is true: "If you can imagine it, you're halfway there."

The power of *imagining* what we want is showing up in brain imaging scans as activating the motor cortex in the same way as actually *doing* that very action. In other words, imagining the action and actually doing the action share the same neural substrates in our brain.

This is awesome news for those of us who love making vision boards, cutting out pictures that inspire us, journaling our preferred future, and writing down goals. Practices that help us think, write, or speak about our desired outcome not only feel inspiring, but science shows that they actually trigger the brain as though we are already experiencing it. These practices are giving us practice for our dream.

Then, Take the First Step. Quickly.

As important as imagination is, recent research also shows that if we stay in that mode we will put our brain in overdrive. Trying to hold the big picture or know all the steps we need to take ahead of time activates the ventromedial prefrontal cortex (vmPFC) which can have a disorienting effect on us if it's continual. (That's the same subdivision of the brain that lit up when test subjects were being chased by a virtual predator!) It's akin to having too many programs running at the same time on our computer, slowing down the actual progress.

To prevent being overwhelmed, as Dr. Pillay shows, our brain responds best when we redirect the activation from the big picture to the current moment.

The very question "What is my next step?" immediately activates the part of the brain that we need in order to move toward that desired outcome. "Actual change (movement toward success)," he says, "really can only occur when we perform a small action that advances us toward our goals." He continues, "Brain activation signifying change in the frontal lobe shows us that actual change is much more likely to occur with small actions than with extensive thought."

Anticipating and Acting in Friendship

Applying this neuro-function research to friendship, here are three steps I challenge you to do as you prepare to put into action all that you desire:

1. **Anticipate the friendships you want:** How can you establish the dissonance you need to remind yourself that at a hypothetical distance there is an outcome you prefer? Give yourself permission to admit, "I want more relational belonging." It might hurt to admit you don't have it now, but being clear that there is a different reality you want will help your brain begin to move you to that point.

Maybe you could create a vision board full of representations of the friends you want or use pictures of you with friends from your past. Magazine pictures can create a collage of activities and experiences you want to do with friends, paint can express the way you will feel when you have the community you want, and poetry could describe the kind of interaction you look forward to participating in. If you're a writer, you could journal about what the outcome would look like with the number of meaningful friendships surrounding you that you want; a photographer might even want to go out and take pictures of women together.

2. Name your first step: When I am teaching, I have everyone list what he or she believes is their first step toward their preferred future. Any first step. It's okay that we don't know our whole plan yet, or even whether or not our dream is plausible—the crucial action is to just name that first step.

Before going to the next step, can you name one thing you can do to move toward the friendships you dream of having?

3. Now, list your 10 to get there. After everyone lists their first step, I then tell them to list 10 steps to get there. They often will look at me with confusion and then break out laughing. It's the classic response. Sometimes our first step is even too vague for us to picture. Remember, we want to be able to picture what we're going to do, as that will trigger us to actually step into it. The smaller the steps, the better. We will begin to prove to ourselves that we can move toward our goal.

So let's take an example. If our goal is to have more meaningful local friends, then maybe we'd think a first step might be to "start meeting new people." And already we can see why many of us never take that step—it's still too big. So what would be ten things that we could do that would move us toward that "first step?" Name as many as you can with as much specificity as you can: sign up for a local cooking class, ask our friend Nathan who used to live in our new city if he can connect us to anyone, join a running club, try to find a business networking association, and so on.

And every time you name a step, ask yourself, "What do I need to do before I can do *that* step?" We just keep breaking every step down to even smaller and more definable steps. Just to find a business networking association to join we might need to: make a list of options, research them, and visit a few of their events before we decide. But before we can even make a list of options we need to: search Google, ask our Facebook friends for suggestions, browse LinkedIn, ask around at the office. And in reality, before we do any of those search options, what we actually need to do is set aside an hour of our week to dedicate to our online research.

You can see the value of being as precise and explicit as possible.

I worked through this process with a client who named "find a therapist" as her first step toward her preferred future. When I prompted her to tell me the steps in getting there it became clear why that was such a hard to-do item to cross off—because it's still ambiguous. After thinking about it, she'd then say, "Well, actually, I guess my first step to finding a therapist is to ask for referrals." Okay, what steps do you need to take to do that step? Continuing another thirty-minute conversation of breaking down every step with ten more steps, she finally thought she'd hit her true first step by saying "Actually, I think I just need to cry first." And true to my word, I responded with, "And what do you need to do before you can do that?" To which she said, "I need to go find a box of Kleenex."

In the end, she looked up at me and said "It feels like a long road to get to that therapist, but this is the first time I've ever had my own roadmap for knowing how I can get there."

That's what we all want for ourselves.

HOLDING OUT HOPE

Making new friends isn't rocket science. But neither is it necessarily uncomplicated. How could it be, when we have ever-evolving humans filled with insecurities and needs trying to find ways of being together? We're complex! So when we get two of us together, it's just double the complexity.

But we don't need to fear complexity. We're not afraid of hard work—we know that it leads to accomplishments we value. We're not unwilling to be uncomfortable—we know that nothing in life is pain-free. Look at the suffering we're willing to endure for what we deem important in the boardrooms, the counseling offices, the health clubs, and the labor and delivery units across this country. We are much stronger than we ever think we are. And we're much more adaptable than we usually give ourselves credit for being.

As we forge friendships with other women, we become more practiced at being loving. And this love—unlike romantic love, which is limited to only one person at a time, or parental love, which is limited to how many children we have—is limitless. We can grow in exponential ways as we open ourselves up to platonic love. Every relationship we engage in will be a life teacher for us, cultivating moments of impatience to teach us patience, frustration to teach us forgiveness, annoyance to teach us acceptance, angst to teach us joy.

We're committing to meet new people, to initiate consistently with them, to contribute positively to the relationship, to increasingly reveal ourselves in meaningful ways, and to forgive when needed.

We're taking the risk. We're growing the love. We're saving the world by practicing the skills that will bless others.

So it wasn't just for my gain that years ago I stood on Polk Street and decided that I was going to embark all over again on meeting friendly local women and developing them into friends who mattered. I did indeed benefit! It's not lost on me that when I'm meeting my friends for tea in a café, I am living my dream. But more than my own gain—and even more than that of my friends who undoubtedly also feel benefited by our friendships—because I have been in relationships where I can repeatedly practice how to give and receive love, I am a better person for this world. I am healthier and happier, but I'm also stronger, more compassionate, more generous, and more courageous. Imagine how this world could be improved if more women experienced these profound friendship gifts.

No, friendships don't just happen. We make them happen. And so much depends on us continuing to do just that.

ABOUT SHASTA

Shasta Nelson is a nationally recognized friendship expert. She is the founder and CEO of GirlFriendCircles.com, the only online community that matches new friends offline by connecting local women in cities across the U.S. She has been featured as a friendship expert on the *Today* show and *The Early Show* and in the *New York Times*, the *Chicago Tribune*, the *San Francisco Chronicle*, the *Huffington Post*, *Martha Stewart Radio*, *Essence*, *Parents*, *More*, *Redbook*, and *Glamour*, among others. Shasta is also a nationally acclaimed public speaker and regularly hosts Speed-Friending and Friendship Accelerator events in New York, Chicago, Los Angeles, and San Francisco, where she facilitates local women getting to know each other.

CONNECT WITH SHASTA:

- Sign up to receive her weekly blog at www.ShastasFriendshipBlog.com
- Watch her "I Have a Theory that Friendship Can Save the World" video, invite her to speak at your event, or see if she's coming to your city at www.ShastaNelson.com
- Join her Facebook page at www.facebook.com/GirlFriendCircles or follow her on twitter at @girlfrndcircles
- Access free worksheets and resources under the Goodies Page at www.ShastaNelson.com
- Watch her short teaching videos about the 5 Circles of Connectedness on YouTube at http://www.youtube.com/user/ShasGFC
- E-mail her and let her know your favorite part of her book at Shasta@GirlFriendCircles.com

ABOUT

girl friend circles.com

introducing women,
inspiring friendship.

I went to bed one night frustrated with how difficult it was for some of my life-coaching clients to find new friends in their new cities and life stages. One of them said to me, "I can line up three dates on match.com for next week, but far be it from me to figure out which women in this city are willing to put in the time to establish new friendships." It brought up all my own memories of how many times I've had to engage in that search, and how exhausting it can feel. Never with the intention of starting a business, I nevertheless woke up the next morning with GirlFriendCircles.com in my head.

GirlFriendCircles.com is a women's friendship matching site for females who value making new friends. It's free to join in most of our 35 launched cities in the U.S., with the exception of some of our larger markets where we ask for a nominal investment to help provide this service. Our community is open to all women over the age of 21.

There are four ways to start friendships in GirlFriendCircles.com. The most popular is through our ConnectingCircles, small groups of women that our system matches up to meet at specific times and places. Most women find a potential friend after only two or three of those Circles! We also provide CalendarCircles, in which our members can post any events of their choosing; ClassfiedCircles for posting specific friendship requests; and ChooseMyCircles, in which any member can search our database and reach out to anyone they would like to meet.

I hope you'll consider joining GirlFriendCircles.com so you can start meeting other women who value new friends in your city. You can also subscribe to ShastasFriendshipBlog.com where I write weekly about my favorite subject: healthy people in healthy relationships.

ACKNOWLEDGMENTS

This book is but one expression of a calling I have long felt—a sense that it is in our relationships that we achieve the most personal growth. And that has been no less true for me. Because of the people on this page, I dared to see how my education in spiritual growth and my passion for healthy friendships could give birth to GirlFriendCircles.com, this book, my speaking and teaching, and any other expression in which I challenge us to love more deeply, show up more authentically, and engage in the work of forgiveness that will ultimately lead us to peace.

I'll start with my husband, Greg, who more than any other human being has co-created a relationship with me in which I am becoming more the person I want to be. I have a deeper heart because of his modeling of love and acceptance for me, and his giving me the space to practice giving it back.

To my family, who loved me so well that I could have this courage: my dad, Jeff Emery; my stepmom, Marilyn; my mother, Jenny McBride; and my stepfather, Jim. To my sisters, Kerry and Katrina, and their spouses, Mike and Jesse: I love you all tons! Also to my husband's entire family, especially his sister, Kari, and her husband, Keith, and his daughter, Natalie, and her husband, Geoff, all of whom regularly and eagerly encouraged me along the way. There are dozens of others I call family whose love means no less.

To my friends, most of whom are mentioned in this book: It's my regret that you are only highlighted as illustrations here and there, but thank you for being more than that in my life. It is most definitely because of you that I am passionate about this subject and wish everyone could call you her friend.

To those who have made GirlFriendCircles.com happen—Jeff, Maci, Caitlin, Rachel, Amy of Big Picture PR, all my entrepreneur friends from Savor the Success, Christine Bronstein of A Band of Wives, my 10/10 group; and all my Friendship Circle colleagues, especially Dr. Irene Levine of TheFriendshipBlog.com, Debba Haupert of Girlfriendology.com, and Rachel Bertsche of MWFseekingBFF.com—thank you. I have higher dreams still for all that we can do together for women.

And most tangibly, to those who have made this book go from ideas to words to publication—the speakers and organizers of the San Francisco Writers Conference; my agent, Sharlene Martin of Martin Literary Management; my editors Diane Gedymin and Christina Huffines; and everyone else at Turner Publishing, owned by the impressive and hands-on Todd Bottorff. With no less thanks for those who gave feedback on chapters along the way: Daneen Akers, Roy Carlisle, Katrina Emery, Lindy Gligorijevic, Scott Moncrief, Janet Mowery, Greg Nelson, and Diane Steenstra.

And to you, the reader, I thank you for the journey we've shared in these pages and wish you only deeper connection and greater joy.

BIBLIOGRAPHY (IN ORDER OF APPEARANCE)

Bertsche, Rachel. *MWF Seeking BFF: My Yearlong Search for a New Best Friend.* New York: Ballantine, 2011.

Levine, Irene. *Best Friends Forever: Surviving a Breakup with Your Best Friend.* New York: The Overlook Press, 2009.

Schappell, Elissa. *Blueprints for Building Better Girls: Fiction.* New York: Simon & Schuster, 2011.

Rubin, Gretchen. *The Happiness Project: Or, Why I Spent a Year Trying to Sing in the Morning, Clean My Closets, Fight Right, Read Aristotle, and Generally Have More Fun.* New York: HarperCollins, 2009.

Gilbert, Elizabeth. *Committed: A Skeptic Makes Peace with Marriage.* New York: Viking Adult, 2010.

Blau, Melinda and Karen L. Fingerman. *Consequential Strangers: Turning Everyday Encounters Into Life-Changing Moments.* New York: Norton, 2009.

Brafman, Ori and Rom Brafman. *Click: The Forces Behind How We Fully Engage with People, Work, and Everything We Do.* New York: Crown Publishing, 2010.

Hagel, John, John Seely Brown and Lang Davison. *The Power of Pull: How Small Moves, Smartly Made, Can Set Big Things in Motion.* New York: Basic Books, 2010.

Christakis, Nicholas A. and James H. Fowler. *Connected: The Surprising Power of Social Networks and How They Shape Our Lives.* New York: Little, Brown and Company, 2009.

Dobransky, Paul. *The Power of Female Friendship: How Your Circle of Friends Shapes Your Life.* New York: Plume, 2008.

Fredrickson, Barbara. *Positivity: Groundbreaking Research Reveals How to Embrace the Hidden Strength of Positive Emotions, Overcome Negativity, and Thrive.* New York: Crown Archetype, 2009.

Strobel, Monica. *The Compliment Quotient: Boost Your Spirits, Spark Your Relationships and Uplift the World.* Littleton, CO: Wise Roads Press, 2011.

Kushner, Harold S. *Conquering Fear: Living Boldly in an Uncertain World.* New York: Knopf, 2009.

Williamson, Marianne. *A Return to Love: Reflections on the Principles of "A Course in Miracles."* New York: HarperCollins, 1992.

Brown, Brene. *Daring Greatly: How the Courage to Be Vulnerable Transforms the Way We Live, Love, Parent, and Lead.* New York: Gotham, 2012.

Nouwen, Henri. *Life of the Beloved: Spiritual Living in a Secular World.* New York: Crossroad, 1992.

Arylo, Christine. *Madly in Love with ME: The Daring Adventure of Becoming Your Own Best Friend.* Novato, CA: New World Library, 2012.

Meyer, Joyce. *Do Yourself a Favor . . . Forgive: Learn How to Take Control of Your Life Through Forgiveness.* New York: FaithWords, 2012.

Smedes, Lewis B. *Forgive and Forget: Healing the Hurts We Don't Deserve.* San Francisco: HarperSanFrancisco, 1984.

Riso, Don and Russ Hudson. *The Wisdom of the Enneagram: The Complete Guide to Psychological and Spiritual Growth for the Nine Personality Types.* New York: Bantam, 1999.

Kelley, Tim. *True Purpose: 12 Strategies for Discovering the Difference You Are Meant to Make.* Berkeley, CA: Transcendent Solutions Press, 2009.

Whyte, David. *The Heart Aroused: Poetry and the Preservation of the Soul in Corporate America.* New York: Doubleday Business, 1994.

Haidt, Jonathan. *The Happiness Hypothesis: Finding Modern Truth in Ancient Wisdom.* New York: Basic Books, 2005.

Chapman, Gary. *The Five Love Languages: How to Express Heartfelt Commitment to Your Mate.* Chicago: Northfield Publishing, 1992.

Buckingham, Marcus. *Find Your Strongest Life: What the Happiest and Most Successful Women Do Differently.* Nashville: Thomas Nelson, 2009.

Pillay, Srinivasan S. *Life Unlocked: 7 Revolutionary Lessons to Overcome Fear.* New York: Rodale Books, 2010.

OTHER RESOURCES

Weider, Marcia. Founder and CEO of The Dream University. www.marcia-weider.com.

Taylor, Arlene. Founder and President of Realizations, Inc. www.arlene-taylor.org.

The Center for Nonviolent Communication. www.cnvc.org.